Praise

'Altogether an exciting story' – *New York Times*

'It has great pace and excitement … taut and extremely well written' – *The Guardian (UK)*

'A ripper … very well written' – *The Age*

'Highly readable … In a word: inspiring' – *Herald Sun*

'A heroic story at a ripping pace'
– *Sydney Morning Herald*

'A rattling good read – something for everyone'
– *Canberra Times*

'A blockbuster' – *The Australian*

'Riveting and well-researched' – *Courier-Mail*

Author Roland Perry OAM is one of Australia's most prolific and versatile writers.

Professor Perry's non-fiction works include *The Queen, Her Lover and the Most Notorious Spy in History* as well as comprehensive works on the two major war fronts of the Great War: *Monash: The Outsider Who Won a War* and *The Australian Light Horse.* He further covered Australia's involvement in the Pacific War of 1941–45 with *The Fight for Australia.*

He is the only author to publish two biographies on the infamous Cambridge University Ring of Spies, who were controlled by Russian Intelligence: *The Fifth Man* and *The Last of the Cold War Spies.*

Professor Perry's other non-fiction international bestsellers include *The Don*, the definitive biography of Sir Donald Bradman, *Miller's Luck*, and *Hidden Power,* about the election and presidency of Ronald Reagan. A brief foray into books on animals saw him publish the classic *Bill the Bastard* and *Horrie: The War Dog.*

Céleste is his thirtieth book and sixteenth biography.

Also by Roland Perry

Fiction

The Honourable Assassin

Programme for a Puppet

Blood is a Stranger

Faces in the Rain

Non-fiction

The Queen, Her Lover and the Most Notorious Spy in History

Horrie: The War Dog

Bill the Bastard

The Fight for Australia [AKA *Pacific 360*]

The Changi Brownlow

The Australian Light Horse

Last of the Cold War Spies

The Fifth Man

Monash: The Outsider Who Won a War

The Programming of the President

The Exile: Wilfred Burchett, Reporter of Conflict

Mel Gibson, Actor, Director, Producer

Lethal Hero

Sailing to the Moon

Elections Sur Ordinateur

Bradman's Invincibles

The Ashes

Miller's Luck: The Life and Loves of Keith Miller, Australia's Greatest All-rounder

Bradman's Best

Bradman's Best Ashes Teams

The Don

Captain Australia: A History of the Celebrated Captains of Australian Test Cricket

Bold Warnie

Waugh's Way

Shane Warne, Master Spinner

Céleste

ROLAND PERRY

ABC
Books

ABC Books The ABC 'Wave' device is a trademark of the Australian Broadcasting Corporation and is used under licence by HarperCollins*Publishers* Australia.

First published in 2016
by HarperCollins*Publishers* Australia Pty Limited
ABN 36 009 913 517
harpercollins.com.au

HarperCollins*Publishers*
Level 13, 201 Elizabeth Street, Sydney, NSW 2000, Australia
Unit D1, 63 Apollo Drive, Rosedale, Auckland 0632, New Zealand
A 53, Sector 57, Noida, UP, India
1 London Bridge Street, London, SE1 9GF, United Kingdom
2 Bloor Street East, 20th floor, Toronto, Ontario M4W 1A8, Canada
195 Broadway, New York, NY 10007, USA

National Library of Australia Cataloguing-in-Publication data:

Creator: Perry, Roland, 1946- author.
Title: Céleste : courtesan, countess, bestselling author / Roland Perry.
ISBN: 978 0 7333 3508 2 (paperback)
ISBN: 978 1 4607 0646 6 (ebook)
Notes: Includes bibliographical references and index.
Subjects: Chabrillan, Céleste Vénard de, comtesse, 1824-1909.
Women authors, French – 19th century – Biography.
Courtesans – France – Biography.
Actresses – France – Biography.
France – History – 19th century.
France – Social life and customs – 19th century.
Victoria – History – 1851-1891.
Victoria – Social life and customs – 1851-1891.
843.8

Cover design by Darren Holt, HarperCollins Design Studio
Cover image: Joseph Desire Court (1797-1865), The Mask, 1843 by DEA / A. DAGLI ORTI / Getty Images; all other images by shutterstock.com.
Typeset in Bembo Std by Kirby Jones
Photo Credits: Text: Page vii: A. Duvivier, State Library of Victoria.
Picture Section: Page 1: Mayer Brothers, National Library of France, Res. Eg4-162. Page 2: Heritage Image Partnership Ltd/Alamy Stock Photo. Pages 2–3: Granger, NYC/Alamy Stock Photo. Pages 4–5: DeAgostini/Getty Images. Page 5: The Protected Art Archive/Alamy Stock Photo. Pages 6–7: Heritage Image Partnership Ltd/Alamy Stock Photo. Page 8: Michael Maslan/Corbis/VCG via Getty Images. Page 9: Lebrecht Music and Arts Photo Library/Alamy Stock Photo. Page 10: INTERFOTO/Alamy Stock Photo. Page 11: Chronicle/Alamy Stock Photo. Page 12: Antoine Fauchery, State Library of Victoria. Pages 12–13: Old Paper Studios/Alamy Stock Photo. Page 14: Granger, NYC/Alamy Stock Photo. Page 15: Nadar Atelier, National Library of France, FT 4-NA-237 (2). Page 16: Céleste de Chabrillan undated, by an unknown artist, carte de visite photograph; National Portrait Gallery, Canberra; purchased with funds provided by Graham Smith 2009.
Printed and bound in Australia by Griffin Press
The papers used by HarperCollins in the manufacture of this book are a natural, recyclable product made from wood grown in sustainable plantation forests. The fibre source and manufacturing processes meet recognised international environmental standards, and carry certification.

Not quite the Mona Lisa. A portrait of Céleste, age 40, at the peak of her writing career in the 1860s. The life she was leading was etched in her face. The artist has captured her melancholy and quiet determination in this drawing, which frequently accompanied newspaper reviews of her work.

For Frederique Lallement
and
Annette and Peter Dezarnaulds,
two lovers of Paris and Céleste.

Contents

PROLOGUE
Young Queen of the Demimonde 1

CHAPTER 1
A Providential Escape 5

CHAPTER 2
Vincent the Predator 13

CHAPTER 3
Saint-Lazare Prison 21

CHAPTER 4
Denise the Dominant 27

CHAPTER 5
A Thespian Born 37

CHAPTER 6
Not Quite Heaven 44

CHAPTER 7
Musset, the Not So Magnificent 49

CHAPTER 8
Medical Road to Liberty 58

CHAPTER 9
Dancing Destiny 69

CHAPTER 10
Horsewoman Extraordinaire 78

CHAPTER 11
Mogador, Courtesan 86

CHAPTER 12
Chariots of Desire and Ire 94

CHAPTER 13
Céleste We Forget 104

CHAPTER 14
Love at First Chivalry 112

CHAPTER 15
Love's Roller-coaster 125

CHAPTER 16
Castle of Broken Dreams 133

CHAPTER 17
Return to the Castle 140

CHAPTER 18
Roulette or Ruin 148

CHAPTER 19
The Riot that Ate Paris 154

CHAPTER 20
Rural Realities 160

CHAPTER 21
Love in the Time of Cholera 167

CHAPTER 22
Richard: Another Fallguy 172

CHAPTER 23
Actress 177

CHAPTER 24
A Platonic Solution 187

CHAPTER 25
Crime of Passion 192

CHAPTER 26
The Lawyer's Incentive 197

CHAPTER 27
Dalliance with Dumas Sr 202

CHAPTER 28
Lionel's Voyage of Discovery 208

CHAPTER 29
Céleste's Haut Couture 210

CHAPTER 30
The Near Gatecrasher 214

CHAPTER 31
Courtesan Countess 222

CHAPTER 32
Croesus *Crossing* 227

CHAPTER 33
Distractions and Dangers 231

CHAPTER 34
Watertight 235

CHAPTER 35
Trials in a Wild Southern Town 239

CHAPTER 36
Memoirs of Another Life 248

CHAPTER 37
A Hanging and Miner Rebellion 253

CHAPTER 38
Whatever Lola Wants … 261

CHAPTER 39
Counted Out 269

CHAPTER 40
Solvency Solutions 276

CHAPTER 41
The Battle for Mémoires 284

CHAPTER 42
Golden Moments; Lionel Returns 289

CHAPTER 43
Lionel Departs; Dumas Inspires 297

CHAPTER 44
The Long Farewell 301

CHAPTER 45
Title Fight: Return Bouts 308

CHAPTER 46
Author–Actor–Producer 318

CHAPTER 47
Working-class Revival 324

CHAPTER 48
Creative Transition; More Battles 328

CHAPTER 49
War Changes and Service 337

CHAPTER 50
Commune with the Devil 342

CHAPTER 51
Muse and Munificence 349

CHAPTER 52
Battling On 356

CHAPTER 53
The Extended Goodbye 362

NOTES 367

WORKS BY
Céleste Vénard, Countess de Chabrillan 374

BIBLIOGRAPHY 376

INDEX 377

ACKNOWLEDGEMENTS 388

PROLOGUE

Young Queen of the Demimonde

When Céleste Vénard strode into Paris's Café Anglais in the winter of 1846–47, heads turned almost in unison to stare at this most celebrated beauty, the City of Light's most sought-after courtesan. The more discerning onlookers searched for imperfections but could find none in this 22-year-old femme fatale. The popinjays at the café were struck by Céleste's sensual face: the large green eyes, her petite nose, full ruby lips and alabaster skin. Her light auburn hair was long and combed back over neat ears so as not to hide any of her exceptional features. Her full figure did not need the corset under the red dress, which only served to accentuate alluring proportions of lush breasts, slim waist and rounded derrière. Céleste's long, slim arms, often noted as the most striking of her many physical features, were fully exposed. She undulated just short of a swivel to a table with her friend Frisette, herself eye-catching but a mere shadow in this moment. Céleste removed her bonnet and off-white shawl, then ceremoniously slid off white gloves to expose her slender fingers.

The young men were nervous about approaching her, even though they were among the wealthiest members of France's aristocracy. Some were afraid because it took courage to accost her, despite the well-accepted fact that women entering the café were seeking paying paramours. Others knew her reputation for saying *Non, Monsieur, merci.* They feared her rejection beyond a drink or a meal. Such was Céleste's fame that this once low-level prostitute could pick and choose any man with whom she wished to take favours, no matter how wealthy or important; an unusual situation even for the well-known actresses of the era. But then she was more beautiful than Empress Eugénie, Napoleon III's Spanish wife; even Queen Victoria, who made a hobby of describing the appearance of notables she met, thought so. It was said that the real princesses of France were the courtesans, who ruled by conquest. Céleste Vénard surpassed these so-called members of royalty. She was more like a queen. She dominated.

The corseted male fops and exhibitionists, with their overly styled hair, tangled cravats, body-hugging trousers and effeminate shoes, stared at the new arrivals but were guarded. Céleste was the unattainable prize, who treated them with neither disdain nor contempt, but who nevertheless rebuffed them with a cold stare or maybe a glance of careless disapproval. Both women knew the onlooking debauched species well enough. These men wanted playthings, not relationships of substance. Their dissolute, privileged lives did not lend themselves to responsibility or work of any kind. Yet Céleste and Frisette remained in search of worthy lovers, who might keep them for a few months, even a year or more in a salubrious apartment. If they met no one suitable, they might at least enjoy a drink, a dinner and banal, flirtatious conversation.

This night it began with something else: abuse. Two degenerate types, knowing they would have no hope of ever dating, let alone bedding Céleste, resorted to obnoxious remarks in an attempt to hurt her, ridiculing her clothes and hair. She returned serve with remarks about their bad teeth and unkempt appearance. This was unexpected. The courtesans were supposed to accept being the butt of this low form of amusement, but not Céleste. She had a tangible power because of her risky, courageous bareback horse riding at the Hippodrome and her fame, which extended back beyond her brave circus acts to her days as Paris's most notable performer at the popular dance halls. She had created her own high-kicking version of the polka, which would later be accepted as the precursor to the cancan. Her outstanding looks and character had made male spectators at the halls, and later the open-air riding circus, fantasise about having her. Her image, active and in repose, inspired myriad artists, poets and writers of the creative period in the mid-nineteenth century, as well as those of the *belle époque* and beyond. They included composer Georges Bizet, who was driven to operatic genius and fury over her with *Carmen*. Henri Gervex was motivated by her to deliver sensuality in his painting *Rolla*; Céleste was the muse for, and in, Thomas Couture's masterful painting *Romans During the Decadence*; and she rekindled public enthusiasm in Alfred de Musset's poetry. The press reported her every performance, and the occasional dalliance.

Her licence to thrill gave her confidence to stand up to her tormentors. Céleste's sharp tongue cut deep.

'You mindless slobs have nothing better to do tonight, eh?' she goaded. 'Alone you are cowards. Together you urge each other on without finesse or finery of words. Your champagne- and gin-soaked brains have shrunk to allow you to squeak out attempted cruelties only, which reveal your idiocy. We don't laugh at you. We scorn your unmanliness, which dare I say, would most certainly reach to physical inadequacies!'

A dozen dandies at other tables clapped at these remarks.

'Who brought this whore to the party?' one of her tormentors asked with a vicious glare of defeat. Frisette wanted to leave, but game Céleste refused. At this moment, a dashing, dark-haired man intervened and demanded reparations from the main offender for his unpleasant remarks. Céleste had never seen the man before. There was something intriguing about him. He had none of the effete accoutrements of the dandies, nor their patronising manner which exposed insecurities. He was chivalrous, and clearly an aristocrat. In fact, he was 25-year-old Count Lionel de Chabrillan, the only man who could possibly take Céleste away from her notorious past. Would he be her first true love, and at last help her forget her miserable childhood?

CHAPTER 1

A Providential Escape

It was 1832 on a winter's late afternoon in France's industrial southern city of Lyon. Eight-year-old Céleste was coming home in the failing light with her small white dog, Lion. She heard movement behind her. Lion barked a warning but Céleste was no match for the heavy-set brute who grabbed her from behind. She was shocked, but when she realised it was her stepfather, Guy, she punched and kicked and screamed. In her fury, she showed surprising strength as Guy tried to hoist her onto his shoulder. Brave Lion snapped at the man's ankles, and he was kicked hard in the side, causing him to yelp and back off in pain. Guy slapped the little girl across the face and head, subduing her to sobs. He then hurried off with her to a narrow passage in the southern part of the city and a working-class brothel, La Belle du Sud, which, given the shuttered windows, appeared closed at least until night. But Guy, his unshaven face masking several scars from bar-room brawls, knew his way around this place. He pushed through the front door, staggered upstairs past rooms where men were indulging their carnal urges with grunts of pleasure and crude language, and into a large, smoke-filled sitting room and bar. There were five prostitutes with clients playing strip poker. Guy dragged the stunned and frightened Céleste into this scene. Four of the women didn't care about the child's presence. But a fifth, Marianne, saw the fear and shock on Céleste's face and protested to Guy, who replied, 'But she's my daughter! I must hide her from some wild men who would take her from me!'

Marianne took the child to her room, leaving Guy to drink and join the card game. Céleste was so distressed that Marianne gave her a sip of sherry to settle her. After twenty minutes of cajoling the girl into telling her what had happened, Céleste opened up.

'He is not my father!' she whispered and repeated it several times. 'He lived with my mother in Paris. He beat her up so badly once that she couldn't walk! She was taken to hospital. When she was better, she had to leave. We came here to Lyon … Guy must have discovered where we were …' Céleste broke down. She was shaking badly. Marianne took her in her arms and comforted her. Through choking sobs, Marianne managed to learn that Céleste's mother, Anne-Victoire, worked in a Lyon silk-weaving factory. After reassuring the petrified child, Marianne locked her in the room. She left the brothel in search of Anne-Victoire. But she could not find her and so left a note at her home, telling her to come for her daughter early in the morning, when Marianne hoped Guy would be comatose from drinking and physical exertion.

Anne-Victoire arrived at the brothel at dawn and was shaken to find Guy still up and cavorting with the women of the house. Although drunk, he was steady enough to attempt to attack Anne-Victoire in the bar room, but not strong enough to push off the other prostitutes, who closed around Anne-Victoire. She escaped the room and hurried to Céleste, who had been alerted by the commotion. They made a dash for it.

The prostitutes managed to restrain Guy, who was in no real state to give chase.

Mother and daughter were forced to move from one friend's home to another to avoid the disreputable Guy. Anne-Victoire still worked at the factory, owned and run by the kindly bachelor Monsieur Raoul, who eventually gave her and Céleste lodgings in his big home next to the factory. It stood on a quay overlooking a river bridge with two large customs buildings at either end. Raoul lived on the ground floor, an elderly lodger lived on the first floor and mother and daughter took rooms on the second floor. But there was nothing Anne-Victoire could do with Céleste during the long hours at the factory, which meant that the little girl had to stay in a bedroom all day.

'I don't want to be locked up,' Céleste protested. 'I want to work with you!'

'You're too young,' Anne-Victoire replied.

'But you said I looked twelve,' Céleste said, clasping her budding breasts. 'I'm taller than girls who are twelve ...'

Anne-Victoire spoke to Raoul, telling him Céleste was ten.

'The law is strict,' he replied, 'I have a few under twelve already and don't want to attract the attention of the authorities.'

'Could you at least give her a trial?'

Raoul relented. Céleste was asked to wind the silk threads over the bobbins and she proved as competent as the older children. She was given the standard ten *sous* (equivalent to a farthing, or quarter penny) a day, and a few extra if she worked overtime when her mother did more than the standard ten hours a day. Even as a child, Céleste loved fashion and she coveted the colourful silk dresses on display in the factory's foyer. Anne-Victoire encouraged her to save her money and buy one for herself. After two weeks' work Céleste managed to do this and it generated her first feelings of pride in being independent.

A month later, Guy discovered their whereabouts and turned up at the house. His appearance had changed. He wore a smart suit and he was not reeking of alcohol when he met Raoul for the first time in the front garden. Cap in hand, he ingratiated himself as much as possible.

'I am reformed,' Guy said, 'I've found God, and good employment.'

'Always a useful combination,' Raoul said, with a trace of cynicism.

'I'll help out around the house as much as you like,' Guy said. 'I love working in the garden.'

Raoul observed him, saying nothing.

'I'll … I'll pay you seven months' rent in advance,' Guy said and added as if crestfallen, 'I just want to be with my wife and daughter. I miss them terribly!'

'There, there, old chap,' the compassionate Raoul said, patting Guy on the back. 'I'll have a word to your wife.'

Raoul later put Guy's case to Anne-Victoire.

'No,' she said, 'he can't be trusted. He's a bullying, drunken oaf!'

'But he says he has changed for the good. He won't be drinking anymore …'

'He's said that before.'

'He claims to have a good job, and to have found the good Lord.'

'That's new.'

'Could you give him a second chance?'

Anne-Victoire looked at her daughter, who shook her head in disapproval.

'No, Mama, you mustn't!' Céleste cried. 'He'll beat you again. He'll never change. Please don't do it, Mama, please!'

Anne-Victoire reflected overnight. She wanted the security

of a man, especially if he brought much-needed income into the house. She relented.

In the first three weeks, they were surprised at his almost civil behaviour. Twice he did not come home at all, and when he did he claimed he stayed away because he was drunk and he did not wish to upset Anne-Victoire. She *wanted* to believe him, but she had wanted to trust her husband, Alain, too, before he disappeared when she'd been pregnant with Céleste. She had made bad choices in partners, which she said in her self-effacing way was due to her own lack of intelligence. Anne-Victoire, thirty-two, a good-looking, shapely woman, had always been attracted to the adventurers and the brash, the braggarts and womanisers, those who took rough pleasure in the moment.

Guy inexplicably seemed to have plenty of cash. He even handed some to Anne-Victoire, but she was wary, even nervous of how he'd acquired it. Guy had never been more than an itinerant labourer. His flash clothes and patent-leather shoes were suspect. Nevertheless, she accepted the money and hid it in a hatbox under loose floorboards in her daughter's room, telling Céleste that when they had enough money they would make another escape.

After a month, Anne-Victoire became suspicious that Guy's earnings were ill-gotten when he locked her out of their room and 'entertained' two tough-looking characters. Through the keyhole, Anne-Victoire saw the three men examining bags of money and other proceeds from a robbery, including jewels and expensive clothing. She was distressed but kept calm, and, the next day at the weaving factory she told Raoul about what she had witnessed. He felt guilty for having believed that Guy had reformed. He then devised a clever if daring plan so Anne-Victoire and Céleste could escape his home.

That evening Raoul asked two of his weavers, both big, strong lads, if they would do him a favour and pose as policemen, come to the house, and act as if they were there to arrest Guy. One pouted.

'You want to get rid of him?'

'He treats his wife and child badly.'

'We've noticed. He's a notorious thug and thief, you know.'

Raoul nodded. 'Dress in your Sunday suits and wear hats,' he said. 'There'll be a small bonus in your pay packets.'

Later that night they came to Raoul's house and pounded on Anne-Victoire's door.

'Guy!' Anne-Victoire whispered, fear in her face. 'You must hide,' she urged him.

'Where?' asked Guy, shaken by the commotion at the door.

Anne-Victoire looked around the room frantically until she spied a cupboard. 'In here!' she gestured.

Guy rushed in without a second thought and Anne-Victoire quickly locked the cupboard. She opened the door to the imposter policemen, who demanded to know Guy's whereabouts.

'He hasn't come home, officer. I don't know where he is.'

'Madame,' one of the cops said, 'I wish to inform you that an associate of your husband has confessed about a robbery. He told us your husband was the ringleader.'

'I know nothing about this, sir, I assure you,' Anne-Victoire said.

The policemen acted as though convinced of her sincerity, and after a few more questions, they left.

No sooner had Anne-Victoire unlocked the cupboard to let out a very frightened Guy than he raced to the back garden and hid in the shed. After midnight he disappeared with a sack full of his booty.

But that afternoon there were threats of another kind in the city of Lyon. Boatmen, traders and workers rioted over high duties for river transport of silk goods. Since the French

Revolution of 1789, Lyon had been an intermittent centre of political unrest. An industrial dispute such as this threatened to engulf much of the city. The initial targets of the rioting were the customs buildings at either end of the bridge. Officials were shot, stabbed and thrown into the river.

Anne-Victoire and Céleste watched in horror from the second storey of Raoul's house as the angry mob swirled around the customs buildings and set them alight. Their inhabitants were burned alive or forced to jump into the river. Many could not swim and drowned. Others who scrambled ashore were dealt with by the bloodthirsty mob.

Belatedly, police on horseback with swords drawn charged into the mob and killed several rioters. This dispersed them, but they were not done yet. Knots of men headed for houses along the quay, including Raoul's. Anne-Victoire and Céleste bolted the door to their living quarters. They clung to each other in fear as they heard men smashing windows and shouting, and shots were fired. When it was dark and the noise of the rioting had abated, Anne-Victoire decided to take Céleste to a friend's house in another part of the city. They were descending the stairs near the first landing when Céleste slipped and fell. Anne-Victoire helped her daughter up and noticed congealed blood on her feet. Both women looked to the door of the first-floor lodger. There was a rivulet of blood running from under the door to the steps.

'They've killed him!' Anne-Victoire screamed and hurried into the street with Céleste. Fighting could be heard only a block away. Police were patrolling the area, weapons drawn, and they escorted mother and daughter to their destination.

A day later Anne-Victoire returned to the house, where Raoul confirmed that the lodger had indeed been stabbed to death. Raoul had been in another part of Lyon on business during the rioting. His home and factory were among thirty that had been ransacked. Silk looms had been broken. Raoul was despairing but resolute. Living in Lyon meant putting up with such events.

Three days after the upheaval, Anne-Victoire was summoned by police to the town hall, which was being used as a temporary morgue for identifying the dead. She was asked to wait in an anteroom with wailing relatives of those who had perished. When called to a window, an official slid items to her. It both chilled and thrilled her to see a wallet and passport belonging to Guy.

'I'm sorry,' the official said, looking over his glasses and trying to sound concerned, 'but your husband is dead.'

Anne-Victoire was too amazed to say that she had never married the man. She examined the wallet. It was empty.

'Would you like to see the body, Madame?' the official asked.

'No,' she replied, 'I'd rather not.'

She did collect herself enough to look sad. In the street she allowed herself an inward smile of elation. *God had smiled on her and her daughter.* This vicious criminal character with whom she had become entangled would never brutalise her again. Anne-Victoire could not wait to tell Céleste.

CHAPTER 2

Vincent the Predator

Céleste was filled with relief when she learned that her mother's tormentor was gone for good. This emotion was overtaken by one of joy when Anne-Victoire decided they would return to Paris. They first tried to live with Anne-Victoire's father, but her stepmother blocked this. However, he did give them enough money to find lodgings. Céleste was delighted that the choice was near the tree-lined and trendy Boulevard du Temple that divided the 3rd and 11th arrondissements in Paris's centre and ran to the Place de la République in Le Marais. It was also just a kilometre from where she was born at 7 Rue du Pont-aux-Choux, where she had lived her first eight years, before the flight to Lyon.[1]

The district was a place for walking and recreation, studded with fashionable cafés and theatres. It was the theatres that the impressionable Céleste loved. She would often steal into a matinee session and become consumed and awed by a crime melodrama, which was a popular theme and reflected Paris's underbelly of lawlessness, potential insurrection and political instability. The shows were so numerous that the street became known as the Boulevard du Crime. These shows, and those that her mother took her to on Sundays, caused Céleste to declare with more forthrightness than an average child daydreamer that she would become an actress. Apart from the glamour, fame and applause, and being the centre of attention, which she craved, there was the fact that she had lived much real drama in her short life. Seeing murder, physical assault, sex and bawdy behaviour acted out was exciting. The formerly threatening activity took on a widely acceptable form on stage, and she wanted to be a part of it.

Apart from the fantasy of the boulevard of dreams, Anne-Victoire was her world. After many disappointments and much foot-slogging, Anne-Victoire found work with a hat maker. She learned quickly, and became among the best of the staff of twenty working at the factory, which was close to their home. The owner of the business paid her a little extra to model the hats at fairs and exhibitions, or when he invited clients to fashion shows in the foyer of the factory. Anne-Victoire was too full-bodied to model dresses, but she was attractive and had the right head shape for hats, which enhanced her looks and led to increased sales for her employer. Her mother's modest success inspired Céleste's love affair with hats and the world of fashion.

Céleste adored her mother. 'No one else loved me,' she wrote in her memoirs. 'I had no friends like other children. I was jealous of everything my mother showed the least signs of liking.'

However, at age ten, Céleste did find one friend in Vincent, a 27-year-old mason, who moved in on the floor above them. He was single, handsome and carefree, with enchanting emerald-blue eyes that twinkled with warmth whenever he saw her. She could sometimes hear him singing in the morning as he prepared to go to work. He was off-key but it didn't matter.

Vincent was happy with life, like no other man Céleste had known. At night she heard him playing a piano, also without much musical talent. Yet again it was of no consequence. Vincent appeared content with his lot. He was always nice to her and often gave her a Belgian chocolate, which he confided was his one vice. Céleste, who was idle most days and did not go to school, began to fantasise about him. She idolised the older man, who represented a sort of father figure. Céleste had never met her father, Alain, about whom Anne-Victoire refused to speak. Her grandfather had remained mute about him, too, which only frustrated Céleste further. She felt deprived, especially when she saw girls she knew promenading on the boulevard hand in hand with their fathers. She knew that abandoned women (or young widowers) and children were not uncommon in war-torn, revolution-divided and strife-riven France. But she resented that she fell into what she saw as an underprivileged category. The only other close older male she had known was the hideous stepfather, the drunken, angry Guy.

Vincent endeared himself further to Céleste on 28 July 1835 when an attempt was made on the life of King Louis-Philippe. It occurred on the boulevard less than 300 metres from her home. In the ensuing chaos, eighteen people were killed and another twenty-three were injured.[2] Céleste had seen a bigger riot in Lyon, but this failed effort to murder a king on her boulevard and the resultant disruption to life in the cafés and theatres shook her world to the core. Anne-Victoire was also troubled. She tried to settle her daughter, but it was the relaxed Vincent who remained calm.

'Everything happens for the good,' he told her. 'The king survived and now his security will be tighter. Paris and the boulevard will move on and be back to normal in a week, you'll see.'

Céleste didn't seem convinced.

'I'm only a floor away if there's any further disturbance,' he told her. 'I shall protect you and your mother.'

Céleste had only heard this kind of assurance once before, from Monsieur Raoul in Lyon. It was comforting coming from someone she admired in every way.

The gallant Vincent was in her life, if in a limited fashion. He told her she was 'the prettiest girl on the entire Boulevard du Temple'. When she reached thirteen and had the figure of a fifteen- or sixteen-year-old, many boys and men would have agreed with this flattering assessment. Céleste was learning a dress sense from her mother that accentuated her beauty. She had not yet acquired the derrière and hip movements, pivoting glide and facial expressions of the coquettes and up-market prostitutes that she saw in doorways and lanes at night. She decided that with greater self-confidence and maturity she would add these accoutrements to her feminine armoury.

Then the hard-working Anne-Victoire and Vincent began noticing each other. This at first pleased Céleste. One day her mother, now thirty-seven, invited him in for an evening meal, which excited the teenager. She dressed as well as she possibly could and pinned back her thick, fair hair in a way that she imagined made her look if not alluring then at least adorable.

She didn't really need to. Her natural beauty and blossoming sex appeal were already turning heads when she wandered the boulevard. Her confidence was buoyed by the main man in her orbit, Vincent, paying her much attention while Anne-Victoire cooked the meal. He even winked at Céleste and passed her a glass of wine, of which her mother disapproved, though not too strictly. Yet as the evening progressed the adults paid more attention to each other than Céleste, who felt left out. It hurt her but not too much because she deluded herself that it was she, the delightful (much) younger female, whom Vincent really wished to be with. *He's only paying attention to Mother to be polite*, she thought.

It was a shock the following week when Anne-Victoire announced she had been invited upstairs by Vincent for dinner. Céleste was not included.

'You left me out because he likes me,' she blurted out. 'I hate you. I'm going to run away. I can't stand it!'

Later Anne-Victoire told Vincent of Céleste's crush on him.

'Really?' he said, as if mildly surprised. 'It's her age. She's discovering the opposite sex. I happen to be around, that's all.'

'It's more than that.'

'Don't worry, it will pass. I'll be understanding.'

This understanding manifested as cuddles and kisses on the cheek, which Céleste realised was a sop for the developing relationship between her mother and Vincent. Increasingly, Anne-Victoire disappeared at night for more than cuddles and kisses, which was obvious from the sound of the rhythmic creaking of floorboards in the bedroom above Céleste's. It drove the girl to distraction. She was tormented and miserable. Whenever Vincent now showed her an apparently platonic 'uncle and niece' type of affection, she pouted and was torn between desire and competing with her mother. Her confusion became stronger when it seemed that Anne-Victoire was now paying more attention to Vincent than Céleste. This hurt deeply. It became unbearable when Anne-Victoire announced that Vincent would be moving in with them.

The excuse was 'saving on the rent'. Céleste was furious. A part of her wanted this most desirable man closer. But mostly she realised that she would be the odd person out in the trio, no matter how much the adults showered her with gifts and blandishments, such as more trips into the country and the theatre. The worst time was at night. Instead of the telltale creaking of floorboards above her, the thin walls allowed Céleste to hear Vincent's grunts and expletives, and her mother's shrill appreciation of his prolonged pounding efforts. Céleste covered her ears and even put the pillow over her head. She contemplated childish ways to make them both pay, such as burning the place down when they were at work, or committing suicide.

A small solution was found when the adults encouraged Céleste to take on a trade. She was bright but without formal schooling or instruction. Anne-Victoire found an embroiderer who agreed to employ Céleste as an apprentice. The pay was poor, but there was promise of at least a token education in the business. Céleste was not overjoyed about this change, but it did remove her from the house five, sometimes six, days a week. Her torment continued at night. She became quiet and sullen, which seemed to intrigue Vincent. He noticed that as she approached fourteen years of age, she was developing a quite exceptional physical appearance. The puppy fat on her face was falling away to reveal an unusual beauty rather than the formerly pretty and 'sweet-looking' child. Her eyes were a little too close for perfection, but they were a penetrating brown, which attracted the blue-eyed Vincent. Even in her early teen years, tall Céleste had the figure of an eighteen-year-old. She was no more the skinny child. Her bust promised to be substantial, like her mother's. Her legs were slender and long, similar to those of the girls in the growing number of Folies Bergère shows. Céleste was spoilt, but her tempestuous, at times wilful nature had an allure for Vincent.

He mentioned to Anne-Victoire that Céleste may be trouble in the near future. After all, the girl was coming up to the age of consent, which was fourteen in France. But Anne-Victoire was not looking too far ahead. Handling Céleste day to day was enough of a challenge. Céleste had settled well into her embroidery work, and like most things she applied herself to, she was a quick and diligent learner. The work was in fashion, which kept alive her dreams of one day being wealthy enough to buy her own fine clothes. She hated the token studies she had to do, but again her agile mind took in the 'history of the embroidery trade' easily, especially if there was a descriptive component. She was semi-literate, but it did not stop her from understanding what she'd read and regurgitating it verbally, with a few embellishments from her fertile imagination. Céleste seemed to enjoy the struggle to articulate a response to any question from the teacher.

She was easily the smartest girl in the small class and this gave her a much-needed boost in confidence. Unfortunately, it was at the expense of the boss's dim and jealous daughter, Louise. This petulant, unattractive girl chided Céleste about her background after she had told Louise of her frightening experience in Lyon and the demise of Guy. Céleste was given such a hard time that she would often arrive home distressed and shut herself in her room. First Anne-Victoire then Vincent would try to comfort her. He was often drunk and in this state his affections bordered on something more than avuncular when her mother was not in the room. It befuddled young Céleste. She was pleased that he flirted with her and jollied her in those times of need. But she was unsure about his attempts to kiss her, not on the cheeks as before, but full on the mouth. His hugs were too smothering and close, and she could smell the stale alcohol on his hot breath. His relationship with Anne-Victoire had killed off his image as the sought-after father figure. And gradually his appeal diminished.

Céleste grew to view her mother's lover as something of a sleaze. But Anne-Victoire was in love with him. He was seven years her junior, warm and respectful to her, and he had steady work. At her age, Anne-Victoire had little prospects of finding a suitable partner. She would do everything to secure this relationship.

Early in 1839, a few weeks after Céleste's fourteenth birthday in December, Anne-Victoire received an urgent message to go to

Fontainebleau, where her father was dying. The family wanted her to nurse him in his last weeks. She responded to the call to look after a man who had always done the right thing by her.

'I don't want to be left alone with Vincent,' Céleste told her mother, 'he's so awful when he's drunk!'

'Don't be melodramatic, dear,' Anne-Victoire said dismissively. 'I'll have a word to him, but he's already promised he won't come home late or drunk.'

The day her mother departed Céleste was in a foul mood. This led to an argument with Louise at work about the design pattern for a new, sleeveless chemise for women. Despite her limited reading skills, Céleste stubbornly maintained she was right about the instructions to make it. Louise, manipulative and envious as ever, tearfully asked her father to adjudicate. Probably to keep the peace at home with his family, the boss supported his daughter. Céleste was so furious that she resigned on the spot, without even asking for the week's pay that was due to her. She stormed home. Vincent's method of consoling her—with embraces and slobbery kisses when sober—infuriated Céleste further. She shut herself in her room. When he left for work she wandered the boulevard and came home late at night. Vincent returned home soon afterwards, this time drunk. He lunged at Céleste, running his hands over her breasts. She tried to fight him off, but he brought her to the floor, his weight pinning her down, and attempted to force himself on her. In desperation, she bit him hard on the forearm. He cried out in pain and fell back.

The second his attention turned to the bitemark, she freed herself and ran for the door. Vincent stumbled after her, but he was in no condition to pursue the fleet-of-foot teenager, who scurried off towards the boulevard.

CHAPTER 3

Saint-Lazare Prison

Céleste kept running until she felt she was safe, ending up in the nearby 4th arrondissement. She didn't dare return to the Boulevard du Temple, where she imagined Vincent would search for her. Céleste was desperate to reach her mother, but she did not have the address in Fontainebleau. It was the heart of winter and it wasn't until dawn that she found a hayloft off Rue Saint-Antoine. Exhausted, she slept until noon, when she was disturbed by a farmer delivering hay. He chased her away, but Céleste thought it would be a useful place to return to. The tightly packed bales afforded some warmth if she buried herself deep in the hay. During the day she stole food from stalls in the nearby markets, but her amateurish efforts as a thief nearly caused her to be caught. On day three, numb with cold, she scavenged in bins but found little nourishment. Beggars and vagabonds in the area had already pillaged the offerings, especially those outside the better cafés.

By the fourth night Céleste was starving and ill. She found a recess at the entrance to the Église Saint-Paul, prayed for salvation and curled up in a ball. A street prostitute, Thérèse, saw her there and took pity on her. The eighteen-year-old had run away from home at thirteen and could relate to Céleste's plight. At sixteen, she had taken the only route she felt open to her, and that was to sell her body. She had registered as a prostitute, which had the flimsy benefit of not being harassed by police if she obeyed the laws of the city regarding her trade. Thérèse's compassion wavered.

'If I'm found with you,' she told Céleste, 'I'll be charged with "corrupting a minor".'

'Why?'

Thérèse pouted. 'There's a law to stop underage girls falling into my "trade of no return". I would get a year in prison for it.'

She observed Céleste, then made up her mind. 'C'mon, let me find you some food and clothing.'

The next day a policeman spotted them in a laneway, huddled against the biting wind. Céleste poured out her story about the predatory Vincent and Thérèse explained how she had found the destitute girl. The policeman was compassionate.

'You should never have done this,' he admonished Thérèse, 'but under the circumstances I admire you for looking after this fallen angel.'

He took the two girls to the local police station and made a report. Céleste wrote a letter, explaining where she was, and Thérèse promised to send it to Anne-Victoire.

'But whatever you do, don't mention what Vincent did,' she advised Céleste. 'Your mother may not believe you.'

Céleste agreed that Vincent would already have put his version of events to Anne-Victoire and that it would be better to tell her face to face.

Céleste was processed at the station. She was then pushed into an open cart, crowded with prostitutes, adulterers, child beggars, thieves, bar brawlers, those who had caused an affray, and those labelled insane. This was a shameful moment for

Céleste. All in the cart were jeered at, abused and even targeted with rotten fruit along the route to the women's prison of Saint-Lazare in the 10th arrondissement, a marshy area near the River Seine, on the road from Paris to Saint-Denis. Ever since the location had been a leprosarium in the twelfth century, it had held an air of foreboding. By the seventeenth century it had become a large fenced-off area, where young undesirables were sent so they could no longer embarrass their families. Witches, thieves, beggars, rapists, murderers, heretics and blasphemers were herded there. The ignoble nature of Saint-Lazare took on renewed vigour thirty years before Céleste's forced visit when it was converted into a prison during the French Revolution and the so-called Reign of Terror, which had been precipitated by violence between political factions. Twenty years before Céleste's arrival it became a women's prison and the inmates since then had maintained its nefarious and odious reputation.

The women were ushered into a long hall of wire cages. The adults, ranging up to the age of seventy, were separated from the juveniles. The latter included a ten-year-old beggar who had befriended Céleste at the police station. These two were the last to be sorted by an official. He asked if they had been in prison or arrested before. Both had not. This was Céleste's last chance to tell somebody in authority that she had a home but had fled after nearly being raped by her mother's partner. But she said nothing, preferring to take her chances in a tough system rather than face Vincent's violent sexual abuse.

Céleste was put in her cell. The next day she was ordered to dress in prison clothes, including a shirt emblazoned with 'Prison of Saint-Lazare', which was a frightening adornment for a fourteen-year-old, and one of many moments she would remember vividly for the rest of her life. The prison-issue garb offended her youthful fashion sensibilities. It included a thick woollen sack-like dress of grey; a blue-striped apron, which would stand out for the wrong reasons anywhere; a black wool bonnet, which coordinated with the dress, at least in its fabric; and a scarf decorated with roses of different hues, which may have been the prison's modest concession to brightening the inmates' lives. It did impress Céleste (as she later recorded) that the colour scheme was bizarre and more in keeping with circus clowns than anything else. But at least she was able to keep her smart and comfortable brown leather shoes.

Things took an odd turn the next morning at 8 a.m. when Céleste was marched to the mess hall of long tables, that each seated twenty inmates. After a short prayer of thanks, she and the others not interned for misdemeanours and crimes were sent to a workroom for two hours of writing, arithmetic and singing. This was the first formal education she had had apart from the brief lessons in the embroidery factory. She felt intimidated, given her limited education in anything other than basic adding up. But she enjoyed the singing, which was of religious hymns of praise, rather than the popular and sometimes bawdy tunes she knew by heart from the shows on her much-loved and now yearned-for boulevard.

The teacher, Mademoiselle Michelle Benard, twenty-five, was a kindly, timorous soul, who had no hope of controlling the unruly class. Céleste was keen to learn and especially enjoyed the writing exercises. She was praised for her efforts, which brought howls of derision from many of the other girls, who were delinquent in every respect and, given the era, without hope of rehabilitation. She referred to them as 'Demons' or 'Devils, with a dog-eat-dog mentality that knew no boundaries'. They appeared to Céleste to be girls who might never have experienced real love. They depressed her and she appreciated the affection and spoiling she had received from Anne-Victoire. It made her pray that her mother would come for her soon.

Céleste received a second reality check in the crowded prison yard in the afternoon of her second day. The fifteen-metre-high walls created a claustrophobic atmosphere and were constant reminders of being shut off from society.

If she thought the younger internees were a problem, she was really put on edge during her first Sunday mass at Saint-Lazare, the big event of the week. It was held in a chapel, which reminded her of some of the tiered theatres on the Boulevard du Temple. The women serving sentences were in a gallery behind a wire fence. These were a mixed bunch. Céleste tried to avoid eye contact with the tougher ones and felt nervous even glancing at them. There were not many smiles or much softness in their faces, which were grim and defeated. They bore the consequences of a life of crime or incarceration. Gnarled ears, scarred cheeks and broken noses were prevalent.

By contrast, wedged in with these worst cases were attractive young women, each with a telltale extra garment—a silk scarf, a cotton vest or camisole poking over the neck of the standard-issue shirt, a lace bonnet, or even in a couple of instances, white cotton socks. These extra garments indicated the women were prostitutes with a connection beyond the confines of Saint-Lazare, usually to brothels. The madams of these places wanted the girls back as soon as they were released. To keep them content with their temporary lot, the brothel keepers furnished them with everything from cash to food, wine and extravagant sweets. Linen, pillows and warm coverings in the cells, even books, were further signs that these women would return to their glamorous yet dangerous and dead-end employment in the brothels, which were a part of Parisian life and on the rise from the 1830s.

Céleste was intrigued and painted this group in a good light in her later memoirs: 'These were the aristocrats of the place. They employed old and uncared-for women prisoners to wait on them and do their work ... on the whole they were generous and paid for everybody.'

Some in this pampered group were also given money by their male clients, whom they would take up with again once they left Saint-Lazare.

At that first mass, Céleste observed them, along with all her other new companions in detention. Below the upper galleries were the older internees. A handful of this group would die in the prison. Most were on light sentences, from a few months to a year. Some were on remand before being placed in less severe institutions. The older women saddened her. She vowed even then that if her mother never came for her, which she thought was unlikely, she would somehow escape from the stifling confines of Saint-Lazare.

Another shocking feature of the prison emerged quickly. Céleste, a virgin, was astonished to see that the girls and women formed special bonds. This manifested during mass with blown kisses and notes passed. At night when the lights were doused the attachments became intimate. Movement on bunks, groans and the odd scream of delight made it clear that sex was the only real joy for the internees, to which the guards, teachers and nuns seemed to turn a blind eye.

CHAPTER 4

Denise the Dominant

A fellow inmate named Denise (known also as Narelle), with the odd surname of 'Onze' (Eleven), made swift advances towards Céleste. Denise was the most overtly sexual inmate. She kept her hair clipped very short, and her looks were rather pretty. She was the tallest of the convicts. Her body was fit and strong. Her breasts were fully developed at sixteen years and her no-nonsense swagger seemed to fit her rustic background. Denise had grown up in France's wine-growing region near Lyon, but when both her parents died from a mystery plague when she was twelve, she had drifted to Paris to be in the care of an uncle, who had taken the opportunity to abuse her physically. So she had turned to street prostitution, which led to four years in Saint-Lazare. No one picked on Denise. She had a reputation for being able to kick like a horse.

Within a few days, Céleste was receiving gifts from her—a small, carved wooden elephant; the sketch of a horse; a ring. Then came a love letter.

Dear Céleste,
I loved you from the first sight of you in the salad basket [cart]. You are the most adorable, beautiful creature that God has ever created. I wish to know you so well, be your close friend; just be with you. All my senses are alerted by your presence …

Céleste was flattered to have made such an impact, but she wanted it from a male, not a female. Denise's alluring, somewhat androgynous appearance muddled her thinking. She was vulnerable and lonely. Her teacher saw the passing of the note and counselled her impressionable new charge.

'Denise has at base a good heart,' she told Céleste. 'She's not a depraved or bad person like some you've no doubt noticed. But she will lead you astray. She's bold and afraid of nothing. Do not encourage her. She'll smother you with affection.'

Céleste was both intrigued and overwhelmed by this sudden, determined attention. The love letters continued until one asked for an assignation at night in the laundry. It meant that Céleste would have to hide after the evening meal and hope that she would not be missed in the dormitory. Denise was waiting for her, standing behind baskets of clothes, holding a small candle, which exposed an eager yet sympathetic smile on the older girl's face. She had brought a bottle of wine and cheese with her.

'How did you …?' Céleste asked.

'I still have good contacts with wine wholesalers in this city,' she whispered, 'and one of them is an admirer.'

Denise poured the wine into wooden mess cups and toasted Céleste.

'To the brightest flower at Saint-Lazare!'

They sat on washed clothes that Denise had laid out and they chatted. Céleste unburdened her problem with Anne-Victoire and Vincent.

'I've sent several letters to her,' she moaned, 'but I'm pained each day the mail arrives and there's nothing for me. I cry every time. I don't know if she's still away or if she's back in Paris.'

'She wouldn't have received the letters,' Denise said with a shake of the head. 'Your would-be rapist, Vincent, would've seen to that. He'd be fearful that you'd expose his attack. I had the same thing with my uncle. I had no one to turn to. I ended up on the streets.' She sipped her wine. 'And here I am.' She leaned across, kissed Céleste gently on the cheek and filled her cup. After more sympathetic chat and a third cup of wine, Céleste felt heady.

Denise, an expert seducer, moved closer and let Céleste pour out her fears, all the while comforting her and not coming on too strongly. Then came a kiss on the mouth, and Céleste fell for Denise's seduction. Denise had spent an hour listening to Céleste's complaints about the physical aggression of a drunken, insensitive male, who had attempted to rape her. By contrast she caressed Céleste into even enjoying her first experience of physical love.

Sensing this seduction, the teacher, Michelle, saw Denise passing more letters to Céleste and reported her to warders. The letters were intercepted. Denise was sentenced to thirty days in solitary confinement. Instead of feeling sorry for herself, Denise sang her way through the extra incarceration and after her release asked Céleste for another assignation. The encounters continued more clandestinely and more intensely.

Denise claimed that Céleste had special (unspecified) endowments that would be great assets for work in a brothel. The encounters left Céleste with a mix of emotions, including pleasure and guilt, and shame for having her first sexual experiences of consent, more or less, with a female. It was not how she had imagined or dreamed of it. Some of her confusion was due to the fact that she had enjoyed it. Céleste wondered if she should confess to anyone, even the prison chaplain, because there was a kind of unwritten taboo about lesbianism, although the sexual sophisticates of the era knew it went on and many indulged in it themselves. But the church would always condemn it if it were ever raised in public, which it never was. The godly argument would be that it was 'against the natural order of things'. The United Kingdom lagged behind French social mores but followed them nonetheless. England's Queen Victoria—two decades later—refused to allow the Parliament to legislate against lesbianism. When asked why by her prime minister, she said she had consulted the royal court physician and her husband, Prince Albert, who agreed with her that, 'Lesbianism is not physically possible, so why legislate against it?'[1]

Over time, Céleste found that the pleasure of it all seemed to override other feelings.

She was comforted when Denise told her, 'I'm bisexual. I like men as much as women. It's just that women understand women's emotions better.' When Céleste expressed surprise, Denise added, 'All my clients are men. You'll meet some of them if you join me in the brothel I'm going to work in, when I'm out of here. Many of them are really nice, and most are rich. I plan to meet and marry one of the richer ones.'

'I've seen them in plays on the boulevard. They're always glamorous.'

'Yes well, the theatre often reflects real life. What would you rather have? That or life in back alleys as a street girl?'

'I love the glamour.'

'And so you should. Someone with your looks should get the best out of life. Believe me, life on the streets is the worst. You're prey to drunks and vagabonds and the mentally ill. The girls end up with some awful disease, or they die of starvation.'

Céleste was cautious. 'I must see how things are at home …'

'With that brute Vincent? You know he'll push himself on you every chance he gets. Predators like him never change, never! Compare that with the well-to-do gentlemen you'll meet. Some are from the aristocracy.'

This touched Céleste. She dreamed of escaping her working-class life. Denise gave her the brothel's address and urged her to go there when life at home became unbearable.

Early in 1840, after a year in the stifling and oppressive Saint-Lazare, Céleste, now fifteen, awoke one morning to a premonition that her mother would come for her. In the early afternoon she heard the bell that heralded visitors. Céleste, in the classroom, insisted that her mother had come for her. To confirm or dispel her urgent feelings, the teacher let Céleste go to the visitors' parlour, with Denise accompanying her. Along the way, Denise reminded her of the most likely scenario if Anne-Victoire was still with Vincent: 'Don't tell your mother about what Vincent did to you.'

'Why not? She must learn the truth.'

'Don't be stupid, Céleste. If as you say, your mother loves this man, she'll side with him, not with you. Love is blind. She's not getting younger. She may see Vincent as her last chance at security. Your version of events may well see you left here.'

The pressure mounted. Céleste felt faint. She had to pause to regain her composure. First among these conflicting thoughts was how her mother would react to her. This, she knew, would dictate her own reaction.

They arrived at the reception room. Denise was ordered to let Céleste enter alone. She walked shakily into the white-tiled room, which was dominated by a large crucifix facing the entrance. Anne-Victoire was indeed there, sitting on a chair.

Céleste's first response was joy. Her prayers had been answered. But within a few seconds other emotions swept over her. Her mother sat stony-faced until Céleste was in front of her.

Anne-Victoire had always doted on her daughter but without being overly physically affectionate. Now her body language registered estrangement. She remained seated and hissed at her, 'You miserable girl! You ought to be ashamed to have made me come here!'

Céleste was stunned. She managed by an exceptional will to control her feelings of shock, anger, indignation and perhaps rejection. Ringing in her ears was Denise's savvy advice not to antagonise her mother by mentioning Vincent's attempted rape. But she went close by saying, 'I hope, Mother dear, you know what brought me here, and that you're not going to reproach me. You must have known I was here. You've taken long enough to come.'

Anne-Victoire showed her own indignation by commenting that Saint-Lazare did not seem to have reformed her. 'I only learned you were here three days ago,' she said, 'and that was the length of time it took me to receive a visitor's permit.'

'But I've sent you many letters over the year I've been here!'

'That can't be true!'

Céleste wanted to accuse Vincent of hiding or destroying them. But in the moment's silence she realised that her mother had been duped again, by Vincent. Céleste steered away from accusing him by asking how long her mother had been back in Paris.

'What were you told when you arrived home? I suppose you noticed I wasn't there?'

'I was told the truth,' Anne-Victoire replied.

'What truth?'

'That you were led astray by some woman and ran away from home.'

Céleste stared in disbelief. The woman in question was Thérèse, whom Vincent must have seen delivering the first letter spelling out Céleste's plight.

'Who told you this?' Céleste demanded.

Her mother's face flushed but she refused to answer.

'How did you know I was here?' Céleste pushed further.

'Three days ago the woman who had you arrested stopped me in the street.'

'Thérèse? She didn't have me arrested. She helped me!'

Anne-Victoire ignored her. 'She told me you were here at Saint-Lazare. She gave me a cock-and-bull story about her calling twenty times but that she hadn't been allowed up and was told that I had not come back.'

It dawned sharply on Céleste that Denise had been one hundred per cent right. Anne-Victoire was accepting her lover's version of events without question, simply because she wanted it to be true.

'And how is Monsieur Vincent?' Céleste asked with a trace of cynicism.

'Well, he came with me,' Anne-Victoire replied, 'he's waiting for me outside.'

This was a declaration of solidarity with Vincent and it forced Céleste to back off. She now implored her mother to write to the Prefect of Police asking for her release. Soon the time for the meeting ended. Anne-Victoire stood, and after a moment's hesitation, leaned towards her daughter and gave her a perfunctory kiss on the cheek. Céleste realised that her mother had made her choice clear: her lover was preferred over her daughter. It seemed to be the most unfair thing ever done to her in her short life, and carried far more pain than Vincent's attempt to rape her. The love between mother and daughter evaporated in that single second of false embrace.

Céleste's hatred of Vincent was now set. She wished all sorts of calamities on him. She made a pathetic vow to get even, knowing that the chance to do so was extremely limited. She was a young girl in trouble. He was a man her mother would probably never leave. Behind the happy-go-lucky singing tradesman that everyone else liked, she saw a lying, manipulative individual with surprising guile and cunning. Céleste decided to wait until she was free before she told Anne-Victoire of Vincent's subterfuge and his attack on her. Otherwise, she feared that Anne-Victoire would leave her in prison for another year, maybe even to rot there for a whole lot longer.

Anne-Victoire did write to the Prefect of Police. Ten days later, Céleste was told to prepare to leave Saint-Lazare. Denise was devastated. She cried and was bitter about the departure of her young lover, who despite the deprivations had bloomed into an exceptionally attractive individual. The stay inside had matured her beyond her years in more ways than just looks.

Denise's deep disappointment caused her to frighten Céleste by warning her that Vincent would come at her again.

'*Une fois un prédateur, toujours un prédateur,*' Denise told her. Once a predator, always a predator.

'Please don't say that!'

'You'll have to face it, Céleste. Men like him don't change. You must leave and register as a prostitute. It'll be your chance for real happiness, and luxury.'

Denise began crying.

'These tears are for you, if you don't avoid an awful situation.'

'I promise to keep it as an option,' Céleste said, hugging Denise, who smiled through her tears.

Céleste said her goodbyes with tears for her warm and tender teacher Michelle, who told her to follow a 'pure path'. But regardless, her teacher said she expected Céleste to achieve much in the life she chose, or was chosen for her.

'You have the gifts of will and determination,' she told her. Not knowing quite what this meant, Céleste was nevertheless buoyed by words of apparent praise from someone she respected highly. She left in the same cart that had brought her to that place of infamy and incident. The two horses that had plodded away, heads bowed, from the police station now took her back there with a little more spring in their clip-clop step, for the cart had only one passenger. She now wore ill-fitting, uncoordinated prison clothes, which caused a few stares rather than abuse. She had given her other dresses and shirts to a girl who claimed she needed them, though no item was ever returned.

Céleste was placed in the tiny police station waiting room. She stayed there for three nights with half a dozen beggars from Alsace. The food was unpalatable and the unsavoury company kept her awake nearly every night.

On day four at 8 a.m. she was summoned by the magistrate on duty, Monsieur Regnier. He wanted to know why her mother had not come for her. He took pity on her and, annoyed at Anne-Victoire's apparent callousness, gave the grateful Céleste enough money to buy food and placed her in a cell on her own. Anne-Victoire, still cold and unyielding, finally turned up just before midnight. She was affronted at the magistrate admonishing her for her tardiness. He ordered her to promise that she would look after her child.

Regnier then lectured Céleste.

'Be careful,' he warned. 'Do not let any of those women you've met get you into trouble again.'

Céleste desperately wanted to protest, but bit her lip and remained mute.

'If you come back here I shall punish you very severely,' the magistrate said. 'Your mother would not be able to take you home again.' He then added the most feared threat he could imagine, saying that if she was in trouble again, he would send her to the convent of Mont Saint Michel for six years. This was no place for fallen angels; the inmates were 'devils incarnate', cutthroats and murderers who would make Saint-Lazare seem like a fun park. And, equally as bad to someone with her looks, he reminded her that at Mont Saint Michel her head would be shaved.

Céleste was most contrite in her promise that she would be good from then on.

CHAPTER 5

A Thespian Born

Céleste was ebullient with her freedom. But Anne-Victoire brought her back to reality on the way home when she followed on from the magistrate's warnings by saying, 'Promise me you'll behave yourself with that poor Vincent.'

Céleste could not hold back now that she was free. She vented against Vincent and told her mother what had happened. Her mother listened in silence. Once home, Anne-Victoire took a gamble and asked Céleste to repeat her version of events to Vincent. He listened without reaction before Anne-Victoire urged him to respond.

'You know that your daughter hates me,' he said. 'I've known her since she was a child, and for your sake I loved her. When she came home she was miserable and I simply tried to comfort her. I don't know what she imagined, but she ran away. It was a pretext.'

Vincent stayed calm. There was something pathological about his cool explanation and the way he then smiled and left the house.

'I can't believe you seem to accept what he just said. He's a liar!'

'No, Vincent is an honest man.'

Céleste was exasperated. After a pause, she said, 'If he stays, I'm leaving home!' She began crying.

Anne-Victoire tried to calm her. In an effort to placate her daughter, she held her.

'Don't be upset,' she said. 'We can find another home and live without Vincent.'

But Céleste was unsure. She was beginning to comprehend that her mother would never leave her man.

Arguments continued. After less than a fortnight, Vincent came home intoxicated, found Céleste alone and made another attempt to give her unwanted kisses. He hugged her, she resisted; he groped her, she threatened to bite him again. Vincent made out that he was only being playful. But Céleste had no doubt that he was trying to break her down so that she would have sex with him. She tried to get away from him and leave, but he stopped her. Seeing that she would not let him have his way with her, he changed tack and asked her forgiveness for trying to rape her. Céleste was in no mood for compromise. She refused to forgive him and said she would tell her mother what he had again attempted. But she wanted to escape his clutches. Vincent was taking a big risk but knew that he could push the situation to certain limits because of Anne-Victoire's dependence on him. Trying to appear somehow gallant, he suggested that he should leave rather than Céleste. This was bluff. He knew that Céleste had nowhere to run. She was now distraught. Her main thought was that she should flee to Denise at the brothel. But she would not be sixteen until the end of 1840, which meant she could not register as a prostitute until then.

Céleste cried herself to sleep that night, unable to remove these 'evil' thoughts from her mind. She began to convince herself that the glamorous life Denise had outlined was far better than suffering in the presence of a cunning, relentless predator. Meanwhile, in the following months, Vincent would go into his 'playful' routine when Anne-Victoire was not at home. He even suggested that Céleste and he run away together. This was a further crafty way of seducing her—letting her think his interest in her went beyond the carnal, and that he loved her. But Céleste did not want him. He revolted her and she certainly did not wish to devastate her mother with such an extreme move.

As her sixteenth birthday approached, Vincent's continued, sometimes rough, advances caused Céleste to dwell even more on the brothel option. But before she seriously considered that doubtful and dangerous move, she wanted to prove to her mother that Vincent was a diabolical character. Drawing on her passion for and memory of all the melodramas she'd seen along the boulevard, she put a plan to her mother.

'Pretend that you're going out for the day, hide in my room and listen. You'll then see who's telling the truth.'

Anne-Victoire at first dismissed such a scheme as juvenile. Céleste nagged her all day until she relented. Vincent returned home at 9 p.m. that night. He had been drinking as usual but was not quite as drunk as on earlier occasions.

'Where's Anne-Victoire?' he asked, his manner weary.

'She just left for the night market.'

Vincent poured himself a drink and sank into a living-room chair. He seemed moody and said nothing.

'You don't even talk to me anymore,' Céleste prompted. He hardly glanced at her.

'You see how right I was?' she taunted him. 'If I had gone away with you, you would already be tired of me.'

Vincent stared hard at her. 'Just try,' he said softly.

'Try what?'

'To come with me,' he said, his voice mellow and enticing, 'to be my mistress.'

'What about my mother …?'

'Arh, forget her! She's weak and flighty. She'll soon console herself.'

There was the sound of something hitting the floor in the next room. They both hurried to see what had happened. Anne-Victoire had fainted. Céleste could not contain a sweet smile of victory. Not only that—she was thrilled that her acting had worked so well. It had been so successful that her audience of one had collapsed. And she could count a second in the audience, Vincent, who had been deceived.

He was unsettled as they fetched water for Anne-Victoire, who recovered, but was in no state to respond to what she had heard. Céleste waited for her to throw Vincent out, but she stayed in bed for a week and he catered to her every whim. Each day he implored her to forgive him. He brought her flowers and gifts. Vincent did not attempt to rescind his obvious subterfuge towards her in his overtures to Céleste. There was no way he could lie his way out of the situation. Instead, he grovelled to Anne-Victoire. He promised he would be a reformed character. He would never approach Céleste again. He did claim that alcohol had a strange impact on him and weakened his resolve. He vowed he would consume less and keep control over his 'natural male urges'.

After a week of this, Céleste was upset as never before when her mother forgave him. Céleste now made up her mind to leave them and go to the brothel, known by the name with the dubious double meaning, 'L'Alternative du Paradis' (Heaven's Alternative).

But it was mid-November 1840 and she was still six weeks short of her sixteenth birthday. Céleste would have to endure what she saw as her mother's cowardice, and the sneering asides from Vincent when out of earshot of Anne-Victoire. Céleste kept her intention secret, wishing her daring move to have maximum impact on her mother. Revenge against Vincent was still very much on her mind. Contempt for her mother's weakness meant that Céleste did not care about the collateral damage, primarily in the form of shame for her family, that becoming a professional, registered prostitute would cause.

However, Vincent had a plan to push Céleste out of the home in an expedient but less harsh way. He was careful how he put it to Anne-Victoire, but he was sure he could find a suitable marriage partner for Céleste, given her outstanding beauty and growing sex appeal. Her mother was interested in the idea. Why not use her assets, which had led to so much angst, to pass her on to someone else? The chosen man would provide for her, taking the burden off them and keeping her away from them at the same time. After all, marrying off daughters was an aim for most parents and there would be no opprobrium in such a move.

They implemented the plan. Several hopefuls with suitable working-class backgrounds similar to their own were invited to the home to meet Céleste. She was not happy, and while polite, was somewhat surly about the matchmaking. She had dreams of rising above this social status, partly because she had seen her mother monstered by Guy, and had been herself maltreated by Vincent. More than that, she had witnessed the riots in Lyon and the working-class perpetrators frightened and revolted her. Céleste was not enamoured of men who drank heavily and liked brawling. She had dreams of partners with finesse, style and good breeding. She had spotted the aristocrats at the theatre and in their carriages. They dressed so well and their women always seemed so ravishing and happy. She dared to dream that she could attract someone of the upper class, unaware of the complexities of such couplings.

Despite the promise of a more egalitarian era in post-Republic France, there was not much evidence of aristocrats who had missed the guillotine wooing the young women of the less salubrious suburbs of Paris. In fact, surviving members of the aristocracy were even more snobbish and precious about their status than their still intact British counterparts (and they remain so). It was true that the rich males of the middle and upper classes had relationships with working girls in brothels and even the streets. But using them for pleasure and company was a far cry from taking them to the altar in front of disapproving family members.

Although women were emancipated legally in France in the tenth century, there was still a sense that women were like chattels (as they were under British law until the late eighteenth century)—owned by the husband once married. Céleste did not wish to be shackled to someone with that outlook. Naivety led her to believe that men with money would be somehow more respectful and gracious with women. This was part of the vision presented by Denise and now it seemed a more alluring proposition than ever. The rough working types that Vincent and her mother introduced her to only enhanced it. She did not like the way they ogled her with anticipation and her strong olfactory sense was also offended by some of them.

Céleste's continued hostility towards Vincent made him anxious for her to be gone. Anne-Victoire seemed to have lost all real love for her daughter. She began to worry that he might walk out on her if Céleste did not leave. The atmosphere was angst-ridden. Céleste remained steadfast in her rejections and each day brought her decision closer.

She turned sixteen on 27 December and was noticeably more buoyant. She chose the next day to leave, in the mid-afternoon, when both her mother and Vincent were at work. Light rain was falling. She decided to take a cab. The driver stood at the carriage door and did a double-take when he heard the address. She climbed in. The driver did not shut the door. Céleste had rehearsed this moment many times, but it had not featured a cabbie not knowing Heaven's Alternative. She checked if he knew where it was.

'Oh, yes, of course I do,' he said with a laugh and closed the door.

CHAPTER 6

Not Quite Heaven

The bordello near the Champs-Élysées was far grander than anything Céleste had envisaged. It was a four-level mansion with a well-manicured lawn and impressive, solid, dark-green façade with an attractive ivy covering. She rapped on the front door and rang a bell. A tall, plain-looking woman answered and looked around it suspiciously. Céleste was nervous and in awe of the moment.

'I'm Fanny,' the woman said with a querulous look.

'Is Denise in?'

'Denise?' Fanny said with a frown. 'There's no one here by that name.'

Fanny showed her into the hallway and left her there. A minute later Céleste was ushered into a room of garish pink décor. A corpulent, grey-haired madam entered the room. She wore a black lace shirt, a long silk dress and a diadem of espensive-looking stones.

'I apologise,' she said, shaking hands with Céleste, 'Denise is called "Narelle" at work.'

The madam paused, chuckled mirthlessly and added, 'Also,

you're stunning and I don't wish Denise to run away with you. She's one of my best girls.' The madam waved her hand at Fanny. 'Find Narelle and bring her to me.'

The madam eyed Céleste up and down. Her expression lightened a fraction.

'How old are you, my dear?'

'Sixteen.'

'Have you registered?'

'No.'

'Then I think you should leave.' The madam sighed. By doing this she was covering herself if Céleste was a police plant. Other brothels had been caught this way when police paid young girls to help expose the use of underage, unregistered prostitutes.

Denise appeared wearing a pink satin dressing gown, filled with swansdown, and a transparent white shirt. As she opened her arms in delight to see Céleste, her gown fell open to reveal a petticoat embroidered in pink to cover her private parts. Denise hugged and kissed Céleste, happy to embrace her friend for the first time in a year.

Pointing to her gold slippers, Denise said with exuberance, 'The luxury surprises you, doesn't it? Stay with me here and you'll have it, too. I've never been happier. You'll feel like a princess here.'

Denise then explained the madam's unwelcoming attitude. She assured Céleste that the madam was most impressed by her and that she wanted her to join the brothel. Céleste was starstruck as Denise led her up four flights of stairs, past a score of wood-panelled doors on each landing and into a bedroom. She was introduced there to three other sex workers. Céleste's enthusiasm fell away when she saw the reaction on their faces. She realised that they recognised a rival in both beauty and charm. They were all in their late twenties, and off-duty looked a fatigued and forlorn threesome. They were in no mood to be excited over someone who might threaten their livelihood and future. This was a minor jolt for Céleste. Another came quickly when she was told she would have to see the Prefect of Police to register in her chosen trade. It was likely to be the tough but fair Monsieur Regnier again. This meant in turn that she would have to face her mother, who had to consent to this drastic move, which could have lifelong consequences, for it was far, far harder to get off the register than on it. Registering had its hurdles.

Denise, enraptured to have her former lover close again, gave her more useful advice. 'You know what Regnier is like. You must show strength as if you're absolutely certain of your path. You want this life. There can be no turning back. If you express this, he can't, under the law, stop you from doing what you want. If you show weakness, he'll throw you back in Saint-Lazare until you see the "error" of your ways. Once you show that toughness, it only needs your mother to agree.' Denise paused and stared at Céleste. 'And she will agree. She long ago made her choice—for Vincent over you. You know she wants to see the back of you.'

Céleste wrote to her mother, asking her to come to the prefecture's office. Two days later Anne-Victoire appeared, this time at the appointed hour. Céleste had rehearsed the words she wished to say to her mother and delivered them with resolve.

Despite what had gone before, Anne-Victoire was overwhelmed to learn that her daughter would become a prostitute of her own volition.

'Are you mad, child?!' Anne-Victoire asked. 'Have you thought of the misery and infamy you'll bring on yourself?'

Céleste hung her head and bit her lip, but said nothing.

'Look, my darling,' her mother said, touching Céleste's shoulders solicitously. 'I know I've wronged you, but we can work this out. We can put everything right.'

'No,' Céleste mumbled and began to cry.

'Come home,' Anne-Victoire implored, 'and I swear I shall break with Vincent.'

Céleste didn't believe her. 'No,' Céleste said again. 'It's too late.'

Céleste was then taken alone before Monsieur Regnier. Again she had to summon strength. She looked him straight in the eye and said, 'I wish to be registered.'

'What? Do you know what you're saying? I have a good mind to send you back to prison.'

'As you wish, Monsieur,' Céleste said boldly, 'but when I come out I shall come back again to ask you to have me registered.'

'Has your mother agreed to this?' Monsieur Regnier asked with indignation.

'Yes, she has. She's in the building. She agrees with this.'

With that, Regnier turned his back on Céleste and said to an attendant, 'Take this girl to the Records.'

In the registration room they wrote down her name, age, physical description, and even her body measurements. Céleste Vénard was now officially a prostitute; a woman who had the right to sell her body for sex under certain circumstances.

She left the room and joined her mother. Anne-Victoire burst into tears and uttered, 'May God forgive us!' She then turned on her heel and walked away without even a kiss for her daughter.

In that moment, Céleste let go of the tension she had been holding. She felt 'all my love for my mother rush back. I wanted to run after her.'

But the madam at Heaven's Alternative had sent Denise with Céleste to make sure she kept her nerve. Denise witnessed Anne-Victoire waving down a cab, and Céleste hesitating at the front of the prefecture's office. Denise went to her and put her arm around her.

'I'm not sure what I've done,' Céleste mumbled, near tears.

'What are you thinking of?' Denise asked. 'Do you want to go home and start all over again with your mother and Vincent? You'd make her unhappy, and yourself, too.'

They watched as Anne-Victoire entered a cab.

'Let her go,' Denise urged. 'You'll never have to worry about Vincent or his type again!'

They watched as the cab pulled away. Céleste felt a surge of remorse and guilt, and had to be supported by Denise all the way back to the brothel.

'You'll soon meet the most impressive gentlemen in all Paris,' Denise told her. 'One day you'll be wealthy enough to have your own apartment ...'

These lovely fantasies weren't enough to console Céleste. To take her mind off her pain, she was given the clothes and other items that would transform her from a struggling girl into a sexual siren. They included a white satin dress and matching shoes, along with a coral necklace.

To Céleste, the clothes and adornments represented the gateway to a new life and potential riches, away from the poverty, abuse and deprivations of her background, which she despised so much. In reality her glittering new acquisitions were claimed by the madam to be worth 1100 francs, which would represent years of labour at her old employ as an embroiderer, and not much less in her new profession. Her joy would have been wiped away in an instant had she known.

Céleste had just four francs in her purse.

CHAPTER 7

Musset, the Not So Magnificent

Céleste was disillusioned with her new life within two months. She met several rich men but none wanted to be with her for more than a night of sex. Some were overly vigorous; others impotent or nearly so. Some talked a lot and seemed to need even her, a sixteen-year-old, as a sounding board, a type of amateur psychological counsellor. Still others were laconic and sullen and said little. There were many that wanted stimulation through such things as spanking or masturbation. A large number wanted fellatio and/or cunnilingus. Denise and the madam had to instruct her on how to handle other fetishes with the feet. And while 'the customer was always right' and had to be pleased, anal sex could be denied to the client. This caused some anguish here and there. Céleste was revolted by the thought of threesomes and foursomes and the odd orgy. But she noticed that the older working women indulged. She asked Denise why.

'They reach the point where they have to oblige for the money. You should do this,' Denise advised her with a cynical laugh, 'because most clients are drunk when they want it and they can't get it up anyway. Then we must be sympathetic and jolly them.'

Again, a lot of the gentlemen were very excited by lesbian acts. Denise talked her into this on occasions because the clients were usually voyeurs rather than participants. Céleste felt comfortable enough for this kind of exhibition. All a performance needed was plenty of fake orgasms, vigorous tongue movements, and lots of screaming '*Oui! Oui! Oui!*' Strap-on wooden dildo action would rarely be demanded by a client, but when it was, the girls learned how to simulate hard action while not hurting each other. These shows appealed again to Céleste's thespian tendencies.

Denise, now eighteen, did not attempt to seduce Céleste as she had at Saint-Lazare for she had fallen in love with a respectable young man named Alex, whom she had met at a dance. She had kept secret her work in the brothel, knowing he would dump her if he knew about it. Céleste was happy for her and somewhat relieved that their past as lovers would be buried. But she was also confused. Denise let slip that she wished she had never been in the brothel now she had a 'real' lover. And yet meeting the right gentleman had been the lure for joining Heaven's Alternative. Denise's success drove home the complications of achieving any aim to snare a suitable partner.

This was part of the reason Céleste became bored and depressed by the daily unromantic transactional activity. Unlike Denise, she had not met anyone she remotely fancied. Where were the men of quality? Those who might sweep her off her feet and beg her to marry them? So far, she had had the wrong types, who either fell about her like love-struck puppies or were sophisticated in manner but utterly indifferent. Some wished to impress her with their manhood by waggling it in front of her as if that alone would make her swoon. This soon became tiresome, especially as the girls were instructed by the madam to make approving noises about the men's equipment, even if some searching was needed to find it in the more hirsute crutches.

Just as she was beginning to regret the choice she'd made, she was ushered into a salon to meet a thin-faced, delicately handsome, fair-haired and blue-eyed man. Céleste guessed that despite his drawn, sad face, he was probably just thirty, which was accurate. She saw him as ghostly, from his thin, pale cheeks, accentuated by a long, narrow nose, to his feline fingers.

He was seated on a sofa when she entered. He ignored her at first and rang the bell hard. Denise appeared and he ordered his favourite drink, a mixture of absinthe, cognac, English beer and egg yolk. When Denise left he looked up at Céleste with a hint of contempt and asked where she came from. Céleste was becoming used to this careless and arrogant manner from the supposed gentlemen of the aristocracy. She ignored the question.

'I don't know you,' the man said, with more than a hint of a temper. When she refused to respond, he swore at her and repeated his question.

'Do I ask who you are,' she said, 'or where you come from?'

Céleste was defiant, telling him she didn't have a birth certificate, if he wanted to see one. Denise appeared with his drink and departed. The man looked curiously at Céleste. After a pause he demanded, though not harshly, 'Stay here, I wish it.'

But Céleste had had enough. She bustled out and went straight to the madam in her book-lined office to complain, with Denise present. But the madam was phlegmatic, saying that she regarded the man as her best friend. He often stayed for more than a week at a time. The madam smiled knowingly, paused and remarked, 'That man is one of the greatest men of letters of this century.'

Céleste was astonished but pretended not to be impressed. 'Then I'd advise him to write less well and talk better.'

Denise spoke up, explaining that the man was the outstanding poet and playwright Alfred de Musset.

'Don't you recall?' Denise asked. 'I told you about him and his grand love affair with the novelist George Sand.[1] Now he's in a relationship with the famous actress Rachel.'

'Ah, yes. Sand, the one you'd love to have an affair with. The one who rejected him for their surgeon, and he never really got over it.'

Denise blushed and nodded.

'That may explain his rudeness to a degree,' Céleste said, 'but it doesn't excuse his behaviour. It's not my fault that he's become a woman-hater because of rejection. I pity Rachel.'

The madam said defensively, 'He wrote the first modern French dramas.'

'He … he seemed somewhat haughty.'

'Both his parents are descended from distinguished families,' the madam added. 'His father is an esteemed writer of history and travel.'

'He wrote a poem, *Rolla*, about a prostitute,' Denise proffered, 'and a debauched member of the bourgeoisie.'

'The girl he had in mind was from an elite place,' the madam said, 'not a low-class brothel that the poem indicated. You see, the man in the poem is of course him. The girl of whom he writes was one of my employees, here in this place. He was hiding the fact, but not so well.' The madam paused. 'His choice of female five years ago when he wrote that poem was uncannily like you, especially your general beauty and your wonderful skin. His choice is now you.'

'But he's never seen me!'

'Oh he has, I assure you, but he was perhaps too shy to make an advance. Now he wishes to make your acquaintance.'

They could hear Musset ringing a bell for attention again. It was prolonged and demanding. Eventual wealth, not artistic brilliance, was what Céleste had signed on for as a prostitute. Denise advised her not to go back but she was intrigued to view this 'great genius'.

She returned to him; he continued to be obnoxious, saying, 'In this house everyone obeys me; you will do the same!'

Céleste was hurt and thought about leaving again when he rang for drinks. She only wanted something 'soft', which caused Musset to swear again. This time Fanny brought sugared water for her and the absinthe mixture for him. He filled two glasses with the alcohol, but she shook her head when he offered one to her. When he pressed her to take it, she grabbed the glass and threw the contents in the fireplace.

'Arh! You are disobedient!' he said, taking her hand and twirling her around. 'I like that, too!'

Musset took some gold coins from a jacket pocket and promised them to her if she took the absinthe. She refused a second time.

'What a charming character,' he said with a laugh. 'As impervious to fear as to self-interest. Never mind. I like you this way.'

He invited her to sit next to him on the sofa and to tell him her story. He was patronising, telling her she had been 'unhappy and persecuted', just like the others in the brothel. The generalisation may have been true, but Céleste did not appreciate his blasé comment.

'Tell me frankly,' he said, his arrogance and narcissism continuing. 'Do you like me?'

'I dislike you intensely,' Céleste replied.

'Then you're not like all the others. They're mad about me, or so they say.'

She maintained her defiance and said nothing.

'I can't bear them,' he added with contempt, 'but you seem original to me. And I like you.'

He offered her the gold coins again, saying, 'You haven't earned it, but I give it to you.'

Céleste refused.

'Leave me!' he ordered as he reached again for the absinthe bottle.

She made her exit, her self-possession and dignity intact. She was disappointed by the experience. Despite being semi-literate and not knowing Musset's works, she respected artists, especially playwrights and poets, who created the melodramas she loved so much. But his behaviour and abuse of alcohol upset her. She wondered why such a talent would drink himself into depression and anger, and visit brothels. It was another reality check concerning the complexity of human behaviour, not dissimilar to her mother's choice of Vincent over her. She was fast understanding that not all matters were black and white, as sometimes depicted on the stage.

The madam knew that Musset was attracted to Céleste, so she urged her to be with him. Céleste said she would not put up with his attitude. She asked how she should deal with it. The madam suggested she be herself, without offending him; she should stand her ground. But the piece of advice that resonated for Céleste was that she would 'learn much' from him. Flawed as he was, Musset was of the class and style of men she aspired to infiltrate; and he was in the business of creativity and drama that appealed to her most. She had always been moved by the glitter, romance and inspiration of the theatre.

So Céleste gave in. Musset's requirements seemed odd at first. He dressed in a purple satin gown and matching slippers and sat on a chair in his favourite boudoir. He made her stand in front of the half-open curtains at the windows that gave the brothel's best view of the apartment rooftops in the area. He made himself tipsy, if not drunk, with his beloved absinthe. So far there had been no physical contact. It was as if he were appreciating the sensual view before savouring it. Musset asked her to take off all her clothes, not in a strip as such, but in a steady way, as if he was interested in every hand gesture, every lithe body movement. It was as if he was assessing her through the five senses. He had heard her laugh and speak, occasionally vehemently; he had bought her the most expensive perfume in the Paris stores; he admired her beauty. There was only the senses of taste and touch remaining.

Musset admired her alabaster skin as if it were a garment, which caused Céleste mixed emotions. She accepted the compliments, but no one had ever been so obsessed about any part of her. Then he touched her arms and neck and face. He was gentle, but it frightened her just a fraction. She did not know where this was going. He stood and touched her breasts. He kissed them gently at first, then he sucked her nipples, still with her standing, motionless. When she went to touch his arms, he put her hands back by her side. Musset sat on the sofa again and examined her pubic hair. He touched it as if he were combing it. Then he leaned forward and pushed his tongue around her vagina. This tickled her. She stifled a laugh, and he half looked up but not completely because he was intent on his new focus. Céleste put her hands on his head, holding on as she stood on tip-toe to avoid the sensation that amused rather than titillated. Musset removed her hands from his head.

After satisfying all his senses, he pulled back the bedsheets and motioned for her to lie back against the large, white pillows. Musset pulled the curtains, lit a small lamp and placed it on a side table with the fastidiousness of a theatre lighting director.

Without a word he then mounted her and was done within twenty seconds.

Céleste certainly learned much from Musset, but not in the way she expected or hoped. It was more a lesson in how to cope with the sensitivity of self-centred males rather than with creativity. And she struggled to understand him. It frustrated her and it showed in her challenges to him. He had no answer to her question as to why he insisted on seeing her.

Musset's renowned poems were in the literary review paper *Revue des Deux Mondes*. Céleste couldn't understand how he could compose such lovely things, which appeared in the morning, and be the same person at brothel orgies at night. His indifference caused her to tell him, 'You're nothing but a drunkard!'

The madam and Denise had explained in more detail about his pining for George Sand, and Céleste had the temerity to raise this delicate issue.

'If one woman made you unhappy,' she told him, 'that's no reason to condemn all the rest of us ...'

Musset seemed to accept her berating. It appeared to amuse him, for after one tirade he asked the madam's permission to take Céleste out to dinner at the fashionable restaurant Rocher de Cancale. Céleste was excited. She wore a new dress to celebrate only the second time she had been let out of the brothel since arriving several months before. It was beginning to feel like a version of Saint-Lazare, the major differences being the company and the exotic attire.

Musset was already on the way to being intoxicated when he picked her up. During the meal he told some bad-taste jokes, some of which were directed at her and her fellow sex workers.

'Did you hear about the farmer's daughter, a prostitute, who went to the fair?' he asked.

Céleste waited.

'She couldn't keep her calfs together.' He laughed. She didn't find it that funny.

'Did you hear about the prostitute who wanted to get an acting job on the stage?' he went on.

Céleste thought at first this was directed at her. She had expressed her desire to one day be an actress.

'She slept with the writer,' Musset said with a distinctly patronising grin.

'I don't understand.'

'No, I suppose you wouldn't. You see, Céleste, if you want a job on the stage, you sleep with the producer or director, not the writer. Writers don't have the power over casting.'

'What if the writer is the director?'

'Nice lateral thought but unlikely.'

He ordered absinthe and was soon drunk. Céleste asked for soda water. After more cynical commentary, Musset reached for the soda water bottle and made as if to fill a glass. Then without warning he turned the siphon on her and drenched her.

Céleste was shocked. She burst into tears at this public humiliation and ran all the way back to the brothel.

CHAPTER 8

Medical Road to Liberty

Denise felt cornered in a world she wished to reject. But she was not confident enough to make the break. Instead, she explained to the madam that both she and Céleste should be allowed more freedom. The madam begrudgingly permitted her to take Céleste to one of the many dance halls, called La Chaumière. The best orchestra in town played a variety of sedate polkas. Ladies outfitted as if they were in a caravan in the Sahara moved in a conga line, protected by male guides in flamboyant white costumes.

The dancing took place mainly outside the vast hall, with thousands of coloured gaslights swaying in the summer night's breeze. Céleste soon drew a crowd by dancing outrageously, with high kicks and lifting her dress to expose her slim, lithe legs. At first she danced with Denise, who did well as a foil for Céleste's liberated movements, which were rarely in time with the tardy music.

They hugged each other at the end of a number.

'I feel so free tonight!' Céleste said. 'It's as if I've been let out of Saint-Lazare again.'

Young men hovered, wanting to approach the two teenagers, but uncertain as to how. One caught Céleste's eye. He was lean and of medium height, with sparkling eyes, jet-black hair, a broad, intelligent forehead and a short-clipped moustache. When her look lingered, he grew bold and stepped towards her. He introduced himself as Adolphe, and then said, 'You are unspeakably beautiful!'

'But you've just spoken, Monsieur,' she said with a laugh. He blushed and Céleste immediately sensed a lack of conceit and modesty in him, which she found refreshing after Musset's self-centred arrogance. There was something reassuring about his shyness, even his insecurity. She learned that Adolphe was a 22-year-old medical student in his final year. She relaxed in his company and was happy not to have to play the innocent, finger-sucking teenager or the dominatrix and cocotte who spanked clients who wished to be treated like little boys. Here was a young man she respected. Still, her sex appeal could not be turned off. Adolphe was dignified enough, but he could not help at times being the big puppy, besotted with her sensual glow, the glimpses of her pert breasts under a revealing bodice, her long, thin arms and perfect legs. She occasionally touched his arm with her fingers, and each time this happened, his body language became emboldened. He seemed to hunch over her as if he were preventing advances from any rivals. Next to the androgynous, taller, striking Denise, Céleste was the most alluring woman at the dance hall. Many other young men, their courage bolstered with alcohol, now hovered, attracted not just to her grand appearance, but also her animated personality. Yet she blocked them all out. Adolphe was the prize at La Chaumière for her, and she was a dream package for him.

There was another important element in this encounter. It was not inside the brothel, where she had to be with someone even if she did not care for him. She and Denise were just like any other females in hundreds of Paris dance halls, hoping to meet their prince charming, or even just Mr Nice Guy.

Adolphe happened to be a good friend of Denise's boyfriend, Alex. Adolphe wanted to visit the girls, but Céleste demurred, having been warned by Denise never to let anyone know they were prostitutes. Denise told him that the next time she saw Alex, she would bring Céleste and they could go out as a foursome.

Soon after this encounter, the madam decided to throw a party for the brothel's regular clients. Céleste was ill. She was running a temperature; her body ran hot and cold. She took to her bed, but the madam ordered her to attend the festivities. Pale and weak, Céleste obeyed, but within an hour had collapsed. A 29-year-old guest named Laurence carried her to the brothel foyer. He revived her with water and chatted with her for half an hour. In her feverish state she told him of her woes and how she'd become entangled financially with the brothel, accruing debts she could never repay. Laurence seemed to remain detached. When she finished her outburst he asked how much she owed.

'A bit more than 2000 francs,' she answered.

Céleste thought her delirious state had affected her senses when he said he would pay off the debt and put her in a self-contained part of his huge apartment. Without waiting for her agreement, he paid the account and called for a carriage to take them away, saying he would send for her personal effects the next day. He refused to let her say goodbye to Denise or anyone else, fearing he would have prostitutes visiting his home.

When Céleste recovered the next day and found herself at this new abode, she realised that her gallant saviour had been true to his word and had acted out of kindness, without any ulterior motive. He called for a doctor to examine her and ordered a valet to look after her. The doctor's examination cleared her of a medical issue and in the time-honoured way of the era, he prescribed 'rest and fresh air'. But a week later, Céleste was too weak to leave her bed. The doctor was summoned again. This time he was alarmed to diagnose the early signs of smallpox, a dreaded, contagious disease that often killed. It caused pockmarking of the skin, especially noticeable on the face. The valet refused to tend to her and the doctor admonished Laurence for taking her in. Chivalrous Laurence refused to throw her out, and he asked the doctor if she could be sent to a nursing home, saying he would pay all the expenses.

Céleste heard the conversation from her room and became even more terrified when the doctor said she could not be moved.

'It might kill her,' he told Laurence and the valet. 'I'll try to send you a nurse.'

The mention of the word 'try' panicked her. What if he failed to find one? A nurse was not a doctor. What would happen? Would she be left to die?

Céleste waited until the three men had departed, then struggled to dress herself. Calling on all her reserves of strength, she left the apartment, hailed a cab and asked to be taken to Saint-Louis Hospital. She fainted en route. The driver, unaware of her condition, carried her into the hospital, where nuns took her into a ward and cared for her.

She went in and out of consciousness, and could not see.

'Poor child,' one tending nun said to another, 'she's blind.'

Despite losing her sight for more than two weeks, Céleste made a good recovery. More than anything, she was devastated by the hideous pockmarks on her face, but the nuns assured her this disfigurement would clear up.

Céleste was most grateful that it did just before her surgeon came through the hospital with six medical students, who were there for observation and instruction. They surrounded Céleste. To her dismay, one of them was Adolphe. When the surgeon moved on to other patients, Adolphe stayed to chat.

'I qualify as a doctor in two weeks,' he told her.

'Congratulations!' Céleste said, reaching up to kiss him on the cheek. 'Have you found a position?'

'House surgeon at the Versailles Hospital. You must come and visit. I mean it.'

This and his lingering look encouraged Céleste to believe he wanted a relationship. It also indicated that he had no idea she had worked in a brothel.

Céleste asked Adolphe to send Denise a note, which she would pass on to Laurence, her good Samaritan. In it she explained to Laurence that she left his apartment because she did not wish to infect him. Laurence gave Denise the few effects Céleste had left at his place, along with 100 francs to help her out. She was again thankful to this man, who restored her faith in humanity.

Céleste's registration meant that, by law she could not lease a room lest she use it for prostitution. This forced her to lie to Adolphe, saying she was too young by law to rent. He happily found her a decent room on Rue Cardinal Lemoine and offered to pay the monthly rent. However, she refused his offer to pay. Instead, she used the money from Laurence, furnished the room simply and invited Adolphe for a candlelit meal.

He brought wine. Céleste began preparing the meal. Adolphe poured their drinks and handed her a glass. He kissed her on the neck. She turned, smiled and said, 'Better to wait until after dinner, no?'

He smiled and bowed. There was none of the aggression and demands of Vincent, or Musset and the other brothel users. At last, Adolphe seemed the kind of gentleman she had wished for. He seemed to have money and would be on a good salary at

Versailles. Céleste would be seventeen in two months and she felt she might be falling in love for the first time.

After dinner he took her by the hand.

'Ready now?' he asked, kissing her. She began removing her clothes, a habit from the brothel.

'No, no,' he said gently, 'that's my pleasure.' He helped her take off her dress, then her undergarments. There was a tender sexiness in his hands, a first for Céleste. At the brothel, clients had undressed perfunctorily. Here was a fit and intelligent young man who wanted to inject more sensual pleasure and romance into an act that had hitherto been made humdrum by men who rarely attracted her, or who she had to wet-nurse through problems in their private lives.

He kissed her with passion and eased her onto the bed. He made sure she was aroused in all the right places. She was soon consumed by him and the basic yet emotionally gripping business of youthful, vigorous coupling. Adolphe was excited, in fact overly so, for he pulled out within a few minutes and climaxed. Céleste was not concerned at his speed. She took it as a demonstration of the strength of his affection. Often at the brothel, no amount of sucking, stroking or dirty language could arouse clients to a respectable salute, let alone ejaculation.

Adolphe apologised. But when she shook her head, smiled and kissed him warmly, he relaxed.

They ate cheese and cake, drank more wine and lay in each other's arms and discussed dreams.

'I want to own a hospital of my own,' he told her. 'I also wish to travel to the United States, and even Australia.'

Céleste laughed at this. 'Why would anyone wish to go to a British penal settlement?'

'I've always admired the French explorers who were there first,' he said. 'I think it would be a fine adventure just to travel halfway round the world.'

'I didn't know about our explorers,' she said.

'Did you know that Napoleon's wife, Josephine, directed them to bring back specimens of both flora and fauna from Australia?' he asked, his face animated. 'I can show you the drawing and painting exhibitions at Josephine's former home, Malmaison, and at Versailles.'

'Oh, I would love that!'

After a few moments, he asked in a languid manner what she wanted to do, suggesting that he was expecting her to say something like, 'get married and have a family'.

'I want to work in the theatre,' she replied coyly, silently predicting that such an ambition would be outside the scope of a respectable bourgeois doctor. When he asked her what she wished to do in the theatre, she looked him in the eye and said, 'Become an actress.'

He laughed, but when she added, 'I'm serious,' he smiled, put down their glasses and began making love to her again.

Adolphe invited her to visit him at his apartment in the grounds of the hospital at Versailles, about twenty kilometres south-west of Paris and close to the beautiful palace. They walked hand in hand through its manicured, symmetrically laid-out gardens. Adolphe took her to see the museum inspired by Emperor Louis-Philippe, which was dedicated to 'all the glories of France'.

Céleste believed that her dreams were coming true. Adolphe was a gentleman interested in the finer things and the culture of France. He was educated and more stable than any man she had met. Most of all he was fun to be with and a good and considerate lover. She enjoyed his company so much that she thought it would be good if she moved in with him. But she decided to wait until he asked her. Adolphe seemed to be very busy at the hospital and

Céleste did not wish to upset the routine, especially as he had just commenced his first appointment as a fully fledged doctor. Her visits to Versailles were rare and he preferred to come to Paris once or twice a week. He would stay the night and leave before dawn to be at work on time. This miffed Céleste somewhat, for she wanted to be with him more, though he quietened her frustration somewhat by leaving gifts and money.

He was surprisingly supportive and encouraging when she made her first moves to become an actress. It was tough going. She visited theatre after theatre, tramping around the streets, including her own earlier stomping ground of the Boulevard du Temple. Directors' assistants regarded her with disdain, perhaps because she threatened their own positions. Whatever the reason, Céleste was learning much about rejection. Finally, a short, plump director of a modest-sized song-and-dance company deigned to see her face to face. His name was Toulouse le Grand, which she thought seemed fabricated, in line with his obvious wig and corset. He asked her what her experience was. She admitted she had never been on stage.

'Nothing?' le Grand said. 'Stand up and turn around slowly.'

Céleste obeyed, uncomfortable with his stare.

'Do you dance?'

'Not really.'

'Sing?'

'Not professionally.'

'Sing something.'

Céleste had a sudden attack of nerves. Her face flushed. Her frazzled brain tried to think of some popular lyrics, but nothing came to mind. His look of contempt and disbelief created a sense of inferiority in her similar to that once generated by Musset.

'You have no experience.' He laughed gruffly. 'And I don't need a tea lady.'

'But I'll learn quickly, Monsieur—'

'This isn't a school.' He chortled again. 'I run a professional troupe, not a kindergarten.'

Le Grand showed her to the door. Outside and alone, Céleste began crying. She wished Adolphe could be there to comfort her. She had to wait three days to see him and by then she was over the director's rejection. Adolphe seemed preoccupied with his own issues, saying only, 'I never understood the attraction to the theatre. No real substance. Unqualified people who think they can perform. Huh!'

Céleste was astonished but not equipped to put another point of view. Instead, she began to learn songs and practise singing them. Denise supported her fierce ambition and applauded her efforts.

A few weeks short of her seventeenth birthday in 1841, Adolphe invited her to a party in Versailles, where he surprised her by asking her to sing. Weeks ago she had choked in front of the unsympathetic director, but the suddenness of this request had not given her time to develop nerves. Besides that, she had practised a few songs and was confident enough to meet her lover's request. There was more than polite applause after her first effort. Some called for more. She obliged. Calm and feeling encouraged, she sang again. Céleste had never had voice training. But she had a very good ear and was a quick learner and clever mimic. This, with her youth, sex appeal and ferocious energy, pulled the audience of about thirty along with her. For this reason, Adolphe seemed pleased and proud of her.

Numbers soon increased. To Céleste's shock and surprise, a well-known up-market prostitute (or *lorette*), Louisa Aumont, arrived. She was twenty-eight years of age, stiff-backed, haughty and assertive. What she lacked in looks she attempted to make up for with extravagant grooming and expensive clothes and jewels. She and other women selling themselves for sex in

Paris's demimonde fell between the street prostitutes and brothel workers, and the grand dames of commercial sex, the courtesans. And similarly to a courtesan, the *lorette* was a kept woman, set up in a private apartment by a businessman, professional or wealthy student. Louisa was typical in that she slid across the boundaries of social acceptability and stigma, and no one dared challenge her morality. *Lorettes* looked down on prostitutes from the brothels, and Louisa was particularly contemptuous towards them. Louisa knew Céleste and saw her as an up-and-coming younger rival. She wasted no time in badmouthing her to Adolphe within earshot of his friends and Céleste herself.

'Didn't I ask you never to invite such women?' Louisa asked. 'Especially that one!'

Adolphe did not say a word on Céleste's behalf. This infuriated Céleste, especially as she realised that Louisa was in a relationship with him. Her presence and attitude made it clear to Céleste that it was Louisa who had been limiting Adolphe to sporadic visits and no commitment.

'If you don't dare to defend me,' Céleste said to the now-flustered Adolphe, 'will you at least have the courage to come away with me?'

Adolphe didn't wish to leave. In a dramatic moment, he was making his choices and letting Céleste know he was more attracted to, and even in love with, Louisa. Stunned and humiliated, Céleste made her exit. She waited in the street for more than two hours, but Adolphe did not come looking for her. Fuelled by emotion, primarily anger at that moment, she began the twenty-kilometre walk back to her Paris apartment. Céleste felt terribly let down. She was in love with Adolphe and had thought this reciprocated. She now realised this was wishful thinking.

This sudden rejection hardened her. She had escaped the dead-end brothel system but had failed to find employment in the theatre. She could look for mundane or menial work, for example as an embroiderer again. But Céleste had been exposed to wealth, glitter and the more privileged classes. She could not imagine herself ever going back to a factory, working long hours in some tedious, repetitive job that earned her a pittance and kept her in poverty.

Céleste vowed to steel herself against all feelings of love towards men like the charming, philandering Adolphe. Instead, she would educate herself as much as possible. She would concentrate on learning to read and write properly. She would acquire knowledge and new skills that would lift her above the likes of Louisa Aumont. Along the way, she would get even with that pompous woman. This new, vindictive streak would propel her, even though, as she dragged her sorry self in the dark and cold through the outskirts of Paris, she did not quite know how.

CHAPTER 9

Dancing Destiny

Céleste knew that she could never return to a brothel or work the streets. Yet she acknowledged that she still had to make a living by selling her body. With the disappointment over Adolphe, she fell into being a lower-ranked *lorette*, with her own modest room to ply her trade. She knew she could not yet aspire to being a courtesan. First she would have to move up the scale of *lorettes*, and to do this she would have to attain notoriety, although not too much to attract the police; or she could try somehow to achieve a measure of fame. Céleste still dreamed beyond the life of a courtesan—to become a performer of some sort, with the theatre at the pinnacle of her ambitions.

She gravitated naturally to the dance halls of Paris, which were open to young men and women of all classes. Céleste loved the glitter, action and glamour, and she was typical of the patrons. The most popular place in 1841 was the Bal Mabille, a modest open-air garden off the Champs-Élysées, which had been set up by Monsieur Mabille a decade earlier. It was a place to eat, drink, dance and be picked up, or to pick up. Bal Mabille was open every night and it was cheap, so Céleste could afford to go alone or with girlfriends. The press loved to report on its goings-on. Few weeks went by without the newspapers referring to someone dancing there. It was not the most fashionable place, not the place for the super-rich and aristocracy, but it attracted so many colourful and interesting people that the press had to report on it if it wanted to keep a finger on the pulse of Paris in this era of growing liberation. Here at Bal Mabille, artists of all art forms, including dancers, came to show off their skills, and the painters came to set up their easels or to gain inspiration for depicting the City of Light.

Céleste saved her hard-earned francs and bought herself the best dress she could afford, along with a colourful bonnet and a fashionable tartan cashmere shawl. She and girlfriends paraded in front of the male peacocks. They set the pace in elegant attire for the hopeful young students, cabbies, barmen, café waiters and bank clerks. If ever there was basic egalitarianism in France, this was its microcosm. Desperate, brave, young and daring Mademoiselle Vénard high-stepped into it. Prominent in the crowd were the *lorettes* such as Louisa Aumont. Céleste had never learned to dance the polka, which was the favourite step of the era at the sophisticated salons of the Faubourg Saint-Germain. The Bal Mabille version was livelier and technique-free, which gave it a vitality and improvisational quality never seen at the salons. Girls with lithe bodies and good legs lifted their skirts high and kicked out. They stayed with the rhythm, yet created steps and movements unique to Bal Mabille. Céleste played with her own version in private and had a vision of performing brilliantly in front of Louisa, Adolphe and his friends.

Bal Mabille had its stars, the couples that everyone came to see dance this exciting variation on the balletic but unemotional waltz. The others followed them like crowds surrounding a street brawl. Céleste observed them with an almost uncontrollable feeling of exhilaration. If she could be in such a couple, she would have her first brush with fame. Such dancers often made the papers, or were sketched by the artists. Where other fans clapped and cheered, Céleste was memorising steps and body contortions. She took special note of one outstanding couple, who always attracted the biggest crowd. The man, Brididi, worked at Bal Mabille and had generated the new craze. He was short with elastic legs and whirring arms. His partner was short, dark and demonic in her movements. He had christened her 'Queen Pomare' after the monarch of Tahiti, which the French had recently colonised.[1] Her real name was Lise Sergent. She was a musical all-rounder who played the piano with skill and sang with panache.

One evening, Brididi and Pomare parted not long after their initial dance, and Brididi began to scour the crowd for another likely young woman.

He had seen Céleste often in his audience of admirers, and approached her, along with two other girls and three men, who were asked to join him in a quadrille, a French-style square dance for four or more. When Brididi asked her to be his partner for this experiment, Céleste told him, 'I've never done this before.' He could see in her face she wanted to try, regardless of the big crowd that would soon surround them.

'I'll teach you,' he said with a confident smile. Céleste handed her shawl to a girlfriend, revealing her short-sleeved silk dress. When the dance began, all eyes soon turned to Brididi and his unknown, alluring new partner. This was different from her athletic, balletic but fun dancing at La Chaumière. Céleste moved forward. The crowd clapped, cheered and urged her on. She squatted at first like a Highland dancer, then stood erect and did her trademark unrefined high kicks, while lifting her dress for a flash of her long legs. Her movements were quick. She was light on her feet. Brididi made a clapping, encouraging gesture with his hands and beamed. He conducted her as they moved around. After ten minutes of this more sedate quadrille trial, they were the only two still dancing.

Céleste showed the zest, vitality, timing and daring that Brididi was looking for. He took a strong liking to her and invited her and Maria la Blonde, also a would-be *lorette*, whom she had befriended inside Saint-Lazare, for a late meal after the Bal Mabille show. They were joined by others and the celebration of the new dancing union went on until 6 a.m. The next day Brididi visited Céleste and had no trouble in persuading her to come to his house so he could teach her the polka. Buoyed by the previous night's experience, she applied herself with unbridled enthusiasm. By the end of a gruelling five-hour session, which went on until 9 p.m., they were both satisfied that she could handle every leap and spin. Céleste drove herself on and on until even Brididi called a halt. She knew that her rival, Louisa Aumont, was very good at this dance. She had not seen her at Bal Mabille, but she knew she would at some point.

Céleste returned to her own room, exhausted but thrilled with the events of the day. She and Maria turned up once more at Bal Mabille, although Brididi had not promised Céleste he would invite her to dance the polka.

Brididi waited until the musical ensemble, at his instruction, started up a polka. He smiled, walked up to Céleste, bowed and reached for her hand. She had a sudden attack of nerves.

'I can't,' she whispered. 'I really can't do this here.'

Some in the crowd urged her to try. Others began clapping. Brididi motioned for her to join him again, and with a kind smile said in her ear, 'You were excellent last night …'

He was interrupted by Louisa Aumont, who was in the crowd with an elderly escort and had pushed her way to the edge of it. She had observed Céleste's hesitation, and remarked loudly and contemptuously, 'Doesn't anyone know this dance?'

Céleste did not have to look around to see who had said it. That arrogant tone chilled her. Pretending not to hear, Céleste had all the motivation she needed. She propelled herself forward and exceeded even Brididi's expectations. The applause was rapturous. An entertainer, if not a renowned dancer, was born. But even as the applause died she heard Louisa's jealous remark, 'How could anyone advertise themselves like that? What a horror!'

Céleste's adrenaline was pumping fast after her performance. She waited until she was close to her tormentor, touched her arm, and said, 'Good evening, Louisa dear. It's a long time since you went to Versailles to see your lover Adolphe, isn't it?'

Louisa went red. She tried to move away, saying, 'I don't know you!'

'Oh, forgive me,' Céleste said, smiling at Louisa's partner. 'I thought Monsieur was your father.'

This time Louisa was too taken aback to respond. She turned away, gripping her escort's arm, but Céleste went on. 'Apologies! I didn't know this was Henri, the old owl you lie to about going to Versailles to visit your aunt. Three times a week, no less!'

Louisa tried to scuttle away, but the damage had been done. Her elderly benefactor was indignant. He stood his ground, looking first at Louisa, then back at Céleste, who turned on her most coquettish smile for him.

'He's not the old monster you paint,' Céleste teased. 'I think Monsieur looks very nice.'

He now seemed confused. Céleste curtseyed and moved off, laughing. Revenge was very sweet when served so decisively. She knew she had lowered herself to Louisa's level, but any guilt dissipated quickly as she began another polka, which lured another group of spectators to her. She radiated energy and some observers rated her better than Queen Pomare. Men swarmed around her, begging for a dance.

Brididi made an off-the-cuff observation that the recently captured Moroccan fort of Mogador in Morocco would be easier to defend than Céleste from her bevy of admirers.[2]

'In fact,' he called to her, 'I shall call you Mogador!'

Reporters and artists picked up on the remark. The press called her 'Mogador' and she had a taste of the fame she craved.

Now the big attraction was the weekly dance-off between the manic Pomare and the vibrant Mogador. But the latter was not satisfied or in any way full of herself. She had bigger aims in life and this success was just a stepping stone to somewhere else, somewhere grander.

Adolphe heard and read about his former girlfriend's spectacular shows and, curious, he went to see for himself. He tried to speak to her, but she ignored him and the young doctor received his first dose of a woman's scorn. She delighted in the attention of many men; some handed her bouquets right in front of Adolphe, who didn't take it well. He tore up the flowers, indicating he was still in love with her. Céleste laughed in his face, but admitted in her memoirs that she still had powerful feelings for him. Nevertheless, she was going to make him pay with declarations, apologies and emotion, and anything else he might concede to her. To her satisfaction, Adolphe demonstrated a seething jealousy.

Later that night, he begged her to come back to him.

'Please, Céleste, please,' he said, 'I love you. I made a terrible mistake in not defending you when Louisa was so insulting. What can I do to make it up to you?'

She considered him for several seconds before saying, 'I'll think about getting back with you on one condition.'

'Yes?'

'You make Louisa apologise to me publicly.'

In the heightened circumstances, Adolphe did not hesitate. He took Louisa over to Céleste.

'I want you to tell Céleste that I'm not your lover and never have been,' he said, pointing at Louisa. 'You also must say you're sorry to have been so hard on her at that Versailles party last month.'

Louisa puffed out her chest. Her expression was defiant.

'C'mon,' he demanded. 'Apologise!'

After a brief pause, she looked at the ground and then up at Céleste.

'I apologise for hurting you. I regarded you as a rival.' With a glance at Adolphe she mumbled, 'We've never been lovers.'

Holding back tears, Louisa scurried off into the crowd.

Exhilarated with the triumph, Céleste kissed Adolphe.

'We can start afresh,' she said, 'but I won't let you forget how you humiliated me; how you forced me to make the long walk from Versailles to Paris …'

Adolphe hated her dancing at Bal Mabille. He begged her to the point of tears to stop, but she ignored him. She was not going to miss her encounters with Pomare, and the gratuities thrust at them for their tornado-like competitions. And Céleste loved the press coverage she was receiving. She and Pomare had backers who would sling them cash for performances. Bets were placed on who would attract the bigger crowds or cheers. One punter thought it would be a good idea if the two famed dancers actually met each other. Money was wagered on who would win a catfight. So it was arranged; however, although Pomare took herself very seriously, Céleste had a measure of humour and vision, even for one so young. She was never going to lower herself to hair-pulling, nail-scratching and biting.

They approached each other. The crowd of fervent supporters fell silent. Then a rhythmic clap began. Céleste stroke forward. Pomare, her black eyes tight and fierce-looking, came a few steps closer. They stood about two metres apart, like gunslingers waiting for one or the other to make the first move. A few catcalls split the warm night air. Céleste took a pace forward, smiled and reached out a hand. Pomare's face relaxed. They shook hands. The crowd clapped and cheered.

Pomare leaned close and said, 'Great to meet you. I always wanted to.'

'Same here. I love your dancing.'

The Bal Mabille competition continued. Mogador and Pomare attracted equal numbers of fans and admirers some distance from each other in the crowded and now ultra-popular garden. They soon became firm friends and visited each other's homes. Céleste was saddened to see that Pomare lived in poorer circumstances. There was no food in her room and Céleste learned that she had forgone meals to save money. Much of what she earned went to her mother to look after her child. The glitter and glamour on the surface amounted to little. In reality the impoverished life she was leading had etched itself into her lovely yet severe face and skeletal body.

That seminal summer and early autumn of 1842 ended for Céleste and Pomare on 30 September when Bal Mabille closed down. Both girls would be out of work. But they had both achieved the press notability they wanted rather than the notoriety. And Céleste had created a provocative, skirt-lifting, high-kicking dance, which would later be known as the cancan, meaning 'tittle-tattle' or 'scandal'. She began it at the music and dance halls such as Bal Mabille, toyed with it often at La Chaumière and made some of the risqué movements her own. On occasions, Céleste went out of her way to wear long skirts, petticoats and black stockings. Her athleticism allowed her to lift the garments and kick higher than anyone else. After perfecting the leg movements, she added arm swings, featuring the elbows moving in and out from the waist. Many observers, including newspaper reporters, viewed the gyrations and skirt manipulations as amoral. The police prohibited it twice. Céleste was careful where she gave performances because she feared the police would use any excuse to send her back to prison. But her natural instincts, exhibitionism and courage to break social boundaries in art saw her perform the provocative dance as often as possible.

CHAPTER 10

Horsewoman Extraordinaire

Almost on the same day in late October, both Céleste and Pomare learned they would gain opportunities in the theatre as dancers. They celebrated with champagne they could not afford at the Café Anglais, which they both loved. Adolphe footed the sizeable bill, knowing he was still paying for his earlier humiliation of Céleste. It forced him to ask her if she would ever forgive him. She replied, 'Never!' She had the good doctor exactly where she wanted him and he had to comply with her wishes or depart. Her newfound fame had given her a certain sense of power. Adolphe could take it or leave it.

One of Brididi's friends worked at the Théâtre Beaumarchais and he lined up an engagement for Céleste to appear in a revue. She would have to learn to dance the mazurka. This had been created in sixteenth-century Poland and made popular in recent years by that country's finest composer, Frédéric Chopin. Céleste's confidence was high after her success with the polka, and she adapted to the mazurka quickly and efficiently. The colourful headgear, military band–style jacket, very tight white britches and long black boots allowed her to display her physical features, primarily, but not exclusively, her derrière and legs. Patrons rushed to buy the front-row 'gynaecological' seats and the theatre was often sold out, especially on Fridays and Saturdays.[1]

Mogador was soon the major attraction at the Beaumarchais as the press and sketch artists were now following her. On the matter of payment, she was promised much and given nothing. The odd patron would slip her some francs after the show, but the theatre management was playing on the belief, accurate enough in Céleste's case, that she would not find work easily as a dancer elsewhere. The theatre owners knew she was registered as a prostitute and therefore under intermittent police surveillance. They were also aware that Céleste had failed to report once a fortnight to the police, who had called on her at the theatre to remind her of her obligations under the *Registration of Prostitutes Act*.

This weighed on Céleste, who was nervous about walking alone in the major boulevards, and particularly Montmartre, where the police paid close attention to any woman, even if they were promenading rather than loitering with intent to solicit for sex.

'Every time a man looked at me,' Céleste wrote in her memoirs, 'I was afraid he was an inspector … My life, dominated by fear, was atrocious.'

Yet despite these general hazards and financial deprivations, Céleste believed she was on the road to becoming an actress. But when Pomare was jailed along with her husband for a crime he had committed, Céleste could no longer stand the parsimonious attitude of the Beaumarchais. She marched into the office of the owner/manager, Monsieur Robert Guichard, and said, 'I want a piece of the gate!'

'Impossible!' Guichard replied.

'Why? You're playing to packed houses.'

'You don't understand, Mogador …'

'I deserve some sort of stipend. Many people come to see me.'

'Mogador, the theatre is closing down in a few days.'

'What?'

'The company has huge debts. The last few months we've kept doors open only to reduce the debts.'

Céleste was incredulous. Flush-faced, she said angrily, 'You mean I've been used to get you out of a stinking financial hole?'

'You may look at it that way if you wish.'

Céleste's brief foray into a legitimate trade on the boards, where she could earn an honest living, would be over after only a few months. It left her in despair.

Adolphe had been furiously jealous of her success, so much so that Céleste had called off their relationship. Now she was alone and it seemed her only choice was to work as a *lorette* once more. To cheer herself up she parted with several francs to have her hair and nails attended to at the parlour of a beautician friend. While sitting in the chair being pampered, she told her story of bad luck and how much she desired to be on the stage. The aged male backer of the parlour happened to overhear her. When the beautician had finished working on Céleste, the old man stood in front of her.

'Do you ride horses?' he asked with a querulous tilt of the head.

'I have, yes,' Céleste lied.

The old man walked around her, stroking his chin and nodding his head. Finally he said, 'You're a fine figure of a young woman. Are you willing to take a chance?'

'That's the only way to make an interesting life, isn't it?' Céleste replied.

The old man smiled. 'I'm looking for an elegant young woman to ride at the new Hippodrome.'[2]

This new Hippodrome was in Montmartre. It was a kind of outdoor circus in an open stadium that would hold 8000 people. The beautician thought it an excellent idea. Céleste had shown courage at the Bal Mabille and on stage. It seemed another, perhaps more enterprising, step into show business.

The old gentleman told Céleste she would be taught by the best riding master in Paris. She would be ready to perform on horseback in a month.

Uppermost in Céleste's mind was her impoverished state and the prospect of not even tips at the theatre.

'How much will I be paid?'

'You'll start with 100 francs a month.'

'For how long?'

'Let's start with a one-year contract.'

'So 1200 francs?'

The old man nodded.

'I accept!' she said with a big smile and shook his hand.

A week after signing, Céleste was being trained by the experienced ringmaster, Monsieur Franconi Laurent. He drove her hard with three sessions a day, starting with a gentle trot on a docile mare, and building within a week to a more challenging stallion. His advice was simple: Céleste should never whip her mount hard enough to draw blood. It was important to cajole the horses in her charge, not yell at them. But she also had to make sure she was respected. A light rein should be kept at all times, and the horse should never be jerked. The ringmaster told her to let the horse know what she wanted.

'If your mount is feeling good,' Laurent said, 'he'll do most of what you want. Try not to dig a stirrup into him if possible. It may be necessary in the heat of competition, but again, don't draw blood. Your heels, as a rule, should be soft. Same with your hands. Your mount will then respond more with what you want. Depending on the horse, sweet words of praise in its ear will help. The animal may well know your voice, if you've practised on it, as you will have. People say horses have the minds of three- or four-year-old humans. I don't believe this. They're more than instinctive animals. They have intelligence and common sense. They have personalities. You, I'm told, are a person of character and personality. Keep your back straight in the saddle. You're not a jockey, you're a grand performer at the Hippodrome, so ride proudly and look confident, even if you're not. Act it. I'm told you want to be an actor, so start at the Hippodrome.'

Laurent was determined to have her ready for the grand opening. But he had pushed her to the limit. Céleste bled from the nose in what a doctor described as a 'slight haemorrhage' and she was prescribed three days' rest. Although not fully fit, she returned to training. There was a troupe of sixteen, from which ten would be selected for the opening night. Her determination saw her chosen for the team after just two months' training. She was to appear in three acts: the grand parade, a race between five riders and finally a stag hunt.

There was not a spare seat in the stadium on the first night. Anybody who was anybody among the city's elite was in attendance.

The parade of ten female riders swept onto the arena to a terrific roar. When the crowd settled to watch the horses prancing around the perimeter, Céleste heard her name called many times as people spotted her. 'Mogador! Mogador!'

A band played. She would have preferred to have been in the first act, but had to wait, mounted on her large white stallion, Pedro. Her nerves built, and she felt the same stage fright as at the Bal Mabille. She shrank lower, as if hiding behind Pedro's long neck and mane. She felt a slap on the shoulder. It was Laurent.

'Are you going to ride like that?' he demanded. 'Pull yourself together, if you please!'

It was just what she needed. She sat up ramrod straight.

'Good, now you look like a broomstick,' Laurent said. 'Get settled into your saddle, body straight but not stiff, elbows in, head high, fingers firm but not hard.'

Céleste was now focused on following his instructions.

'That's better,' Laurent added, 'and don't be afraid, you've a good mount.'

He patted Pedro's head and remarked about Céleste to an inquisitive spectator nearby, 'She's my pupil; she's good …'

The first act came to an end. Céleste lined up with the nine other riders and their mounts for a 600-metre race of two circuits of the arena. A starting horn sounded. Pedro got away well, but Céleste found herself fifth after half the first circuit. She looked over at the other riders. The two in the lead were leaning over their horses' necks in jockey-like positions. This was not the stiff-backed equestrienne positioning that Laurent had insisted on. Céleste leaned forward.

'Go Pedro, go!' she said, sharply, not shouting. She did not use her whip, instead she dug her left heel in with every word to him. The seventeen-hands-high Pedro got the message. He lifted, and was soon lying third behind the two who had led from the start. Into the second circuit, the spectators were on their feet, shouting. Many had bet on Mogador because she was the only performer they knew. A chant went up for her from one section of the crowd. Céleste began to pass her rivals. Her heart beat faster. She began to think she could even win the race.

Céleste took a risk and cut a sharp corner, nearly hemming herself against a barrier, to squeeze through ahead of the second-placed horse. The crowd roared. It inspired her. She spoke to Pedro again, this time saying almost gently, 'Go for it, boy! Go for it!'

'I shut my eyes and left everything to the horse,' she said, 'and just dug my heel into his left flank.'

Pedro responded and pegged back the lead animal, a big chestnut Arabian stallion. Pedro's head was now bobbing with effort. His rider, eyes still closed, held on. With the finish tape only twenty metres away they were dead level, but Pedro found an extra strong stride to end up ahead. Céleste heard her name being chanted again, around the stadium this time. She opened her eyes and found she had won.

She patted Pedro, said sweet things in his ear, and then paraded around the ring to sustained applause from an appreciative crowd. She was more thrilled than at any other moment in her life to that point. Bal Mabille had been exhilarating; the Hippodrome made her ecstatic. She walked up steps to a dais to receive the victory bouquet. The cheer was the biggest of the show and demonstrated she was the crowd favourite.

A proud Laurent helped her prepare for the final event—the stag hunt—where a deer was released and chased down by dogs and mounted horses. Céleste noticed congealed blood on Pedro's left flank. In her frenzy to win, she had dug her heel in too sharply. She patted the horse, made a fuss of him and apologised. Then she gave him four sugar lumps and if the horse had been miffed at her treatment of him, all was now forgotten.

The hunt began with the release of the poor stag, who wandered about in a daze at all the noise and movement. Then the dogs were let loose. They had been cooped up for forty-eight hours, their handlers believing this would cause them to be hungry for the chase. But the dogs were over-excited at being freed, and with the crowd laughing at their wild antics, they obeyed no orders. The stag was the last thing on their minds as they zipped about the arena at a frenetic pace, with a couple even dashing past the disoriented and almost stationary stag. Céleste led Pedro into the centre of the arena, but there would be no chase. Instead there was farce. The crowd seemed to enjoy the chaos, as if it had been planned as an amusing end to the afternoon's events, with only circus clowns missing.

That spectacular first day lifted Céleste's self-confidence higher than ever before. And feeling more secure thanks to her year-long contract, she moved nearer to the Hippodrome to the more distinguished Faubourg Saint-Honoré.

CHAPTER 11

Mogador, Courtesan

The continued Hippodrome success lifted Céleste's reputation from being a notable in the dance halls to being a high-profile Parisienne, simultaneously famous and notorious. Her courage, fiercely competitive spirit and speedily acquired skills as a horsewoman attracted people and press attention. This gave her a strong image, and independence of a sort. With that weekly advertisement, Céleste felt certain her popularity in the complex world she lived in and was creating for herself, was the key to gaining access to the richer, better-bred and more worthy partners available now, not just those in France. It caused her to always take risks in the races, and in so doing she discovered she had a high pain threshold. Falls, crashes with other competitors, hitting barriers and other mishaps were a weekly event. The riders marvelled at their luck.

'Every day accidents happened in which we might have been killed,' Céleste noted, 'but generally we escaped with a few bruises. I would rest for a week and then go on again, more wildly than ever.'

So alluring was the Hippodrome show that many young women lined up to join the troupe, which made those already in the troupe take even greater risks. Some of the races were choreographed to an extent, to make them more spectacular, and despite the desire each rider had to win, there was a good camaraderie.

Pain and fear, the ringmaster told them, were not to be displayed. The audience did not pay to view frightened and vulnerable performers. This was Céleste's attitude by nature.

After a month, the organisers devised more daring races, including a steeplechase with formidable hedge barriers that would never be allowed at any normal horse race. Céleste was now on a lovely and highly spirited chestnut mare named Grace.

'She would tremble for an hour before going on,' Céleste noted, 'and when the gate was opened, she was already in a full sweat.'

One day Grace was more anxious than usual and Céleste almost beat the horn to start the three circuits of about 1000 metres. It had high hurdles every 200 metres, a big commitment for both rider and mount. She and Grace led the field by a long way down the straight on the first circuit. Then Céleste felt herself tilting to one side.

'I wanted to stop,' she said, 'but I was right in front of a hedge. [Grace] jumped. I tried to throw myself to the side so I would not be dragged under her feet. I fell on the track, past the hedge.'

All those coming up behind jumped over Céleste. She covered her head as other horses galloped by, but she was not trampled on. Céleste felt the pain from a strained foot, though her commitment to her image and the show overrode it. She examined her foot, decided that no bones were broken and looked around for Grace, who had galloped off. Céleste brushed herself down and signalled for stewards to bring the horse to her. In full view of a clapping, cheering public, she mounted Grace, patted her and spoke words of reassurance to which the horse had become accustomed. Céleste trotted back into the race, aware that Grace might now baulk at the next hurdle. She took it carefully and the brave mount cleared it easily, drawing a roar from the audience. They finished the run last but received the biggest, most prolonged applause.

All such incidents added to her popularity. Céleste felt it was time to wipe her name off the dreaded prostitutes' registry. She made an appointment with the Prefect of Police. Her reputation had preceded her. He knew about her performances at the Hippodrome.

'It's too soon,' he told her.

'Why?' she asked, 'I haven't worked in a brothel for some time. I have regular work, as you're aware, Monsieur.'

'But what happens if the Hippodrome closes down?'

'What do you mean?'

'You'd be out of work. You'd have no regular, respectable employment.'

Céleste had no answer to what the harsh but experienced prefecture was alluding to.

'You'll be monitored and we'll note your progress or otherwise.'

This threat had a poor impact on Céleste. She worried more than ever about police surveillance and possible efforts to entrap her, send her to jail again and make sure her name stayed on the registry. One night her concierge told her that a policeman had visited and demanded she take down her garden window boxes from her balcony or she would be fined. Céleste obeyed the directive, believing she was being watched.

She suspected that some members of the establishment and police were mean-spirited about her fame and success.

They seemed to object to the fact that a young woman from *nowhere* could weave her way up through the social ranks, propelled by her skills as a dancer and glorified stunt jockey, and her sexual charms.

Justified or otherwise, she was nervous, sometimes paranoid, that every approach to her might be a ruse by the police. Scores of young suitors, including rich local dilettantes and foreign noblemen with abodes in Paris—which was fast becoming the city to be in—wanted to meet her. Having Mogador on their arm at any social function was a prize, a testament to their virility. They employed female intermediaries, forerunners to agents, to arrange introductions. She accepted their blandishments, gifts and invitations, but she rejected them.

She commented in her memoirs that the inclination among the *lorettes* and courtesans was to always accept an offer.

'Nothing gave me greater satisfaction,' she wrote in her diary, 'than to say "no".'

This increased her exclusivity. The men she chose had to be special, and she had to like and respect them. This made her one of the most established and sought-after courtesans in Europe.

But she did say 'yes' to a couple of titled noblemen from other countries. Perhaps this was because she believed this would enhance her status without offending wealthy families in France, who might object to one of their own involving himself with a woman of her background. Or maybe her motivation was that she hoped one day to be a woman with a title herself, which might help her expunge the past. The most notable of her choices was the Spanish Duke of Osuna, Mariano Téllez-Girón, who was a decade her senior and a dissolute type, intent on working his way through inherited riches.[1]

Many of Europe's male aristocrats of the era prided themselves on *not* working. They were openly disdainful of those from their class who had some employ even in the prestigious diplomatic corps or armed services, or anyone who had to earn a living. They preferred to be known for their hedonistic lifestyle, whoring and partying.

When Mariano met Céleste through an *entremetteuse* (agent) who Céleste trusted, he was busy spending away a vast fortune buying land and art, investing in buildings in Paris, and furnishing his castles in Spain. The duke was thirty, unmarried and with no intention of bothering about that institution. At some point he would have to consider it so that the family assets would be passed down. But like many of his male companions, that would only be a formality, a necessity at a future time that would not curb his gluttonous and conspicuous consumption of anything money (or credit if they ran out of funds) could buy.

Mariano was always mixing with the very pinnacle of European nobility and royalty. He represented Spain at the crowning of Queen Victoria in England in June 1838. Whenever the Spanish needed someone from their upper ranks to represent the nation as a wealthy nobleman rather than a diplomat, he was recruited. Céleste chose him, too, and he was the first society notable after Musset with whom she took up. He showered her with gifts, starting with a brand-new ornate, maroon-coloured carriage, with horses and a driver. Riding the boulevards in style was the most public of advertisements that she was now in the top echelon of the demimonde courtesans, much higher than former rival Louisa Aumont. Another present was a large second-floor apartment on the Rue de l'Arcade. Mariano was short, balding and overweight and he found it a struggle, climbing five flights of stairs to reach his new paramour. Arriving at her door, he would be out of breath and in need of a stiff drink. It didn't always augur well for sex. (It seems dancing a polka was enough to have Mariano clutching his chest.) Céleste was more of a status symbol for him, as he was for her. Not that Céleste cared. She was not in love with the duke, though her affection was often lifted by his largesse, such as the installation of a new piano in the salubrious new apartment.

Mariano loved his opera and music and was delighted to pay for expensive lessons for her from a friend of his, the Italian master Pederlini. They proved more costly than anyone anticipated. Pederlini had a friend, the well-known Italian tenor Monsieur Bettini. Aged thirty-two, he was dark and tall, although with a developing paunch that would eventually rival that of the duke. He, like the duke and Pederlini, had been smitten by the brave and attractive Mogador in her Hippodrome performances. He invited her to sit in an expensive box at the opera to watch him make his debut. This was a show of finesse that the duke, who was away in Madrid, never quite displayed.

Bettini enchanted Céleste with his first big performance at the opera. He worked on her diligently and she succumbed to his charms. They made passionate love at the Rue de l'Arcade nest where the duke had ensconced Céleste.

They were discreet. There was something vaguely theatrical about the liaison, which may have been why it appealed to Céleste. Bettini would creep up the stairs after dark and leave before dawn. She watched him at the opera, but they did not frequent cafés or salons together. Bettini thought himself a cook and insisted on creating the meals during their assignations at her place or his on the Rue de Richelieu. Sadly, his culinary skills were limited.

'I could never bear macaroni,' Céleste said, 'which was the staple dish. I detested cheese and it was used on everything.'

Céleste was not in love with him or his cooking, she simply enjoyed his attention and flamboyance. Also, he was more fun than Mariano.

Céleste was always loyal to her female friends, from the unfortunate Lise/Pomare to the depressed Maria la Blonde from Saint-Lazare. Josephine, a companion from Théâtre Beaumarchais, fell on hard times after a failed relationship with an actor, who drained her of her limited wealth. Céleste generously invited her to her apartment, gave her jewels and dresses to partly restore her self-esteem, and secured a riding job for her at the Hippodrome. But this only made Josephine envious of Céleste's apparent success at everything, including men. Her emotions boiled over into spite and she informed the corpulent Mariano of Céleste's affair with Bettini.

Céleste threw Josephine out, but had to see her each week at the Hippodrome. The duke was miffed. Yet the experience was no more than a blow to his ego, when he thought money bought everything, including love and loyalty. He ended the relationship with Céleste, though he was decent enough to allow her to stay in the apartment rent-free, keep the maid, and use the carriage for another three months.

The benefit of their split was a more open relationship with Bettini, who now wined and dined her away from their apartments, and she did her best to avoid the macaroni and cheese ('like his mother used to make') that he always ordered. However, she did appreciate his partying. One night she arrived at his place to find him and his friends eating macaroni and cheese, and finishing their first glass of wine.

'Here is my one vice!' Bettini said, holding and kissing her.

'Why do you put up with a comment like that?' a large, middle-aged courtesan, Françoise, said in a tone of mock indignation.

'It's not an issue,' Céleste replied with a smile. 'I am of course wicked, but I think it's better for me to be in the company of cultivated men.'

'Bettini, cultivated? Bah!' Françoise laughed. 'But we all agree he has a magnificent voice.'

'He has good taste.'

'I agree that he's not a boor,' Françoise said, turning to Bettini and raising a glass to him, 'although he is a complete narcissist. But at least he's witty.'

'Better than a dullard!' Céleste said, and they both raised their glasses to him. 'He lives the hedonistic life of the artist. But this creative era provides for it. And I like it.'

'You're a discerning type,' Françoise observed. 'We both enjoy the pleasures of the flesh ...'

'More the benefits of the associations this brings, such as pleasures of the mind, and the refinement of art.'

Françoise gestured to the up-market crowd in the apartment.

'You can certainly gain that here tonight.'

'Exactly.'

Moments later, Bettini and his friends pushed up the windows looking down onto the street. Bettini, another man and two women began to sing. Within a minute a crowd had gathered below them. Soon there was a traffic jam as people stopped their carriages to listen. Police appeared, but instead of moving the traffic on, they stopped to listen and marvel at the spontaneous show from Bettini and company. After they'd had their cultural fill, they hastened up to the apartment.

'Please, Monsieur Bettini,' one of the cops said, 'you must close the windows. You're causing traffic chaos!'

Bettini shrugged and obeyed the directive. Then he went on singing with the others.

CHAPTER 12

Chariots of Desire and Ire

The 1847 season at the Hippodrome opened in stifling heat in early July. It was Céleste's third, and the competition was stiffer, the stunts more dangerous and the conditions worse. She dreaded the steeplechases in which she had already fallen badly on three occasions and doctors had bled her. This was the arcane method of easing bruising, by draining blood from around the affected area. It was a fatiguing business and she hated it more than the actual falls. Her pay of 100 francs a month had been reduced and she was not earning money commensurate with the risks she was taking.

Céleste asked for a raise. It was rebuffed. The owners knew there would always be young women and men lining up to join the troupe, and many performed for nothing in the hope of making a name for themselves. The time and investment in training had been condensed since the opening. Céleste noted that this did not matter to the show's administrators, as long as they made money.

'They despise the ones who make them rich,' she said. 'If it were not for the police keeping an eye on them, four out of every ten [performers] would be killed. No effort was made to avoid accidents.'

The performers were given lame horses that fell when pushed to win. This created crashes that the public came to see. The Hippodrome now resembled a Roman colosseum, and in that light the organisers revived the concept of the ancient chariot race. But their approach would have made even Ben Hur cautious.

Céleste was horrified by one steeplechase she witnessed. An Englishman failed to clear a ditch four metres deep. The horse had to be put down, and the Englishman was knocked out. His teeth were smashed and there was a big gash on his forehead. When he recovered consciousness, a doctor ordered him to lie down. But aware that the police were in attendance a director had him removed from the arena and sent to hospital. Céleste claimed this was to avoid the event being banned. She protested, abused the director and said the man should be sent to her apartment. But then another director stepped in, agreed with Céleste and said, 'Take the poor man to my apartment.'

Accidents like this occurred in every show. Céleste was asked to try out for the event, but without any instruction on how to prepare the horses or negotiate the jumps. She was forced to accept the advice of unreliable jockeys. The good teachers were too expensive for the Hippodrome owners. The cheaper choices were 'shady characters … who were almost always tipsy'.

Céleste was aghast when the jockeys took off at breakneck speed. It took her a dozen circuits to master the hurdles, which were very high. By the end of the training her hands were bleeding.

This was the moment she lost her enjoyment in performing. She wanted to quit the Hippodrome, but she felt trapped. She cared little now for the fame it had brought. There was no point in carrying on until she was badly injured or dead. But as ever, she wished to have a measure of independence, which reduced her need for benefactors for her sexual favours.

This dilemma forced her to accept the even more dangerous chariot race early in the season. The act, featuring the three best riders—Céleste, and two other young women, Louise and Angele—was the most deadly ever devised at the Hippodrome. The costumes were magnificent.

'I wore a red Phrygian bonnet with gold stars,' Céleste wrote, 'a white, gold-embroidered knee-length tunic, slit to the hips, buskins and a great cloak over the right shoulder, pinned to the left side by a cameo brooch.'

Céleste was not aware that both Bettini and Mariano (well separated) were both in the packed audience and enraptured by her stunning appearance, bravery and dignified, daredevil efforts.

The three chariots criss-crossed each other. Occasionally, wheels bumped with a grating sound heard above the din of the crowd. The women, standing upright in the Roman tradition, used long whips and were lucky to keep their feet. The event was staged up to a point, but on the home straight it was a genuine race, and Céleste, showing the grit that had helped make her a superstar of the show, forged to the front at the finish line. Huge garlands of flowers were handed to her on a dais.

Bettini and Mariano were not the only men in love with her. Probably every man in the stadium, and not a few women, fell at her feet that day. But appearances can be deceptive. As ever, Céleste delivered that glittering smile as she acknowledged the chants of 'Mogador!' 'Mogador!' The heat and tension, however, were debilitating. She had a severe headache and went home to bed.

Bettini arrived at her place, just wanting to be near her. Within half an hour, the maid, her voice full of anxious excitement, announced, 'The duke is at the door!' Mariano seemed to have overcome the humiliation of Céleste cheating on him, and he wished to pay his respects. After all, he was still paying her rent and had not yet taken back her carriage.

'Oh my goodness!' Céleste exclaimed to Bettini. 'I don't want him to see you here.' She pointed to a small cubicle at the foot of her bed and asked him to hide in it.

Bettini frowned and refused.

'Get in,' she ordered, 'or I shall never see you again!'

Bettini cursed, swallowed his dignity and squeezed into the cubicle, muttering expletives. Then the duke burst into the room.

'Why did you keep me waiting in the anteroom?' he demanded.

'Oh, the egos of you men!' Céleste said. 'I was using my footbath. My feet are so sore after the race. And I'm getting used to walking again.'

'What? You have the carriage.'

'Yes, but on a whim you could take it away.'

The duke looked mystified. Then changed his expression and said, 'You were magnificent today. You handled the chariot so admirably.'

'Thank you, but it's given me a terrible headache. I think I have a migraine coming on.'

'Céleste. You must come out to dinner with me.'

'I must?' she said, hands on hips, adding cynically, 'All you great lords are amazing. I find "you must" really charming! How do you know I don't have another engagement? I haven't heard from you for two weeks.'

'I'm rich enough to have you go back on your word to others,' Mariano said, reaching a crescendo of pomposity that left Céleste speechless. 'Get dressed and be at the Café Anglais by six.'

He swept out before she could protest.

The farce continued. Bettini burst out of the cubicle, seething.

'You cannot have a heart to live with a man like that!' he said, pointing at her. 'And I thought you had a big one. That man doesn't love you!'

Bettini fumed in fractured French. 'I will escort you to the Café Anglais, then leave you. Forever!'

'I am *not* joining the duke, but not for your sake. I really do have a headache. I want to be alone, to rest.'

Céleste nodded to the door and said firmly, 'Please leave, now.'

The duke came the next day to check on her. He was 'cold and dour'. He could not understand anyone who did not bend to his will. But Céleste believed that, because she did not give in to his frequent whims, the duke had a certain affection for her. Despite the rift caused by the affair with Bettini, Mariano still wanted some sort of relationship with her.

In mid-July, Céleste awoke to a lovely summer's day after a night out with Pomare, with whom she kept up a strong friendship. But for some reason she felt uneasy, then depressed. The maid took one look at her and thought she might be unwell. Something was wrong. Céleste could not eat breakfast. She confided in the maid that she had a strong sense of foreboding.

'I'm appearing at the Hippodrome today,' she said, 'and I have an idea I might break my neck.'

The maid attempted to console her. But Céleste knew that the acts were becoming more and more dangerous. The first two acts went off without incident. Céleste relaxed a fraction, though just before the chariot race she asked her two competitors, Louise and Angele, not to press too hard because she wasn't feeling well. Her mental state was fragile. Angele was sympathetic, saying she should not worry; they had all experienced that sort of feeling.

The superb weather ensured a packed house, which for the first time included her mother. Out of curiosity, Anne-Victoire had bought a ticket. She had heard rumours that the star attraction, Mogador, was her daughter.

The riders began as usual, floating their chariots seamlessly across in front of each other in turn, the timing perfect as they built speed. Céleste had just overtaken Louise and was about to overtake Angele. They reached the curve on the track near the stables.

'Out of the corner of my eye I saw Louise riding very close to me,' Céleste said. 'I was about to whip my horses to spur them on when I felt a powerful shock.'

A wheel of Louise's chariot had become tangled in the back of Céleste's chariot. A hideous grating sound rang out around the arena. Louise seemed to panic. Instead of stopping, she whipped her horses to pass Céleste. This dragged Céleste's chariot with her. The shaft jabbed her horse on its right side, causing it to rear against a post and whinny in distress. It fell over backwards, forcing the other horse down with it. The animals tried to get back up but instead tipped over the chariot. Céleste still had hold of the reins, but one of the horses hit her shoulder and she let go in terrific pain. The horses kept struggling to move. They dragged the chariot and Céleste, who was facedown in the dirt, for about thirty metres. One of the chariot's wheels ran over her thigh before a steward managed to stop the horses. One of them had a broken leg and was put down in full view of the gaping audience.

Someone pointed at the motionless, prone Céleste and called, 'Mogador's dead!'

Onlookers were distraught. Women cried. People climbed onto the arena fence to see what had happened to Céleste as doctors examined her.

'I opened my eyes,' she recalled, 'I got to my knees, then stood up. I ran my hand over my right thigh. I pushed people away. I wanted to make sure I had no broken bones! I managed to walk but with agonising pain, leaving a trail of blood behind me.'

Céleste saluted the crowd, took a few more steps, then collapsed.

'I was revived, then bled twice,' Céleste said. 'The blood was not coming out.'

Studs on the wheels, designed to prevent skidding on the track's curves, had lacerated her thigh, leaving a wide ring of purple flesh. Her knee was dislocated and fluid was building up around the cap.

The Hippodrome doctor prescribed compresses to poultice her wounds. She was taken to her apartment and helped into bed. After six days of rest, the wounds had not improved. By chance, a young admirer she did not know dropped in to see how she was. The man decided she was not receiving the right attention.

'I'm going to send you the best surgeon in Paris,' he declared and left. The next day at 9 a.m. a very oveweight man arrived, announcing he was the surgeon the stranger had sent. He removed her bandages, then pressed so hard on her knee she screamed. He then examined the thigh wound, which had partially scabbed over. Gangrene had begun to set in. The surgeon placed two fingers either side of the wound. Céleste thought he was going to squeeze again and she begged him not to.

'Now don't be childish,' the surgeon said. 'Do you wish to keep this beautiful leg?'

At that moment, Anne-Victoire entered the bedroom, crying. Céleste had not seen her for four years, since their last meeting at the prefecture's office.

'Mama!' Céleste cried.

The distraction allowed the surgeon to open the wound. He mopped up the blood with a towel while Céleste protested angrily. She pulled her leg away.

'You really hate me, right?' he said with a laugh. 'Well, I'm not here to be liked. I want to make you well. Now, I must check the bone and burn the flesh.'

'Never!' Céleste yelled. 'You'll never touch me again. I'd rather die!'

Anne-Victoire moved close and placated her. 'Be brave, my darling, be brave!'

Céleste, ashamed of showing weakness, obeyed. She placed her foot on the surgeon's knee to brace herself as he rummaged in his bag for a scalpel. He then spread the flesh apart and scraped the bone. It was excruciatingly painful for Céleste, who clung to her maid. Next, he cauterised the wounds and dressed them.

The surgeon instructed Anne-Victoire and the maid to put an oil cloth under her and a wooden rod on top of the injured knee. They were to fill a still with ice, which would melt onto the wound, day and night.

When the surgeon left, Céleste, with mixed emotions about seeing her mother again, asked how she'd known she was injured. Anne-Victoire explained how she came to be at the Hippodrome.

'Every day [after the accident] I received news about you,' Anne-Victoire said. 'Then I heard that your leg might have to be amputated. I couldn't stand it any longer. Here I am. Do you mind?'

'On the contrary,' Céleste replied, which was as far as she would go in embracing her mother's sudden visit.

Anne-Victoire moved into the apartment to care for her. Céleste was keen to know if she was still with Vincent but dared not spoil the moment by asking her.

Two days later, the surgeon came to cauterise the wound a second time. Once done, he patted Céleste's cheek and said with a satisfied smile, 'The wounds are pink. I was afraid of gangrene but you are saved. You'll keep your leg.' He paused and added sombrely, 'If at all possible, give up this profession.'

Céleste was tearful and most grateful. 'Sir, how can I repay you for the care you've given me?'

'You don't owe me anything,' the cheerful roly-poly surgeon replied. 'I'm no longer practising. It took an incident like this to get me out. I'm too fat! I cannot climb stairs anymore.'

He left Céleste without telling her his name.

Anne-Victoire and Bettini both urged her to take the doctor's advice and give away her daredevil acts. She listened but was stubborn, saying she would ask for a raise at the end of the season. If she didn't receive it, she would quit.

Céleste recovered in six weeks. She returned to the Hippodrome for the last show of the season and was affronted to see that she had been replaced. Infuriated, she demanded she be given her costume and a place in the chariot event. This was granted, but despite her physical fitness, her mind was still scarred. She marched out to her chariot to grand applause, for she was still a drawcard and well remembered.

'I was very emotional,' she recalled, 'I lost my head and stopped at the second lap.'

This breakdown almost caused another accident as the chariot behind nearly crashed into her. She slowly guided her chariot out of the arena. The crowd applauded politely, unaware of the reason for her withdrawal.

A few days later, Céleste arranged for a meeting with the director and asked for a raise.

'Why should I give you a raise?' he asked. 'Do you not manage your own affairs? What do a few hundred francs more or less mean to you? I plan to decrease personnel. I have more women than I need.'

The director had seen her breakdown. He had decided that Mogador had lost her nerve, and he had plenty of younger no-name performers he could use. On balance, he reckoned he could do as well without her. He stood firm and Céleste left in despair. Her mother tried to console her. Anne-Victoire recalled a recent fire at the Hippodrome and speculated that the business may have been in financial difficulties. The novelty was wearing off after three years of success.

Céleste returned the next day to pick up her things, hoping against hope that the director would show some compassion and keep her on. But compassion was not in big supply among the Hippodrome management.

No one even gave her a polite goodbye.

CHAPTER 13

Céleste We Forget

Céleste's life changed when she left the Hippodrome. She no longer had that grand stage on which to perform. With it went the attention, and she learned as she approached twenty-two years of age that fame was fickle, and so were the people who had attached themselves to her because of it. Duke Mariano lost interest and faded from her life. Bettini remained a distant companion, though he found his thrills in his own fame bubble. Young male admirers, who had fought to be with her, now disappeared. Her satisfying position of being able to choose her companions reverted to her hoping for paying paramours. Reluctantly, she faced the prospect of a return to prostitution, even if at the higher level of the courtesan, but not before hoping for a reprieve from a Dutch baron, who had courted her a year earlier. He wrote to her from The Hague and invited her to visit him there. She consented and travelled to The Hague in January 1846, but she was so disappointed with the country and the baron that she made a hasty return home soon after.

The baron had proved a dud. But another opportunity was provided by her mother, who suggested they open a dress shop together. Anne-Victoire was keen to help her daughter move away from what she saw as a sordid, dangerous world. The timing seemed right to Céleste and it appeared to be a sensible road to reconciliation for the both of them. There was still no talk of Vincent, and Céleste had not asked.

The two women found a suitable shop on Rue Geoffroy-Marie. Anne-Victoire would stay in the flat at the back. Céleste took a third-floor apartment above the shop and hired a new maid from Nantes called Marie, who Céleste described as 'short with cat-like eyes, a big nose and a dumb but honest look'.

Céleste sold most of her expensive possessions, including jewellery, to obtain the shop. It attracted plenty of customers to begin with, but most were from Céleste's circle. They bought on credit and Céleste found she couldn't refuse them. Anne-Victoire took charge and was more cautious about new accounts.

Early on, Céleste learned that Vincent was still on the scene. It infuriated her. The sales girl told her that a man fitting his description would leave the shop via a back door whenever Céleste came down the stairs. Céleste at first wished to confront her mother, but decided to let it slide. This time, Anne-Victoire had put her daughter ahead of the interests of Vincent, which she had never done before. Eight years of him and his drunken behaviour would have swayed her to do this. But she still needed a man, and if the dress shop didn't survive, a breadwinner. Céleste, who was maturing fast, pretended she did not know Vincent was slinking around. At least, she thought, he had the good sense to stay out of sight.

Early one Saturday morning, an hour before the shop opened, an unknown man rang the doorbell.

'Answer that please,' Céleste told Marie, the maid, 'and tell whoever it is I'm not in.'

Marie obeyed.

'I have orders to pick up your mistress,' the man said.

'What?'

'To arrest her.'

'She … she's not in,' the maid said.

'Tell her that if she doesn't go to the prefecture before noon tomorrow,' the caller said in an officious tone, 'I shall have her picked up by the guards.'

Marie reported the conversation. Céleste was embarrassed, saying that the man must have had the wrong address.

'Don't tell anyone about this,' Céleste said. She was in despaired, believing she would be jailed for a month at least for not having reported regularly to the police—a stipulation of being registered as a prostitute that would not go away. She was at a vulnerable point. Her slip from fame and from being so desired had affected her more than she thought it would. The baron had let her down, and now the dress shop was struggling.

Céleste was ashamed and weighed down by her past, from which she was forever attempting escape. She was overwhelmed by the thought of how the neighbourhood would respond if she were arrested. Céleste was running a respectable business and trying to shed Mogador. Jail would mean terrible publicity and humiliation.

The torment was too much. She decided to take the only route away from all that, a route that several girls and women she knew had taken. *She would commit suicide.*

It was drastic but Céleste did not act like a desperate woman. Instead, she planned her own demise *precisely*. She knew that the police would not arrest her the next day, which was Sunday. They never worked on the Lord's day of rest. That gave her a day to tidy her affairs as best she could and carry out her self-destruction. The maid would be out and her mother would not open the shop.

On Saturday night Céleste spent a few hours writing letters to her best friends. At 11 p.m. her mother came in to her apartment to say goodnight.

'Oh, you're writing to our suppliers?' Anne-Victoire asked.

'Yes.'

Céleste didn't even think to kiss her mother. She had suppressed her anger about Vincent's proximity, but it welled up at this moment and stopped her from expressing something, even a kiss, that would at least leave Anne-Victoire with some small sense of reconciliation, amid all the pain that the suicide would bring. Céleste had vivid memories of those times of abuse, which were even more horrifying now, with time, not less. As a young adult, and at this moment of extreme depression, she lay the blame for the path she had been forced to take with her mother and her mother's hated partner.

Céleste arose at 10 a.m on Sunday. Outside was a fine mist, almost like fog. She summoned her maid and told her to hand-deliver a letter across town.

Once Marie had left, Céleste went to the woman's room and moved out all her things. She put white sheets on the iron bed. Then she went out and purchased two small clay ovens. Back in Marie's room, she locked herself in, plugged the keyhole, put coal in the ovens and lit them. Céleste then sat on the bed and prayed, asking God and all those she had hurt to forgive her. She felt dizzy as she put more coal in the ovens. She was transfixed by the blue flame they emitted. She struggled to stand and looked in the mirror.

'How horrible,' she recalled later. 'My head was puffy; the veins in my forehead were swollen; my lips were blue; and my hair was standing on end.'

But the thought of death suddenly scared her. Céleste wished to live. She wanted to call for help, but her voice failed her. She tried to run, but her legs gave way. She fell to the floor. The room, even the floor was getting hotter. She sweated and wanted water. Then she blacked out.

Marie could not find the letter's recipient, so she returned dutifully to her mistress. Céleste was not in her room. Marie entered the kitchen. Then she noticed smoke coming from her own room and thought it was on fire. She tried to open the door, but something was holding it closed. It was Céleste. Marie managed to push the door open and found her mistress. She had fallen with her mouth facing the gap underneath the door, which gave her enough air to stay alive—just.

Marie dragged Céleste clear of the room and put out the ovens. She then rushed to find the local doctor, who came at the double. He and Marie put Céleste in her bed and he revived her. She was tearful and distressed, and still worrying about the man coming to arrest her. Soon her room was crowded. Anne-Victoire was there, as was another doctor and the neighbours.

Marie cared for her over the next few days. Céleste had a headache, worse than anything she'd had before, and a nagging cough that took some time to abate. She fretted every day that the police would come. But as the days slipped by, she began to realise that the whole thing had been a cruel hoax.

After recovering, Céleste began to resent her failed attempt to end her life. The dress buyers stopped coming once Anne-Victoire refused to give them credit. But the goods had been 'sold' and the shop had to pay for them. It meant that nothing was saved. Céleste had no funds to pay the rent. She had invested almost all her assets in setting up and maintaining the shop. The landlord threatened to throw her out. Those to whom she owed money bullied her and said they'd sue and seize what little property she had left.

A few old friends kept her amused but not enough to give her a zest for life or even a reason to carry on. Then one day a man, clearly a servant from his striped trousers, knocked on her door, and finding her in, motioned to someone in a pretty carriage drawn by two horses. A gaunt woman emerged, helped by the servant, who was asked to wait outside. The woman lifted her face veil with one hand and extended the other to Céleste. She wore diamond earrings and rings.

It was Lise/Pomare. She had come from Nice with her elderly, wealthy count to see a doctor. Céleste was upset by her appearance—her pallid complexion and ill-fitting, far-too-white, false upper teeth. Lise asked if Céleste thought she had changed.

'Yes,' Céleste said, recovering quickly, 'you're beautiful!'

'Everyone thinks I look ill,' Lise said, pleased with her friend's comment. 'It seems I am dying of tuberculosis.'

Lise put on a magnificent front and insisted on going to a ball with Céleste a few days later. Her count had forbidden her from seeing Céleste, probably because this would exhaust Lise too much. But when he left Paris for a few days Lise dressed flamboyantly in a pink lace domino, with a black headdress and roses in her hair, and went to the ball with Céleste. But she was pale and practically immobile. The ball crowd was abuzz at the deterioration of the former flame of the Bal Mabille.

'What are they saying about me?' she whispered to Céleste.

'Oh, they are so impressed with your appearance!'

'Please don't make it up, Céleste. I know I am but a shadow of my former self.' Lise paused, then added: 'I am dying and I am afraid.'

Céleste protested that she was mad to say that and tried to lift her spirits. Lise watched the dancers twirling about and her manner brightened.

'She was following them with her soul,' Céleste later observed. 'She seemed to be inhaling the lives of others.'

Lise wanted to waltz. Céleste didn't dare refuse her. She asked a male friend to dance with her.

'Hold her tight,' Céleste whispered to him, 'very tight.'

Lise began dancing and then stopped, leaned up against a wall and said in a hoarse voice that she couldn't carry on. She gave a dry cough and brought up blood. She was haemorrhaging. Céleste took her back to where she was staying. She had a fever and in her delirium said she wanted to go back to the ball. Céleste switched off all the lights to calm her down and she eventually fell asleep.

Lise's condition worsened in the coming days. When the old count heard she was dying, he did not return to her. He withdrew her allowance and said he 'would not spend more money on a girl who only had another month to live'.

Céleste went to Lise's room the next day and all the doors and windows were open. Lise had died overnight. Céleste kissed her, knelt and said a prayer. When she dropped by a day later in pouring rain, she could hear the nailing of the coffin.

'There were only two people in the funeral procession,' Céleste wrote, 'me and my coachman … when the last lump of dirt was thrown on her, a cross with her initials was dropped in.'

The experience upset Céleste deeply. She was sad to lose her closest friend and to see how she had been treated at the end.

It depressed her to think that despite her own rise to greater heights in life, she could be heading for a similar end. Like Lise, Céleste had no steady man in her life, their mothers were both mostly estranged from them, and they were both in debt. Again, Céleste cursed the fact that she had not succeeded in her suicide attempt. She now felt at a lower ebb than ever before.

As if to try to rectify this, she returned to Lise's grave a week later in the hope that someone, perhaps Lise's mother, or the count in some pang of guilt, had put up a tombstone. But there was nothing. Lise had been abandoned in death 'as she had in the last illness'. Céleste ordered an iron railing and marble monument with the following inscription:

Here lies Lise Sergent, born 22 February 1825, died 8 December 1846. Her friend Céleste.

Céleste buried her memories of Pomare and Mogador, though not necessarily forever. A few smaller newspapers made some tasteless comments, even jokes about Lise's demise. One cynically said, 'Much will be forgiven her because she loved so much.'

Céleste wrote in her memoirs that it should have read: 'She might be forgiven because she died as a good Christian and because she suffered so much.'

Céleste was projecting again, fearing that one day something similar would be written about her. Guilt and thoughts of redemption were playing on her mind.

CHAPTER 14

Love at First Chivalry

Céleste never ceased to mourn Lise, but she had to get on with her own life, which meant trying to find suitable benefactors. Courtesans rarely went out alone and so she found a new friend, Frisette, who would accompany her on the interminable rounds of cafés, restaurants, gambling halls and parties, with the most notable meeting place being the Palais-Royal. Frisette was pretty and spirited, but no competition for Céleste, for this new pal's lover was none other than the energetic dancing dervish Brididi from Céleste's days at Bal Mabille. Céleste wasn't interested in him, which comforted Frisette, and Frisette in turn would not entice any prospective beau away from her new best friend.

One evening in the late winter of 1846–47, they went to the fashionable Café Anglais, where the richest dandies congregated in large numbers, increasing the chances of success for the young women who flocked there. The dandies originated in London, and they migrated to, and were mimicked in, Paris after the defeat of Napoleon at Waterloo in 1815. The difference between the dandy Anglais and the dandy Francais was the dress. The French version went for more extravagance, with taller top hats and more colour everywhere. Their long hair was curled and coiffured. Their bright blue frockcoats were corset-tight. Cravats were outsized and ruffled and trousers were skin-tight to show off what they had or had not. These were the true peacocks of the human species, who loved to ponce around Paris as if in open cages, while the rest of the population could watch this special zoo. As a rule they were a dissolute and degenerate bunch, whom Céleste was familiar with thanks to the Duke de Osuna. They were busy spending inheritances, with many going through the funds due to them long before they received them. As with the duke, they were without ambition or any real experiences of life beyond the drinking, whoring and gambling that threatened to exhaust even their large lines of credit. Consequently, most were weak and unreliable types, who often lacked character or serious mental development.

Céleste despised them and she could not always hide it. She was motivated by the hope that some of their generosity might trickle or even flood towards her. But this hope now was devoid of any thought of love or marriage. The treatment of Lise had hardened her against trusting or giving her heart to any man. She was glad of this emotional shell on this typical night at the Café Anglais. It usually made her impervious to the insults, slurs and put-downs these rich Parisian dandies hurled her way, as if it were their right. But on this particular night, in the raw emotional aftermath of Lise's death, Céleste was in a combative mood.

When supper was served (with the dandies always picking up the tab), Céleste found herself next to a small, thin man with bad teeth, and opposite a tall, handsome man, who was admiring himself in every possible mirror, including the large silver food dishes. Both were boastful, embarrassingly self-centred and devoid of any intelligent conversation. The smaller man began to bait and put down Céleste in the most unimaginative way.

'Whose hair did you borrow tonight?' brought mirth from the good-looking man opposite.

'And that dress! Surely on loan from the local poor house!'

He continued on beyond anything that might be thought of as fun, except by his friend opposite, who Céleste thought had to be stupid to be amused by Mr Yellow Teeth. She dubbed him 'daddy-long-legs'.

The goading continued. The short one tried teasing her about her efforts at the Hippodrome. Her backhand return was, ''Tis a pity your breath matches your fangs.'

The women were supposed to absorb the teasing or abuse without riposte, but not Céleste. Soon she was receiving more, and louder, laughs than the tormentor. Defeated, the weedy one lost his temper.

'Who brought this whore to the party?' he asked.

Daddy-long-legs, with a 'grin of idiocy', urged his companion on.

Frisette could see trouble coming. She whispered to Céleste that it might be better to leave. Céleste refused. 'No doubt your title is a recent one,' she told her abuser. 'If there were no women like us, what would you do? I've paid my fee by listening to you, and I am staying!'

The table fell silent. Pressure from the beaten dandies would normally call for the women to retreat. Any amusement at the banter had dissipated. Bitterness now hung in the air along with the thick smoke of cigarettes, pipes and the odd cigar. Minds had been dulled by too much champagne. Suddenly, an observer intervened.

'Really, gentlemen,' he said, with a tone of firmness yet familiarity while stroking his moustache. 'Haven't you gone far enough? Will you not stop this?'

All eyes turned to the speaker. He was handsome, tall and well built. He was elegantly rather than garishly dressed. His lively brown eyes flicked with the hint of a smile to Céleste and then with something more serious to the would-be tormentors. 'Neither your usual good taste nor your generosity seem to be in evidence today,' he told one of them. 'There are two of you ganging up on a woman! One would already be too many.'

Céleste could hardly believe her ears and eyes. Here was the most attractive man in the café sticking up for her with a firm, authoritative eloquence that hinted at reserves of determination. He was not foppish like the others.

The weedy offender paused at this mild challenge, but seeing that everyone seemed to support the stranger, he backed down a little.

'If I've hurt Mademoiselle's self-respect,' he said, 'I'm quite willing to make amends to her.' Admitting he was wrong to tease Céleste, he said, 'I have the good sense to pay for it … as you are her self-appointed champion, you may name the price.'

The stranger replied sharply, 'Fifteen Louis!'

No one uttered a gasp, but this was the equivalent of 300 francs.

'Right, fifteen Louis it is. She shall have it tomorrow.'

'Tomorrow is too late.'

There was another silence.

'But I haven't got that amount on me,' the weedy tormentor said.

'Never mind. The café manager will lend them to you.'

The stranger called for Vesparoz, the café manager, who soon returned with the fifteen Louis.

'Give it to Mademoiselle,' the weedy one directed.

Céleste refused to accept it.

'Give it to me,' the stranger said. He turned to Céleste, smiled and gestured politely for her to join him. Céleste hesitated, but his kindly manner persuaded her. She sat beside him.

'You really did not need to do that,' she whispered, touching his forearm.

'Oh, yes I did,' he said softly. 'I realise you can look after yourself. You gave as good as you got. But there should be no such games when a gentleman addresses a woman. There should be respect.'

He was distracted by the weedy one making another comment to his daddy-long-legs friend and their subsequent forced laughter.

'For every insult you make from now on,' the handsome stranger addressed the two men, 'it will cost you fifteen Louis.'

'There won't be anymore,' the weedy one mumbled with an apologetic gesture.

After a brief chat, the stranger was taken aside by a dandy who wished to talk 'business'. He excused himself to Céleste.

'Can we continue this later?' he asked, taking her hand and kissing it.

She nodded and smiled. His chair was taken by Frisette.

'Do you know who that is?' Frisette asked, wide-eyed. 'Only one of the most eligible, sought-after bachelors in Paris: Count Lionel de Chabrillan.'

'What do you know about him? Is there a countess?'

'No, but plenty would like to be.'

Céleste glanced over at Lionel. She smiled but said nothing.

'I used to date one of his best friends, Count Roland de Napoli. The Chabrillans are a rich and very powerful family, descended from the Knights of Dauphine.'

'Should I be impressed?'

'Yes, you should be,' Frisette said with a grin. 'Lionel's father was attendant to Charles X.'

Céleste wrinkled her nose, as if she wasn't overwhelmed.

'Wait. It's the mother you should know about. She's the matriarch. She was the daughter of the top French diplomat to Constantinople at the height of the Ottoman Empire. Their real wealth may have come from that association, but I don't know much about it. Lionel's elder brother, Marie-Olivier, holds a position at the Council of State. I don't like him. Met him twice. Treated me like dirt. Of course, a girl like me is dirt to someone from the aristocracy. He has two sisters—'

'I don't care about his siblings,' Céleste interrupted. 'Tell me more about him. He's quite beautiful.'

'He's the poor little rich boy of the family; the youngest, only twenty-five. Bit of a failure in the eyes of the family. His mother got him a job in the French Legation in Copenhagen. That didn't last long. Roland told me that all Lionel wanted to do was own land and a castle in Berry.'[1]

Céleste glanced across at Lionel again. He gave her a coy smile.

'But what is he doing now?' she asked.

'Not much,' Frisette said. 'He's a bon vivant, an inveterate gambler.'

'Gambling at the track?'

'Yes, but mainly roulette. He's obsessed with it. Do you play?'

'No. I must learn.'

They both laughed.

'Is he a womaniser?'

'Strangely, no, not really. He's had the odd mistress. I've seen him at the usual dandy haunts with a stunning partner. But remember I only know a bit about him.'

'Interesting.'

'He drinks only the best champagne. I recall that.'

'Very interesting.'

They both laughed again.

Other men, including her two abusers, asked Céleste for a dance, but she rejected them. They were attracted to her feistiness, it seemed, as much as her outstanding physical appeal and natural sensuality. But Lionel had not approached her to dance. She caught him looking at her. *He must like me*, she thought.

Céleste was confused that he did not pursue her, but she was not going to die wondering about it. She summoned courage and walked over to him.

'I really wish to escape the men pestering me,' she said. 'Could you take me home?'

'With pleasure, my dear,' he replied with a languid grin, 'but only after you've danced a waltz with me.'

Céleste was too overwhelmed to speak as he put his arm around her waist.

'He held me to him and I felt his heart beat,' she wrote in her diary later. 'I closed my eyes and let him lead me. I knew a flash of happiness that passed like lightning.'

This was a pure spark of romance she had never felt before. It was heady. The tough shell around her had been broken down in a few moments and she was in a quandary. Lionel took Frisette home first and then drove to Céleste's place.

'Really sorry to have put you to this trouble,' she said.

'It's a pleasure,' Lionel replied. 'I wouldn't have dared ask you. I didn't want to be the third one to persecute you.'

He pressed the fifteen Louis into her hand.

'You must take it,' he insisted. 'It's yours.'

She had forgotten about it. Her thoughts were on the romance of the moment.

'I'll call on you at four p.m.,' he said, looking into her eyes. He did not kiss her. Instead, he gave her a lingering handshake.

Céleste wrote that her head and heart were filled with images of the count. 'How foolish of me to have lost hope in life!'

Céleste's luck seemed to be turning. She had written the week before to her Dutch baron, telling him of her recent financial and other woes. Guilt-ridden over the poor way he had treated her in The Hague, the baron sent her 2000 francs. This, coupled with the 300 windfall from the rude dandy, was a small fortune, at least for Céleste. It would have taken her more than two years to earn that amount at the Hippodrome. She would now be able to pay off her debts and live for a time without working. But before she could contemplate fully this sudden change of luck, at 4 p.m. as he'd promised, Lionel arrived from his apartment in salubrious Faubourg Saint-Germain at her place on Rue Geoffroy-Marie. He was in an attractive phaeton led by two high-stepping black horses. Céleste came out to greet him as he disengaged the carriage and tethered the horses himself, rather than asking his two servants to do it.

He invited her to dinner at a 'clubbish' restaurant off the Champs-Élysées. When he knocked on the wooden door, a panel slid back. The manager then ushered them in to a dining room, full of discreet cubicles with purple couches to lounge in rather than chairs. The other diners were up-market, she thought, from their dress, manner and the way they scrutinised her. She was both charmed by the atmosphere and intimidated. Her feelings of inadequacy and her class background made her self-conscious in such an environment. But when she looked at Lionel, he seemed relaxed and very pleased to be escorting her. They sat next to each other on a couch. He asked for champagne and a waitress took their food orders. Céleste was astounded to discover he knew her history, and she had the courage to mention her misgivings.

'But my background is very …'

'I don't care about your background,' he said with a dismissive wave. 'I care about you. That is what matters.'

'Shouldn't you be with someone, you know … from the aristocracy?' she asked, going to the brink.

'That's what my family keeps telling me,' he said with a languid smile. 'They don't know my feelings. And anyway, what's so special about the women of my so-called class?' He paused to light a cigar. 'None of them have your courage. The way you rode at the Hippodrome! You have such guts!'

'Is that important? My courage?'

'It goes to character.'

'But you don't know how afraid I was before I entered the arena.'

'A matador would be a fool not to be afraid before a bullfight. I see the results of your fortitude. That is what counts. You dare things no man I know would do, unless mad.'

'Maybe I'm crazy …?'

'Not from my observation,' he said, touching her hand tenderly.

'Do you know I was once in Saint-Lazare? Were you aware I worked in a brothel?'

He laughed. 'I didn't know, and I surely don't care. I see what you are now. Not what befell you in the past.'

'But doesn't someone's past dictate their future?'

'If you let it,' he said, looking into her eyes. He flicked ash and puffed smoke to a whirring roof fan. 'I've heard rumours about your past: the prostitution. I was told by jealous friends.' He leaned forward. 'I don't think you realise that every man who has ever seen you perform has fallen in love with you.'

'Ah, an image! They've fallen for an image, something unreal.' She sipped champagne that had just been poured and asked, 'Have you?'

'Yes, I have, but not an image. I've fallen for the real person,' he said with a shyness that made her feel more comfortable with him.

'You're telling me you love me?'

He nodded. 'I am.' He smoked for a moment. 'And how do you feel about me?'

Emboldened, Céleste told him, 'I love you and will go on loving you for a long time.'

'I feel the same,' he said, and kissed her on the lips, long enough to turn heads at other cubicles.

'You are my first true paramour,' he said, sounding pleased to announce it. 'I lose inhibitions with you. I love your vivaciousness, your fierce independence. I cannot believe your courage at the Hippodrome! I loved your counter-punches at the Café Anglais. You didn't really need me. You were more than a match for those idiots.'

'But you did intervene …'

'Yes, because I wanted you to notice me.'

'I don't care why. I only care that you did.'

'I've never seen a courtesan dare in public what you did. You hit back. You defied …'

'My class? My station in life?'

'No. You defied what is expected from courtesans.'

Céleste began to dare believe that the dream would last. She trusted Lionel like no other.

Céleste always believed that the way men had sex with her gave clues to their character. Lionel was the best experience she'd had, or felt she'd had since Denise at Saint-Lazare. Denise had shown tenderness and consideration, but she was female and Céleste had been just fourteen, and extremely vulnerable after the rough, frightening treatment from Vincent. Looking back eight years, she did not reproach Denise but she did resent being taken advantage of. Though she had no lesbian tendencies, she did not regret what had happened. Denise had aroused her physically, even though Céleste had no deep feelings for her. Lionel managed both. He was gentle, almost apologetic in the way he treated her, but she encouraged him to be stronger by her own actions and movements, not her words. He responded the way she wanted and liked. He was caring by nature and this was apparent in bed. There was none of the rough-house or the voyeuristic in him.

She enjoyed making love to him and it deepened her already extremely strong feelings. She would not have cared if he'd been a poor lover. But he was more than adequate in every sense. More than anything it was his tenderness and sensitivity that impressed her. Céleste spoke of her 'rhythm' with Lionel. It had happened fast but it was this 'fitting together' in harmony that affected her. She didn't know how she had reached this point in her life without knowing what real love was on so many levels.

Céleste now trembled at the thought of losing it.

Lionel didn't like her neighbourhood so Céleste rented an apartment in a more acceptable district at Place de la Madeleine and turned the dress shop over to her mother. Two months into the relationship she was invited to a dinner party at an apartment. While the wine and champagne flowed, she heard open reference to a woman called Zizi. She asked a friend, Albert, who this was.

'Oh, you didn't know?' he said. 'She's Lionel's mistress.'

Seeing her expression of surprise, he added, 'And this is her apartment. Or at least it's one he pays for.'

Suddenly, dreams of being with Lionel exclusively collapsed. She kept her head, although she was itching to challenge him.

Céleste waited until people had left the dinner table before she cornered him.

'Zizi isn't exactly my mistress,' he said. 'It's true that a woman I've known for a long time lives here. But this apartment belongs to me. I intend to leave her, and when I do, I shall let her have all that is here.'

He didn't sound defiant or defensive, just matter-of-fact. Céleste was now herself defensive. Lionel had appeared too good to be true in this 'game of high stakes', as she called it. No matter what he said from now on, Céleste remained 'buried in just one thought: *He had a mistress!*'

The dinner party went on, the tension obvious between them. The champagne was now acting as a 'singing syrup' with Lionel's friends. Céleste learned that Lionel had a lot of debts. He was a classic dandy, tearing through the family inheritance long before it was his; there would be nothing left to inherit if he continued on his present course. Céleste liked the idea that he could end up impecunious.

'His ruin would bring him closer to me,' she later wrote. Céleste was ruthless in her thinking and her intent. She saw Lionel as her main chance for happiness in life. His riches were not as important to her as the man himself. Her furious efforts would now be fuelled by jealousy, although in moments of despondency her more brittle side would cause her to consider walking away. Against her better judgement she accepted his offer to go to the races at Versailles the next day.

They did not even go to bed and at 6 a.m. a landau arrived for them. With more champagne, Céleste enjoyed the day, although not when Lionel said farewell to her after the last race. He was leaving for Saint-Germain, where he said he had business. Lionel's friends then embarked on some mischief by inviting Céleste and a female friend she had come with to join them for dinner in Saint-Germain.

'We arrived at the Henri IV Pavillon,' she noted, 'and saw Lionel there. But when he saw me he took off.'

Lionel's friends thought this most amusing.

'Now why would he leave like that?' one asked, drawing big laughs from the others. Another, not much more sympathetic to Céleste's feeling, commented bluntly, 'Well, he's between two fires, Zizi and here, but it doesn't matter.' He turned to Céleste. 'You'll dine with us. I shall say that you're my mistress.'

This brought more mirth from Lionel's companions and Céleste regretted coming. As they dined, Lionel, who was on his own and *not* with Zizi, approached and held her hands, but her response was cold. Later, Céleste caught him looking over at her when she let the man next to her kiss her hand and her neck. This caused him to march over to her again. He stood in front of her, stared into her eyes and asked her to come outside.

He led her into a garden and took both her hands in his and asked, 'What is the matter, Céleste? You seem to take pleasure in torturing me.'

'You have a mistress!' she retorted. 'Do you want me to cry in front of her? I'm free. I want to forget you …'

'To forget me? Why? Is it my fault that before meeting you I had a liaison? I cannot abruptly leave her without a reason. Be patient.'

CHAPTER 15

Love's Roller-coaster

Lionel sounded sincere. She wanted his dedication to her and his gentle dumping of Zizi to be true. She decided to wait and see if he was indeed being honest with her. She believed he did intend to break with Zizi but was being a gentleman about it. Still, having aroused in him an emotion Céleste knew well—jealousy—she continued to take up invitations. One important one had been issued by another count before she met Lionel. She decided to go to this event, a ball put on by the Jockey Club, the most exclusive club in Paris, yet did not enjoy the night. Some of the women behaved snobbishly towards her.

'Mogador!' they remarked in mock horror. 'A circus rider; a woman who danced at public balls.'

Céleste was immune to the jibes.

'Women of that class were no different from the rest,' she observed in her memoirs, 'only their price was higher.'

Her compensation, even minor revenge, at the ball was to have most of the young aristocrats flock to her. On the dance floor they wanted to show off their skills with a woman whose capacities in all variations of the waltz, from the traditional to the pepped-up, were legendary. Céleste even went into her high-kicking cancan routine and had all heads turning.

When she next saw Lionel, she made a point of telling him about the Jockey Club event. Tactically, it was to see his reaction; an unsaid declaration that she could play the chess move of dating former acquaintances, too, if Zizi continued to be on the scene. A bit more jealousy from him would reassure her. Too much jealousy would torment him. Lionel surprised her by simply and casually asking if she'd had a good time.

This confused her. In her emotional state about him, her first thought was that he didn't care, which meant her ploy had backfired. Later, Céleste wondered if his attitude might be one of resignation, signalling that he might be submitting to her. She decided to give these thoughts time to percolate.

Lionel took her to the gambling halls. He continued to throw away money he did not really control. Céleste was appalled but maintained her cool. Every 1000 francs less, she judged, meant he would be drawn closer to her world of struggle. She fantasised that then her strengths in coping would help control the situation between them, that it would give her a certain power, though she did not want to actually dominate him.

Lionel declared his love by buying her a fabulous diamond-encrusted ring. It was not for engagement, but just because he wanted to. There were other gifts of expensive clothes and trinkets for her slim wrists and elegant neck. They kept coming and she accepted them without a word of protest about his profligacy. She did not care that this was hurtling him faster and faster towards a financial abyss. Céleste knew that she could never drag him from his addictions, especially roulette. She observed Lionel sitting with dissolute, like-minded cronies night after night in halls that held a permanent mist of smoke as the rich players puffed their way into oblivion, often wordlessly.

There was not much discourse as spin after spin of the little red pea mesmerised Lionel and his mates. And if he won, there were low-key reactions, for rich dandies never made an obvious display over pocketing winning chips. This was partly because they did not want to demonstrate any form of relief or rescue due to a really big win, say a 36-to-1 shot coming in. It was also because these young men, who were on average no more than twenty-five years old, had been playing long enough to know that even a string of big wins would be followed by a run of even bigger losses. They joked that their money was disappearing faster than the smoke dispersed by the roof fans, and there was bravado among them for being 'good losers'. And that was one thing they were excellent at.

Céleste observed and absorbed all this without criticising Lionel directly or in her memoirs. She knew that this ruinous compulsion was unstoppable. She heard of mistresses and wives privately complaining about the dandies' waste. They were ostracised. It was the right of a member of this peacock menagerie to orchestrate his own demise, publicly and for all the newspapers to record and the various social sets to gossip over. It was an essential part of Paris's elite of the period. Céleste felt no guilt in being part of the money drain on Lionel through her grateful acceptance of his generosity. She claimed she never encouraged it, although her gratitude and barely contained glee at his largesse were tacit approval of it.

Despite the subtle ongoing contest between them, Céleste was always fortified by the way he made love to her. If anything, their intimacy seemed to become more passionate rather than less as their tempestuous relationship blossomed. Lionel seemed more concerned with her needs and satisfaction than his own.

Céleste had a nagging, prevalent worry—that she was more crazily in love with him than he was with her. The more they were together and had such compelling sex, the more she understood that she was under his spell, even if he didn't quite recognise it himself. Count Lionel de Chabrillan had her body and soul, and she was fearful that his love would one day evaporate, like all her other affairs.

As the weeks progressed, she began to dream the impossible dream for someone of her class; something that everyone from her background and many in Lionel's might hate her for. Like the 50-to-1 long shot he so preferred to back at the Versailles racetrack, she dared to imagine being the Countess de Chabrillan. Reason told her that the longer they were together, the shorter the odds would become. Alternatively, the relationship could come to an abrupt end, which was too terrible to contemplate.

One night the valet came to her apartment at midnight to tell Lionel that his father, the Marquis de Chabrillan, who had suffered from cancer for six months, did not have long to live. The Marquis was sixty years old[1], but it was still a big jolt. Lionel left for the country right away. Céleste was keen to help, but as she had not been invited to go with him, and as it was a private family affair, she could only write to him.

After weeks of letters he finally replied:

My dear child,
Thank you for your kind thoughts. I am suffering a great deal. When shall I see you again? I have no idea. I was expecting it for a long time. I did not think it would happen so soon. You will understand that certain sorrows need solitude.

As the days dragged by Céleste herself had to suffer in silence. Then he wrote saying the marquis had died and that he wanted to mourn at his country estate in Berry. Céleste suspected that he was not yet ready to introduce her to his family, perhaps, she worried, because they would not find her acceptable. Reality struck, at least when thinking about the future, and she did not let thoughts about marriage intrude again. In this time of grief and family consolidation, she felt certain she would remain outside the close circle of relatives.

Céleste wrote to Anne-Victoire at the dress shop. When there was no reply, she discovered that it had closed down. Neighbours told her that her mother had gone to live with Vincent again, a fact that did nothing to lift her spirits over Lionel's prolonged absence.

Her friend Frisette comforted Céleste by saying that Lionel would not be with a mistress at this time because he and the family would have duties to fulfil. But she was less comforted by two of Lionel's dandy friends. Henri told her, 'Lionel has just inherited. That's good for you.' The other friend, Georges, was less certain that Céleste would benefit.

'He's going into mourning in the country,' he told her, 'and now he must think about getting married.'

Céleste was taken aback by this comment but kept an outward calm. What did Georges mean? Was Lionel thinking about marrying her or Zizi, or someone else?

'You've seen him?' she asked.

'At church,' Henri replied. 'He really loved his father, but it's the best thing that could have happened to him.'

Georges was surprised at Henri's candour. 'Is it ever a good thing when one's father dies?'

'Sure, when a person has debts! His father had an income of 400,000 francs, but there are three other children besides Lionel who will also inherit.' Henri, forever candid and blunt, turned to her and added, 'Do not let this go, Céleste.'

Again, Céleste was astounded by such a comment. She had been preoccupied by Lionel leaving Paris and going to the country. But the last remark jolted her.

'I am not in love with his fortune!' she said indignantly.

Henri and Georges laughed at her reaction.

'Still, do not let go of this, Céleste,' Henri repeated.

This hurt and left her in a quandary. If she tried to see him it would appear as if she had an ulterior motive. Yet, she mused in her own defence, she had moved out of her apartment because of him. She had also spent a lot on furnishings, from a large bed to a leather chair, to meet his demands and tastes, although Lionel was not aware of her efforts and she would never have told him. After the discussion with his friends, she was left with the stark realisation that Lionel had left without even saying goodbye. Céleste was devastated. She had no idea where he was, only that he had gone to his newly inherited property.

Four months of 1847 slipped by before more news came from Georges and Henri. It cut even deeper. Lionel had inherited his 100,000-franc share of the marquis's estate, but this hardly covered his debts.

'His only chance of solvency,' Henri informed her with his usual forthrightness, 'is to marry an heiress and to settle down on one of his estates.'

Céleste's pre-Lionel bitterness returned. She reproached herself for being privately pleased that he was running down his fortune at the roulette table. She turned to Frisette, now her closest confidante, telling her that she wanted to forget the 'ingrate'.

'Let's party and have a good time!' Céleste said.

They went gambling at the halls she had grown to know so well with Lionel, but Céleste was an even worse gambler than he was, and she was soon losing what meagre funds she had. Georges found her battling at a card table one night. He took her aside and, finding her so sad, gave her Lionel's address and suggested she write to him. She demurred over this and was not confident enough to write. Then her luck changed.

As ever, innumerable men wanted her favours. Her desirability had been elevated by her relationship with Lionel, who, despite his wealth-squandering, was arguably the most desirable bachelor in Paris, given his title, looks, charm and good nature. Céleste discarded or ignored potential suitors, partners and other assorted prospects with the same care she might have displayed for an empty champagne bottle. But one very thin, refined, perhaps too effete–looking Russian prince, Jean, persisted. The more she rejected him, the more he tried to please her. Céleste told him she could never love him. He kept asking her out and sending her gifts. Céleste remained aloof. After several months of refusing Jean, she relented and slept with him. She practically snubbed him in bed by making their coupling a humourless, unfeeling occasion. But Jean, fifteenth in line to the Russian throne, was so excited that he promised her anything she wanted. She was adamant that her desires did not include him, but she accepted his eager offer to pay off her debts. The funds kept coming, enough to give her some security again.

This reversal gave her the confidence to write to Lionel.

My dear friend,
In writing to you thus, I do not wish to level reproaches at you … I have loved you and a love like mine is most insignificant. You have the right to trample it.

You trod on my heart. Since your departure, I have been losing myself in gambling establishments, killing my memory of you by wearing myself out.

I was mad to love you so much. I knew you could not keep me. With a little reasoning on my part, I could have healed myself. Heedlessly you crushed me. That was mean! I have a better opinion of myself. I did not know I was capable of such love.

I need nothing. I am almost rich now. I wish you all the happiness in the world, and I forgive you your neglect.

Céleste posted the letter. Then she counted the hours until she knew it would be with the count and placed her hand on her heart. She was putting much store in him responding and the strain showed. Her nerves were not helped by the sad death of the sister of her maid, Marie. Then she learned from Georges and Henri that Lionel had rented a house for Zizi at Saint James in Paris, which indicated that he was still looking after her, and the relationship was not over.

All these events caused Céleste to have heart palpitations. Her doctor prescribed rest and strong doses of digitalis. But instead of taking his advice, she stayed up at night and became increasingly distressed over her lost love. She became unwell when winter set in.

'I had to be bled,' she remembered, 'and I took to my bed. One night I was thinking of Lionel. I picked up the bottle of digitalis tincture. Instead of drinking a few drops, which always soothed me, I swallowed the whole bottle.'

This act made her seriously ill. Céleste's memoirs indicate she was confused over why she did this. Perhaps it was less a suicide attempt and more a moment of weakness caused by depression. Or perhaps it was literally a cri de coeur, for as every day of late 1847 slipped by and she did not hear from Lionel, Céleste had to face the reality that their relationship was over.

CHAPTER 16

Castle of Broken Dreams

Céleste took weeks to recover from the drug overdose. Her Russian prince did not desert her and she was waiting for him at her apartment one night when there was a commanding knock at the door. It was Lionel.

'How can you leave a man out in the cold like this?' he asked, as soon as she opened the door. 'It's freezing!'

Lionel took her in his arms and kissed her with passion. Céleste was speechless. Lionel bustled in as if he owned the place, followed by a friend, Martin.

'You're dining with us tonight?' he asked. 'I warn you that I'm spending three nights in Paris, and I'm hiding out at your apartment. Do you still love me a little?'

There was another knock at the door.

'If this is my replacement,' Lionel said, laughing and keeping up a bluff, 'I'm going to throw him out!' He had a fleeting acquaintance with Prince Jean.

Keeping up the bravado, Lionel ushered Jean in and offered him a chair. He then rang for the maid. Jean did not seem to know how to behave. Nor did Céleste. She stood by the fireplace in the living room as this charade unfolded. Finally Jean departed after realising that Lionel was staying and Céleste was not making a move to get rid of him. Céleste felt compelled to offer the travellers dinner, and she had Marie prepare it. When they had finished Céleste left the dining room, pretending she was giving Marie an order. She hid outside the door and listened to what Lionel said to Martin.

'What do you think of her?' Lionel asked.

'Oh, she's fine,' Martin replied. 'I like her better than the one you took me to see yesterday.'

Céleste returned to the dining room a few minutes later. She didn't wish to admit that she had been eavesdropping, but she could not disguise her disdain for Lionel's behaviour. He picked up on her change in manner and asked, 'What's the matter? You seem strange.'

That set Céleste off.

'Me, strange! You're the strange one,' she shot back. 'What sort of provincial manners have you brought back with you? You throw my friend out, and you say I'm strange! I assume you can act this way when you're with Zizi, who's in your pay. I think you're rude!'

Unsure of what had triggered her outburst, the two chastised men said they would go to Lionel's apartment. Céleste made no move to stop them. At that moment she felt she 'loved him less'.

The incident caused her heart ailment to flare and during the night she coughed up blood. The doctor was called and Lionel and Martin turned up to see her when she was being examined.

Lionel asked what illness she had.

'She has a stubborn head!' the doctor replied. 'She does the exact opposite of what she's told to do.'

'How can she be made well?' Lionel asked.

'If she can be taken away from her busy life in Paris,' the doctor said adamantly, 'I'm sure she would recover.'

Lionel and Martin continued to visit her each day. After four days Lionel told her to pack a suitcase.

'I'm taking you to the country,' he declared. 'I shall hide you the best way I can. If you're spotted, people will assume you came for Martin.'

Céleste only really registered the fact that he was taking her with him. She was overjoyed as she filled a trunk. She didn't care if he was only looking after her out of pity. Even the thought of going with him to a country retreat lifted her spirits. She felt also that this demonstrated a measure of compassion in Lionel, which she had rarely if ever experienced from a man. Generosity for favours was one thing. A real sense of caring for her wellbeing was another thing altogether. It was a most attractive trait to her and at that moment renewed her hope in the relationship. It also gave her something to work on.

They took the train to Vierzon in the province of Berry. It was the nearest station to Lionel's estate near the town Châteauroux, 100 kilometres away. Lionel's coachman and valet drove them by private surrey. It was very cold, having snowed the night before, and Lionel closed the carriage windows. Locals peered in to see who was being driven in such luxury, but, Céleste later noted, 'our breath soon formed a curtain against the curious'.

The highway was terrible and the weather was freezing. Just outside a small village they hit a bump. The coachman was thrown from the carriage, which clattered over him. Lionel leaped out to control the horses, and just managed to stop them from heading off the road into a deep ditch. The carriage pulled up. The coachman had bruising on both legs and was unable to walk. Lionel unhitched the horses and hurried to find the local doctor, who came with a stretcher. The coachman was taken to the doctor's surgery, where he would stay the night, and Lionel was forced to find another coachman in the town to continue the evening journey. As usual, Lionel had enough gold coins with him to keep everyone content—the injured coachman, the doctor and the new driver.

This incident took two hours. Soon after continuing on their journey they left the highway and hurtled along an even worse road, with the new coachman keen to reach the destination in quick time. After an hour, Céleste could see trees forming an arcade above the road. The carriage stopped with a yell and a jolt. They had arrived at Lionel's castle.

'The moonlight had emerged from behind clouds to illuminate a beautiful 300-year-old chateau set in snow-covered grounds and featuring looming towers and rugged battlements,' she recalled.

A servant came out carrying a lantern and Lionel led Céleste inside. Martin disappeared into a wing of the vast building while she was taken through a grand hall and up a stone spiral staircase to a large room in the main tower. Another servant was lighting a fire in a nine-metre-high recess. The room had red brocade curtains and was adorned in carved wooden columns.

Only a week earlier Céleste had been depressed about her life. Now she had been transported into a fantasy world for princes and princesses about which she had only read or dreamed. She couldn't help expressing her surprise at the beauty of the castle, which had been maintained in a fifteenth-century style, with all the features that this entailed.

Céleste marvelled at it all but her joy was short-lived when she heard terrible, shrill screams, as if someone was being murdered in the battlements. An amused Lionel reassured her that ritual killings had never been carried out in the ancestral home, as far as he knew. She was just hearing the owls that come out to play in the moonlight.

Céleste, steeped in superstitions, like most people of the era, said, 'I'm sorry about that. Owls bring bad luck!'

The next day, Martin showed her the way downstairs and through several living rooms, including one for billiards, until they reached the dining room. Lionel joined them and after the meal Martin was assigned to show her around the estate.

Céleste was astounded at the number of staff, with a seemingly endless stream of coachmen, stableboys, stablehands, farmhands, cooks, gardeners, valets, grooms, stewards and keepers, not to mention the horses and hounds. She was in awe of the cost of upkeep for such a mighty property.

Céleste deduced that there was only one solution if Lionel were to keep the enormous estate: he had to marry a rich woman, who would absorb the losses from running his land. She realised, too, that he was not a good businessman and was easy prey for swindlers, dodgy deal-makers and money lenders, who kept giving him funds at exorbitant rates.

'He was blindly rushing towards his ruin,' Céleste concluded in her memoirs, and putting a sympathetic spin on his circumstances, said, 'He was too generous at heart to keep track of his money. He was kind.' But perhaps to protect herself she added, 'He had moments of cruelty. He would say unkind things to me.'

Her days at the castle were difficult. She had been thrust into Lionel's private world and developed a sense of inferiority, not helped by his mood. A tall butler followed her every move during meals, which lasted two hours. It was not so bad when the butler stood behind her, but when he loomed in front, correcting her choice of utensils, she became too frightened to eat anything and preferred to go hungry. Her normal instinct would have been to tell the badgering butler to desist, but she felt humbled and less inclined to lash out. Lionel was short with her, too. She accompanied him when a farmer visited to discuss business.

'Go to your room,' he told her. 'I don't need to have everyone see you.'

The ambiguity in this comment upset her. Did he mean he was ashamed of her? Or was he telling her to keep her nose out of his business dealings? Either way it was a put-down, which incensed her.

The next day she received a letter from Marie saying her absence in Paris had created a rumour that she was dead. Marie suggested that her mistress return home. Céleste raised this with Lionel to test if he wanted her to stay. He was irritated.

'Who the devil do you think will take care of you?' he asked. 'Your friends from Bal Mabille? I'd like to think you care very little for them.'

'It doesn't matter if my friends are from Bal Mabille or elsewhere,' she snapped. 'They're thinking about me and I'm grateful.'

Lionel waved a dismissive hand at her.

'You see?' she said. 'You brought me here and you regret it! Well, I shall leave tomorrow.'

Lionel didn't say anything, which was a signal that she should depart. The next day, he again did not try to keep her there.

'I don't regret bringing you here, Céleste,' he said, 'since you're feeling better. I love you very much. But I must get married.'

It was a simultaneous kiss and slap on the face. When she didn't respond he added, 'One of my relatives wrote to me on the subject. That's why I'm letting you leave.'

Although she had been forewarned of this, it still hurt.

The next day he took her to Châteauroux and she bought a coach ticket to the train at Vierzon. When they kissed goodbye, she noticed his eyes were moist. This and his abrupt departure left her clinging to the thought that he still really cared for her.

Céleste felt the contrast of her 'happy love and gratified vanity' on arrival in a splendid carriage to the cold, bitter disappointment on leaving in a rickety, crowded coach. Her happiness and pride were left behind at the ornamental gates of Lionel's castle.

'With a thud,' she later wrote, 'I have fallen back into the mediocre reality of my bohemian life.'

CHAPTER 17

Return to the Castle

Céleste had not given up her quest for Lionel. He had responded to her efforts to make him jealous before and she planned to try again. She invited Prince Jean to take her to Le Havre, a port and seaside resort on the French coast. He, too, overcame his humiliation at his previous dismissal and agreed. Céleste was craftily honest in telling Jean of her split with Lionel, but she made it clear as before that she was still in love with the count. Jean didn't seem to care, as long as he could be with her.

Leaving Paris gave her a useful excuse to write to Lionel.

Mr dear Lionel,
The reasons for our separation were so good [appropriate] that you saw I was resigned to it. However, one must not require of human nature what it cannot achieve! I think of you more than ever! Thanks to your good care, I have regained my health. I have reclaimed Jean's friendship. I shall be here for a few days. If you were to have something to tell me, you could write to me. Keep me in your thoughts.

Céleste.

Céleste was a good gambler on life, and in this case she was betting on Lionel finding it impossible to forget her and difficult to find a replacement. Céleste had just turned twenty-three, yet her knowledge of men and their behaviour was that of a woman twice her age. At the back of her mind also lingered the cold and tactically efficient thought that Lionel would fall so far in life that he would land at her level, putting them on an equal footing.

In February 1848, it seemed likely that King Louis-Philippe I, who was seventy-four, would be deposed and replaced by a provisional reformist government.

Louis-Philippe's reign—the July Monarchy—had been dominated by many former Napoleonic officials and by the wealthy elite, including Lionel and his father the marquis. The main cause of the unrest and demand for reform was that only one per cent of the population had the right to vote, and only those who owned land could decide who ruled and how.

Reforms by the new government—the so-called Second Republic—meant that the largesse of bankers, money lenders and others dried up. This diminished Lionel's attempts to court a wealthy woman. He was forced to stave off bankruptcy and an embarrassing state of insolvency by selling off what he could from the estate.

Not surprisingly, the plain-looking young countess who was thrust in front of Lionel by his family was not impressed by this denuding of the estate's superficial extravagances. She refused his rather desperate hand in marriage. Yet still, Lionel did not appear frantic. His only sign of anxiety was over Céleste's letter indicating she was back in a relationship with Prince Jean. Lionel regarded him as foppish. But young Jean, unlike Lionel now, seemed to have endless resources with which to shower gifts on Céleste. This bothered Lionel, and he wanted to see if his relationship with her could be renewed. He was still in search of a marriageable benefactor, but the absence of his vibrant, wilful, independent, at times feisty lover made him yearn for her. As he told friends, her 'Celestial pull' always attracted him. This was in spite of his family, especially his overbearing and interfering eldest brother and his countess sister, who were horrified at his obsession with Céleste, whom they regarded as a common circus performer with a doubtful past.

Céleste was frightened by the mood in the Paris streets in early 1848. She was no different from most women of the period, discouraged from an interest in politics, which was considered part of the man's world. When walking with Frisette, she became concerned at people congregating in the streets as if ready to do mischief and worse.

'I don't like this,' Céleste said. 'It reminds me of the trouble in Lyon when I was a child.'

When the two women reached the boulevards, where crowds were bigger, there were whispers, then cries of, 'Reform!'

'What reform?' Céleste asked a group of people milling on the sidewalk. They shrugged without answering, except for one young man who said, 'Everything! There must be change! It's progress!'

'Don't like this,' Céleste whispered to Frisette. 'I think there will be bloodletting ...'

In front of the Café de France on the Boulevard de Bonne-Nouvelle, they bumped into a group of about fifty young men. Some of them recognised the former Hippodrome performers and called their names, saying, 'Hooray for reform and beautiful women!'

The cry did not seem connected, yet delighted the two women, who had no interest at all in change. A crowd built and surged around them, like a tornado in search of an epicentre. Céleste became anxious and pushed Frisette towards a friend's house nearby. She let them in and opened the window. The rush and jostle of people again reminded Céleste of Lyon. It continued until around 6 p.m., when many in the crowd headed home.

'Everyone must dine,' Céleste noted in an endearingly French observation, 'even those who wage war.'

Frisette suggested that they, too, have dinner. They parted at 10 p.m. Céleste heard an explosion when she reached Rue Le Peletier. A man warned her not to go to her home at Place de la Madeleine because the reformers had fired on the Ministry of Foreign Affairs. The main culprit in the eyes of the rebels was Foreign Affairs Minister François Guizot. He had resigned in the days before (on 22 February) but now the mob wanted some measure of revenge beyond his departure. They attacked the ministry.

Céleste took a different route and began to worry about Lionel. She knew that a revolution would not be kind to the nobility, which might be forced to go into hiding, leaving their possessions and their estates to the rampaging lawless. She wished that Lionel was with her so she could help him. As if to heighten the sense of danger, she noticed that a local pharmacy on Rue de Caumartin had been turned into a temporary first-aid post. Once she reached home, Céleste wrote a panicky letter to Lionel, mentioning everything she had witnessed and warning him not to come to Paris.

She went to bed but could not sleep, even with a dose of digitalis. Marie was up and too nervous to retire. It seemed that the street was alive at 4 a.m. Then there was a knock at the door. The insistent banging seemed familiar. Céleste urged the concierge to open the door. It was Lionel. He had come from his estate the previous afternoon only to run into the Paris mayhem.

'Why are you here now?' Céleste asked. 'It's dangerous!'

'I'm going to join the National Guard,' he said. 'Someone must protect the king and the government.'

The two slept together until 7 a.m. when Lionel disappeared to join the first legion of the National Guard. He was immediately involved in the fighting as the reformers attempted to burn down the Guard's post at Madeleine. He arrived back at Céleste's place at 5 p.m. exhausted and aware that this fresh revolution was well underway.

'There's no hope for the king or the government,' he declared. 'You're not safe here. You must return to the castle tomorrow.'

Any resolve about resisting him evaporated, but this time Céleste felt their affinity was stronger and his attitude needier than before. On the trip back she was relieved when the train reached the halfway point.

'So what are your marriage plans?' she asked him.

'I've been rejected,' he said matter-of-factly.

'Surely this isn't the end of your family's search for a match for you?'

He smiled carelessly but did not answer. There was no sign of the more usual temper tantrums.

'I couldn't rise to his level,' she wrote in her diary, 'and he blamed me for having to come down to mine. And yet out of affection for him, I had changed.'

She felt she was doing all she could to accommodate his world.

Once at the chateau, Lionel was more open with her about his financial woes. They wandered a field close to the chateau, talking.

'Only one room has not been diminished by the need to sell things off,' he said despondently, 'and as you can see, most of the place is in disrepair.'

'I haven't seen any farmers,' Céleste observed.

'They're leaving because they can't pay the rent. It's all a terrible downward spiral. My creditors are becoming more demanding by the week. I'm borrowing 60,000 francs at a rate of twenty per cent. But the money is scarce because of the revolution.' Lionel pointed to the northern farm sheds a kilometre away. 'The most depressing thing is the Belgian farmers. My father brought them here decades ago. Their families have been here for generations, but disease has forced them to leave.'

'The Fever?'

Lionel nodded. 'Farm hands are falling ill. They can't afford to buy enough food—nutrition—to fight it. They're slowing up and being struck down. I've given money to some of them, but it's not changing things.' He paused and sighed. 'It's very sad that this means my best land lies vacant. Worse, I'm presiding over the demise of this wonderful estate after twelve generations. It's all very depressing.'

King Louis-Philippe I and his family fled to sanctuary in England at the invitation of Queen Victoria as the threat of voting reform (in the form of 'The Chartists') and even revolution reached the United Kingdom. The upheaval in France spread. Uprisings occurred in the provinces. Noblemen's property, ever the symbol of inequality in Europe, became the target for attack. Chateaus in Berry were under siege, and some owners and their families were murdered. Lionel's property remained unscathed. He was universally liked in the region, yet she begged him not to go out. He ignored her for there was still much supervising to do, even in this period of decline and inevitable ruin.

One morning she became most nervous on seeing forty men approaching across the fields. She rushed inside to warn Lionel, who was in the study with Martin.

'They're waving guns and rifles!' she cried. 'Quick, we must hide in the basement.'

Céleste scurried to the cellar, thinking Lionel would follow. She heard shots and shouts for several minutes. When the noise subsided, she cautiously ventured out to find Lionel calmly smoking a cigar.

'What's happened?'

He pointed to the garden where the men had congregated and were drinking wine that Lionel had given them. A peasant, clearly the leader of the pack, wandered over to the terrace in front of the chateau.

'Stay calm,' he told her, 'everything will be alright. Listen to what I have to say to them.'

Lionel approached the leader of the band of peasants, who removed his hat.

'Do you think we could plant a tree of freedom, squire,' the leader inquired politely. 'We only want to have some fun and drink a toast to your health. If this offends you, we won't do it.'

'On the contrary,' Lionel said, remaining his relaxed, unruffled self, 'I would be honoured. But please don't plant it in my garden. Anywhere else in the fields will be fine.'

Céleste was proud of the affection and respect the locals had for Lionel, but was unsure how long it would last.

Céleste's hurried departure from Paris left her with bills to pay and Marie was sending a letter a day to remind her. She asked

Lionel for 200 francs to return to Paris. After much pocket-smacking and fiddling in wallets and in drawers he declared he did not have the cash and that he would have to borrow it for her. In that embarrassing moment Céleste realised she had more money than him.

CHAPTER 18

Roulette or Ruin

After she had paid her debts, Céleste had just 100 francs. She had assets, mainly in the form of jewellery that Lionel, Jean and others had given her. But she was loath to sell the pieces, especially anything from Lionel. Frisette suggested they go to the gambling halls and try their luck. Céleste was unsure at first. She was always concerned that the police would find any excuse to put her back behind bars, and the gambling halls were illegal. Nevertheless, after some persuasion she decided to take the risk and they rode a late-night carriage to a grand multi-storey house in Rue de l'Arcade. The two women puffed their way up six flights of red-carpeted stairs bedecked with lanterns.

The hostess was La Pepine, a pale-skinned, thin woman of thirty, her face framed by curly black hair, which gave her a wild look. Despite having accompanied Lionel and others on many roulette sprees, Céleste had never played the game herself, except to kiss the chips when a drunken character in her group was in search of some luck.

The banker arrived. He was Italian and wore a black suit with a white tie. He gave sharp orders to La Pepine and soon a dozen players, mainly young men, surrounded the table, ready to play. Seeing Céleste's hesitation, La Pepine suggested she follow the bets of an old suited gentleman, who wore war medals. She claimed he was lucky.

Céleste took a gold Louis from her purse and placed it on red near the decorated old man's money. She had just a few francs left.

The banker commanded, 'Place your bets, gentlemen! Place your bets!'

He spun the wheel and the mesmerising pill dance began with its *clip-clip* sound as it bounced around. Players held back as if they could somehow sense on which of the thirty-seven numbers it would land, or on which colour, red or black. Céleste watched with far more concentration than she ever had while at Lionel's elbow. Her money was in the game here.

'No more bets!' the banker said, and scowled as two young men flung coins down a fraction of a second after his order. The wheel slowed its spin. All eyes watched the pill stagger towards a stop.

'The black loses; the red wins!'

Céleste had won. She was about to cash in her modest win, when the decorated gentleman suggested she let them ride on the next spin. She had no wish to be called a coward by anyone at anything. She looked away as the wheel spun. Then the cry went up from the banker: 'The red loses; the black wins!'

Her easily gotten gains had been quickly taken from her. She placed a bet on red again, and it came up a second time in three spins. This time Céleste took her meagre profit into another room. La Pepine, whom she had judged as 'devilish', advised her to keep betting but to retire most of her wins each time. This was in contrast to the reckless betting at the table, and Céleste took the advice.

After two hours she had accumulated 2000 francs in gold in a cautious but calculated lucky streak, where La Pepine's wise counsel had worked. It was past 2 a.m. and the losers—most of the players—were showing strain and fatigue.

Céleste, full of zest, observed that the rouge on some of the women companions had faded. The losers, who until then had ignored her, were now 'letting their bad humour show' as they chatted to her in the hope that her streak might rub off on them. She felt sorry for one tall young man named Bresival, who searched his pockets, placed his hand on his forehead and looked at everyone in apparent despair.

'Would you like a few Louis?' Céleste asked him in pity. He grabbed at them and lost the lot inside five minutes. Céleste was about to give him more when La Pepine brought the players chocolate. She stepped on Céleste's foot and frowned at her disapprovingly. Bresival continued to watch Céleste, hoping for another handout, but she did not make eye contact again. Perceiving this as a snub, Bresival went berserk and had to be restrained as he attempted to destroy the roulette wheel, screaming that he'd been robbed.

It was 4 a.m. and Céleste felt it was time to leave, but not before telling La Pepine that she would like to see her again. The devil had proved more of an angel in Céleste's first ever attempt at roulette, where she joined the euphoric ranks of debutante winners.

There were 4000 francs in her purse.

The next day Céleste went around to all the merchants to whom she owed money—for jewellery, fabric, furnishings, dresses, shoes, bonnets and her carriage hire. She had ridden on credit and the minor ruse of not being at home when department stores such as Ville de Paris, Chaussée d'Antin, Trois Quartiers and Au Siège de Corinthe had delivered her purchases. This meant she would not receive the bill for another six months, though it would always come laden with high borrowing rates. It now gave her enormous pleasure to clear what she owed in one triumphant sweep around Paris. It put her in a good mood and she could not resist going on a spending spree, this time paying cash for four dresses, some undergarments and a purchase that delighted her most: a travel bag trimmed in silver.

Her roulette success had excited Céleste and she could not wait to return to the gambling table. But her motivation was more love and largesse than greed. Céleste wanted to have a swollen bank account when Lionel returned to Paris. She was still worried about the illegal nature of the gambling. However, the eternal pull of getting rich quickly without any labour of mind or body saw her respond to the siren call of that house on Rue de l'Arcade. This was aided by La Pepine, who told her to bring only 100 francs, and if she was to lose that, to stop playing. It was advice that went against the interests of La Pepine's employer, the banker, whom she feared and detested.

In the real world of money shortages, the French government was allowing people more time to pay off debts, landlords were reducing rents by a third, pawn shops would not lend anything over 100 francs, and commerce was generally on the decline. The so-called reform had been limited. Workers lost jobs despite government guarantees that its newly created workshops would lift unemployment. Bread prices rose. The government was accused of corruption. In the rarefied world of the Parisian gambling houses, gold, silver and bank notes were weighing down the roulette tables, and Céleste wondered where it all came from as she took the risk a second time.

She proceeded cautiously again, this time noting all the high rollers and how they played. She observed those that won regularly and how they managed it. She was most intrigued by one short, calm, cigar-smoking man who placed his bets in groups of ten chips at the low-number end of the table. Instead of going for the long shot of 36-to-1, he concentrated on the more discreet 6-to-1 chance. Céleste began to work the high end of the table in a similar manner. Her streak continued, though not as spectacularly as the man at the other end, who had to wrap both hands around his wins to drag them off the table. Céleste had already forsaken the fifty-fifty bet on black or red that had stood her so well on the first night. She would never be in the reckless class of those piling chips on one number, but she was beginning to believe she had some sort of magic touch. And money had never been made so easily, certainly not in her profession in such a short time. Céleste had made another 3000 francs in just ninety minutes and had received a wink from the little man, which indicated he knew she was more or less copying his moves. His only gesture of excitement was to puff more vigorously on his cigar, and Céleste copied this low-key reaction by not jumping up and down as she had the first time. Yet her glee was noticed by an elderly woman next to her. She scoffed at Céleste, telling her she had once won 100,000 francs on a single bet. The woman boasted she'd had a carriage and magnificent diamonds.

'I don't remember experiencing as much joy as you over these few Louis,' she commented with disdain, 'women are really degenerating!'

Céleste was in a good mood but not enough to accept such gratuitous and open insults.

'You should keep quiet about these treasures that have not served you well!' she retorted.

They were interrupted by the doorbell. Play froze.

'It's the police!' some of the gamblers cried. The banker moved swiftly.

'Open!' he ordered a servant, who pushed a button. The table, roulette wheel and all the money disappeared into a trap door in the floor. A rug was hastily placed over the trap door and a trembling La Pepine stepped to the door. The illegal enterprise was set up in her name, despite the banker owning and controlling everything. If there was a raid, she would be jailed, not the banker. She opened the door to be greeted by two slightly embarrassed young men. They had forgotten the password to be let in.

Loud, nervous laughter followed. La Pepine needed a stiff drink. Céleste was so spooked by this false alarm that she decided to leave with her cash and never return.

CHAPTER 19

The Riot that Ate Paris

Lionel returned from the country in mid-June 1848 as the Second Republic government's control broke down after it decided to close the workshops that it had been setting up since February. The idea of work for all was a good one and had been applauded nationally at first. But like many innovative concepts, it proved difficult to implement. The jobs were often low paid and dead-end, and the workers began to revolt. The workshops did not have enough funding. The money for them was supposed to come from taxing landowners, who refused to pay or, as in Lionel's case, could not pay. He was receiving no rent from his farms.

Lionel once again joined the National Guard, now more than 40,000 strong. The worker insurgents numbered 60,000 and, to swell their ranks, went from house to house recruiting more for their cause. But their tactics were counterproductive as they threatened to kill those who would not fight with them. They put up barricades and rioted throughout Paris. The grand City of Light went out as all the theatres and entertainment places such as the Hippodrome were shut down. Labourers descended from everywhere and Paris became an armed camp.

The insurrection began in earnest on 23 June 1848 with clashes between the National Guard, led by the ruthless General Louis Cavaignac, and the insurgents, who raided city armouries in desperation as their ammunition ran low.

Céleste's neighbourhood was quiet, mainly because the boulevards were too wide to put up barricades, but she began to hear alarming stories about other parts of Paris, including Le Marais, where her mother lived on Rue Saint-Louis, on the Right Bank of the Seine. The area was hit hard by the rioters. Houses were being attacked and burned down.

Céleste had lost touch with Anne-Victoire. She decided to risk entering Le Marais to find her, but she needed a special police pass to do so. Céleste, with trusty Marie, who insisted on going with her, had difficulty reaching the local police commissioner. They were blocked at several streets. Céleste pleaded with the police en route, and was finally allowed to see him.

To her delight and relief she found that the commissioner was a fan who had seen her perform at the Hippodrome many times. He tried to dissuade her from going, pointing out that hundreds of people, including many innocent bystanders, had been killed or injured. Céleste remained polite but firm. She wanted to rescue her mother.

Other officers urged the commissioner to let her have the pass.

'You know she's brave,' one of them said. 'Let her have it.'

The commissioner agreed reluctantly and told her to be careful. He suggested she take a circuitous route along the less-known and uncrowded streets to the Right Bank.

When they finally reached Le Marais and Rue Saint-Louis, Céleste could just make out her mother's house, but to reach it, they had to climb over a tall barricade, which would be an act of supreme courage. Onlookers shouted that people had been shot attempting this. Climbers were obvious targets for both the police and rioters. Céleste asked Marie to stay behind, but she was giving new meaning to the term 'maid of honour'.

Both women said a prayer, crossed themselves and bravely clambered up and over the barricade stretching across the street.[1] They held their breaths as they landed on the other side. No shots seemed directed at them. Then they ducked for cover as rioters came charging down the street towards them with police firing in pursuit. The rioters just managed to slip into a house, apparently unscathed.

Céleste and Marie scurried along to Anne-Victoire's building.

They were shocked to see it was partially demolished. There were police and others milling about the entrance foyer. Two women were weeping. Céleste soon learned the building's concierge had been shot dead the night before while trying to stop the rioters from forcing their way in.

Distressed, Céleste asked, 'Where is my mother …?'

She was interrupted by a male voice behind her. It was Vincent.

'Céleste!' he said. 'Your mother's fine, thank God! She's upstairs. Go up and see her.'

Céleste was a whirl of conflicting emotions. Her mother was not harmed. That lifted her. Seeing Vincent brought back a rush of negative feelings. Until there was some justice or retribution for his behaviour, she would never forgive and forget.

She hesitated, torn between comforting her mother and being in the presence of a man she wished dead. After a few seconds, she turned on her heel, Marie close behind her.

'You're not going upstairs?' Vincent asked.

'No,' Céleste replied, 'I've found out what I wanted to know.'

Lionel had arrived from the country.

'Céleste, darling,' he cried when she opened the front door. 'I missed you so! I worried about you.'

His concern cheered her. She now considered Lionel to be everything in her world, her father, brother, best friend and lover. Despite the blow-ups and recriminations, he was the person she knew best, who made her laugh more than cry and, despite everything, the one she trusted. Although Lionel was fickle at times, Céleste had faith in him. He had misled her rather than lie to protect her feelings as he sought the right social and financial partner. She believed in his basic integrity and compassion.

The riots had drawn people together as the death and injury tolls mounted. Seeing Vincent still with her mother, Céleste felt estranged from the only family she had. That left her Lionel, the one person to whom she gravitated and would be lost without amid the current danger. She would give him her last franc if he needed it.

'I want you to have the rest of my roulette earnings,' she said.

'I wouldn't dream of taking them,' he said with a mock frown. 'You, the girl who was so bored by the game, the game that you detested so much, when you watched me play …'

'Lose!'

'Yes, you win again. I'm a gambler and loser. But you must show me how you did so well.'

'Never! It would set you on the path of self-destruction again.'

'But how I need the money now,' he said with a shudder. 'I'm in Paris to secure a loan via my business manager. I think it just may tide me over at the estate. Or at least until the crisis subsides and the economy improves.'

Lionel failed to secure the loan. He was depressed and had to return to his estate. He asked her to join him, this time for a prolonged period while he tried to make the estate profitable.

'I love you very much,' he told her, 'but I'm not rich enough to keep you in Paris.'

His next utterances were about him not having enough furniture in the castle, and how 'one day when we're separate and I get married, I shall pay you what I owe you'. But these words were superfluous.

He had stated his love for her and he wanted her to live with him. For someone with her determination, tactical skills and passion, it was the moment of infinite possibility. She was well aware of his state of mind and ongoing confusion. Lionel was asking her to live with him and yet saw the relationship ending. The pragmatic issues—his status, privileges and money—were still placed above his heart and emotions. But Céleste knew the true makeup of the man. She had experienced his passion for roulette, his estate, hunting and her, and felt certain that his heart would rule his head if he were given the right encouragement, environment and circumstances.

Céleste again did not think twice about the offer. Four hours later she had asked her landlord to rent out her apartment and her bags were packed. Yet she took the precaution of securing a Paris pied-à-terre at 42 Rue de Londres. It would serve as a fallback if things did not work out. She also persuaded Lionel to accept 500 francs in gold coin, which was what remained of her roulette windfalls. He took them and then in a typically whimsical, romantic and profligate manner, he bought her a piece of jewellery worth 3000 francs. His name may not have been good enough to gain a loan, but it was still good with jewellers for the hire-purchase of an expensive luxury item. Céleste had a mixed reaction to this extravagance. She loved the gesture, yet at this moment it offended her that he should waste the money she had given him. Instead of reproaching him, she acted pleased and so avoided spoiling his joy at the act of giving.

The rebellion continued for five days until 28 June, and by the time Céleste and Lionel left Paris two days afterwards, reports were coming in of 10,000 dead and injured in the riots. A further 4000 insurgents were to be deported to Algeria. The city's recovery from the upheaval would be slow. Céleste knew that for a while she would not be missing much in Paris's alluring night-life. She also now believed the biggest challenge of her life was less a dream than a strong possibility. The downtrodden teenage girl from the working class was now a woman of twenty-three who might just become a countess.

CHAPTER 20

Rural Realities

Céleste busied herself at the chateau as her life changed from party girl and courtesan to almost being a squire's wife. She gave it her own twist by setting up an embroidering frame at which she worked most days. She also did good works in her unofficial role, giving away gifts of her handiwork, sweets and luxuries such as sugar to poor local children. When the hunting season began she accommodated Lionel's wish to entertain many guests at the castle. Despite her industry as embroiderer and hostess, she had plenty of time for relaxation and developed a passion for reading. The Chabrillan library was extensive, with all the modern classics. Céleste became immersed in the complete works of George Sand, especially because this woman had been the lover who jilted Alfred de Musset.

It was an inspiration if not an epiphany.

Céleste already had a store of life stories that could match that of any writer. As the months rolled by, reading became the mainstay of her rural existence, which had begun to bore her. Lionel was in his element, still living well beyond his means. Her boredom and his delusional lifestyle began to irritate her.

She started to question the way he was throwing away money on hunting and all its extra expenses, particularly the free-loading guests, who consumed his wine and devoured his food night and day when they weren't chasing wild boar and deer. This turned into a nag. They began to argue.

For a time Céleste avoided being alone by joining the hunting, which occurred three times a week. She was up there with the best of the male riders, but after a while the physical strain became too much and the effort affected her health. She and Lionel were becoming estranged, as Céleste spent most of the days and evenings alone in a large, draughty living room. She finally was her direct self.

'I'm bored,' she told him. 'Couldn't you be with me more often? I don't like country life; I'm used to the bustle of Paris.'

'Why do you stay, then? Am I keeping you against your will?'

'I'm here because I love you a lot. I agree to stay because the time you spend here is supposed to save you money. But hunting incurs tremendous losses.'

'I will go on hunting as long as I wish! If you're bothered by this you're free to go. As for admonitions, I don't tolerate them from anyone!'

It was the first time he had spoken to her with vehemence. It hurt Céleste, who had his best interests at heart. But this had been the most defiant rejection of her solid advice yet. He followed her up to her bedroom and was astonished to see her begin packing her trunks. He wanted to know why she was leaving. She replied that he was effectively throwing her out for the good and accurate advice she had given him.

'I'm telling you again,' she said. 'This way of life is ruining you. You won't be able to continue without adjusting another fortune with yours.'

He stood there frowning and mute, like a spoilt boy who refused to face facts.

'That means you'll have to marry,' Céleste went on. 'Then you'll send me away.'

'Your nerves are distraught,' Lionel said, veering away from the point.

'I don't like the country!' Céleste repeated more forcefully. 'It's a grave where my vivaciousness is being buried. What interest could I possibly take in what's around me?'

'I do nothing to hurt you!'

'Yes, but what does it mean to me that the poplars are growing and earn twenty *sous* a year?'

This angered Lionel.

'I let you sleep in my mother's bedroom! You, Céleste, who just a while ago went pale when looking at her own past in the mirror.'

She ignored this comment, which was not the first I-dragged-you-out-of-the-gutter barb from him.

'My interest is in dancing and the theatre,' she said. 'I want to leave.'

Lionel divulged that his family was alarmed that Céleste was living with him.

'Not a day goes by that I don't receive a letter asking me to send you away,' he added, going red. He paused, caught his breath and said, less aggressively, 'You're my weakness. If I have regrets, I forget them when I'm kissing you.'

She felt conflicted.

'Please don't leave me!' he implored her. 'No one loves you more than I do.'

She hesitated.

'I'm going to Paris in a few days. Wait and go with me.'

'Alright,' she said, without enthusiasm.

In the few days she waited, her maid, Maria, was found to be courting one of Lionel's butlers.

'You must fire her,' Lionel insisted. 'She led him on. He's a simple soul.'

'It takes two to dance the polka.'

'Fire her! It's bad form to have staff carrying on like that.'

Marie was given her marching orders. It hurt Céleste. The woman had been loyal for several years. Now she was being banished for an affair, which made Céleste feel guilty about the double standard.

She remarked mournfully in her memoirs, 'My life was becoming a voluntary restraint.'

On the way back to Paris, Lionel admitted he was using the opportunity to take Céleste away from his estate to *pretend* to his family that he was leaving her. The pressures, he explained, were intense and he had to 'go out in society' as his family wished. He was taking their relationship underground; he would rent his own apartment and see her once a week. He said he would give her money on each visit.

Céleste accepted this haughtily. She hated this sudden relegation of her relationship with Lionel to that of a courtesan, but she agreed to it for the time being. She reflected that he had declared his ongoing love and at least she would see him regularly. She decided that she would go to a Saturday-night ball at the Jardin d'Hiver, a glitzy place on the Champs-Élysées.

He stayed with her during their first days back in Paris. On the night of the ball he watched her dress.

'There's something missing from your attire,' he said, handing her a box containing a magnificent diamond cross. Céleste took it but with no joy. She believed it was a goodbye gift, a thought supported by his next remark.

'Keep a place for me in your heart once you're spinning in your pleasure circle.'

He drove her to the home of Victorine, a friend who was accompanying her to the ball. All Céleste could think of was picking up an admirer handsome enough to make Lionel jealous.

As usual she had no trouble.

One young man asked permission to call on her the next day at 4 p.m. He sent ahead a big bouquet of flowers with a note. Céleste left them on the table and Lionel saw them when he came over just before 4 p.m. He read the card.

'This gentleman is the son of a stockbroker,' he commented. 'He's very nice, but they say he's dumb. Not your type.'

The doorbell rang at the expected time. Lionel took the bouquet, opened the window that looked down into the street and dropped it right on the head of the caller. The embarrassed young man turned, went back to his carriage, rubbing the top of his head, and was driven off without looking back.

Céleste was pleased. It suggested that Lionel was jealous and still loved her. But the next night he took off for a ball of his own, and from midnight onwards Céleste suffered at the sound of every carriage clip-clopping by.

When he was out the next day, she found the key to his desk, opened it and found letters from his mother.

> *Are you finally done with this woman? I hope you are not seeing her anymore. Think of your future. Mademoiselle de Brillard wishes nothing more than to marry you. But she wants to make absolutely sure that you no longer have unfortunate liaisons.*

Céleste also found an unfinished letter from Lionel addressed to an uncle of the woman in question.

In asking for the hand of Mademoiselle de Brillard, I know what I am committing myself to and I am too forthright a man not to fulfil my duty. As for Mogador, it is possible that I was seen speaking to her in the street. The poor girl has not done me any harm, and I don't know why I would pass by her without looking at her.

Dear friend, you know what my life as a bachelor is like. One must find distractions. I found this one. What do you want me to do? One does not drown the girls one has lived with. As soon as I am married I shall leave with my wife. Do what you can to get Mademoiselle de Brillard to decide.

Céleste cried. She placed the letters back in the desk and locked it. Later she could not resist taunting Lionel with the letters' contents. He turned pale.

'I'm yielding to the wishes of my relatives about Mademoiselle de Brillard,' he said.

'Why didn't you tell me?'

'Why trouble you with something that has no hope of working anyway?'

'I don't believe you!' Then she asked, 'What did you mean when you wrote "if only one could drown the girls one has lived with, things would be easier"?'

'I didn't say that. How dare you read my personal mail!'

'All's fair in love and war.'

'Letters not addressed to you are sacred.'

'Don't deny your real emotions and talk such rubbish.'

'We should never see each other again,' he said. 'I'll settle 20,000 francs on you and return the furniture you bought for the castle.'

The next day he sent the few items she had at his apartment with a cold note repeating his final pledges. Céleste cried continuously in an emotional outpouring over this apparent end of the affair, although deep in her heart she did not believe it was over.

Both liked histrionics. Céleste was more determined and better at it.

CHAPTER 21

Love in the Time of Cholera

Céleste occupied herself during this period of grief over Lionel by hiring a new maid. She interviewed more than a hundred applicants and narrowed down her choice to those who were married and who could sew dresses. The first criteria was to hopefully avoid a repeat of the minor scandal that occurred over Marie and Lionel's butler at the castle. Céleste chose a stout sixteen-year-old named Caroline, who said she was married to a coachman. After a few weeks Céleste noticed her new employee seemed to have put on weight around the waist, but the girl denied she was pregnant. Not long after that she learned that Caroline was in the hospital at Faubourg Saint-Honoré, giving birth. Céleste rushed to her and quickly ascertained that Caroline was not married, which was the reason she had hidden the pregnancy. Céleste was sympathetic and guaranteed she could return to her job when she was fit and ready. A relieved and delighted Caroline asked Céleste to be her daughter's godmother.

Céleste visited Caroline at the Beaujon Hospice after she had given birth. The baby girl was so frail that Céleste was sure she would not survive. The father was present and he asked Céleste to hold the child at the baptism the next day. Céleste obliged.

She had the responsibility of naming the baby and called her Solange, after one of the young peasant children on the estate who had often visited her. Céleste suddenly felt an attachment to the child that went beyond her duty.

'On the way out of the church I held her against my heart,' she recalled. 'I felt like running away with her as if she were mine.' Céleste had decided that she would not have children, believing they would interfere with her various career choices. But at moments such as these her compassion and maternal instincts emerged.

Céleste returned Solange to the hospice and then went in search of a nursemaid for her. The following day she visited Caroline. She looked pale and hollow-eyed.

'Oh, Madame,' Caroline managed to whisper hoarsely, 'the nursemaid must come today. Death is in this room! Since your last visit, five women and four children have died.'

When Céleste looked across to the other side of the room, she saw a young woman holding a small baby in her arms.

'She was trying to nurse him,' Céleste wrote in her memoirs, 'but he would not suckle.' Céleste asked a medical orderly what this meant. The orderly looked skyward without replying, indicating to Céleste that this baby would soon die, too. Céleste slipped five francs into the orderly's hand and, pointing to Caroline, said, 'Take good care of the woman over there.'

'Oh, you're the daughter's godmother?' the orderly whispered. 'Take her out of here, now!'

This was uttered with such urgency that Céleste realised something significant was behind the directive. She returned to Caroline, saying she was taking Solange for care to a nursemaid on Rue de la Victoire and would take her home at night. The desperate Caroline was relieved to know that Solange would be out of the hospice and Céleste comforted her further by promising to return to see her the next day.

Céleste marked the date in her diary: 19 March 1849. When she returned as she'd promised, she found the hospice in turmoil. Rooms on every floor had been rearranged. Women in labour had been moved from the first floor to the third. Céleste and all visitors had to submit to scrupulous cleaning of the hands and face, as did the medical staff. She asked a nurse why. The woman confided that seventeen women and children had died in a week.

'Mortality was two-thirds more likely in women who had just given birth,' she was told. Céleste was frightened by this revelation, then puzzled. What was the correlation?

'The problem has spread on the floor where these birthing women are,' the nurse said, looking more and more plaintive and nervous.

'What problem?' Céleste asked.

The nurse moved close, leaned near her ear and whispered, 'Cholera!'[1]

Céleste was frightened. Even the name sounded sinister.

'The doctors are sure of it,' the nurse said, and seeing Céleste's alarm and confusion added, 'All the medicos know is that it's spread through water and food, which has been contaminated by human faeces.'

'Can it be cured?'

'Only by extreme sanitation, Mademoiselle, and clean drinking water.'

While they whispered together, workmen were rolling barrels of water into the foyer near them.

'If you care for your poor friend,' the nurse said, 'take her away from here!'

'Tomorrow her husband will bring her to me,' Céleste said. 'Have her release card signed.'

The following day, Caroline had to be almost carried into Céleste's home.

'She seemed so changed,' a startled Céleste recorded. 'Caroline's eyes were sunken; her cheeks hollow; her lips black. I put her in my bed and sent for Lionel's doctor.'

The doctor came and examined Caroline. Then, looking sombre, he took Céleste aside.

'Send the child away before she sees her,' he instructed. 'The child must not come near her.' The doctor left. Céleste put some powdered camphor in Solange's clothes, bonnet and booties. Then she took the baby to Caroline.

'I handed her to her mother,' Céleste recalled, 'so she could hold her one last time.'

The action was humane and compassionate, though it was a risk because nothing short of burning a body infected with cholera could get rid of the disease completely.

'I was nervous,' she recorded.

Then Solange was taken away by the new maid, a German teenager with instructions not to go near Caroline, even if she pleaded to see the child again.

The doctor monitored the patient for three days and told Céleste there was no hope for her.

'Since her husband is at her side,' the doctor added, 'leave and go to your friend's house. I've done all I can.'

Céleste stayed the night at a girlfriend's house. She dreamed all night about Caroline, woke early and made her way home.

Caroline was lying in front of a roaring fire. She seemed rigid and cold, her eyes closed. Céleste took her hand.

'Caroline, can you hear me?'

'Kind mistress,' Caroline said, her voice feeble. 'I was waiting for you.'

Céleste reassured her she was staying and that she was sending for a priest.

'We shall pray together,' Céleste said softly. Caroline's husband went to the local church. The dying woman motioned for Céleste to come close.

'Will you take care of the baby?' she asked, her eyes pleading. 'You're all she will have.'

'Yes,' Céleste said with conviction. 'I shall take care of her.'

Caroline struggled during the prayer. The cholera struck hard. She contorted. The priest, her husband and Céleste fought to keep her from rolling off the bed.

'She stiffened and fell back,' Céleste wrote in her memoirs, 'her mouth and eyes open.'

Céleste placed one hand on Caroline's forehead and one on her own heart and swore that she would raise the infant.

'I will make an honest woman of her,' Céleste added poignantly as if to reassure the priest.

She knew this was a big undertaking. Caroline was correct. Tiny Solange would have no one else. The father was not Caroline's husband. He was married to someone else and had kept the affair secret.

'Without me,' Céleste wrote, 'the poor little girl would only have the Foundlings Home.'

CHAPTER 22

Richard: Another Fallguy

Céleste took responsibility for her adopted daughter, but it did not change her lifestyle. Adele, the new maid, took charge of Solange while the mistress of the house attempted to avoid thoughts of Lionel and make herself available as one of the top courtesans and actresses in Paris, along with Thérèse Lachmann, Caroline Letessier, Alice Ozy, Alphonsine Plessis and Apollonie Sabatier. Céleste met a young Englishman named Richard Maylam, who she dubbed 'handsome and too good-looking for a man'. Richard became her main partner. She made it clear to him, however, that she loved another, and he would become irked by talk of 'Lionel this ... and Lionel that'. But Richard, being besotted with his quasi-conquest of one of the decade's superstars, put up with playing a distant second in her affections. He accepted the situation and demonstrated a certain humility and grace. These were the unwritten rules of this so-called Romantic Age, where the top women reigned over this artificial world of partying and licentious behaviour, fashion, and in the modern parlance, the 'A-list'. The pleasure and honour of escorting and bedding these women could lead to the massive denting of egos.

Richard seemed so enchanted that he didn't care about the possible trade-off for squiring Céleste about town. And she was always honest with him, after charming him into submission.

The more she was away from Lionel, the more her passion magnified his positive qualities. Céleste put aside his born-to-rule arrogance and petulance; his put-downs about her background and life; his bank account– and asset-withering lifestyle; and his incompetence at most things, except hunting. She thought only of his being a gentleman in the smallest details. He had a quick mind and was 'kind, generous and honest'. He was 'so exuberant in ardour and imagination'.

Richard did not quite measure up, although she found him 'sweet and kind'. He was generous, too. He set her up opulently, paid for her sometimes extravagant accumulation of clothes, shoes and jewels, and made sure she was invited with him to the best parties. This created the opportunity for her to stand tall among all the Paris princesses of the late 1840s. The artifice was at its peak. Céleste was on top.

Now settled in to yet another new apartment, this time at 24 Boulevard Poissonnière, Richard and Céleste were walking to a nearby restaurant, the Maison d'Or, when they were confronted by Lionel. He stopped in front of them and asked if he could have a private word with her. Richard realised it had to be her long-term paramour and was irritated. He agreed, most reluctantly, to her polite invitation that he carry on to the restaurant and she would follow.

Lionel apologised for the interruption but claimed he had to talk 'business' with her.

'I should have known that when one leaves a woman like you for just a few hours,' he began in a cutting tone that Céleste knew well, 'it's necessary to write ahead, to avoid running into others.'

Céleste diplomatically ignored his remark.

'You had the right to leave me,' she said, 'and I had the right to replace you. I have no fortune. I'd rather die than ask you for anything.'

'So, you don't love this man?'

'No, unfortunately.'

'Then stay with me. Don't have dinner with him. You owe me that much. I've broken off everything. I can't live without you. If you go out with him, I'm leaving and will never see you again.'

Céleste had heard this kind of declaration before. She called his bluff by telling him she still loved him but that she could not stoop so low towards Richard.

'I'm going to dinner with him,' she said. 'After dinner I shall write and tell him I can't see him anymore.'

'Go,' Lionel said, 'I shall wait for you.'

Richard was overjoyed to see Céleste walk into the Maison d'Or but was soon deflated by the news that she was going to see Lionel after the meal. Richard asked for the truth and she confirmed that she still loved Lionel.

'I can't compete against him,' he conceded, and told her to leave. 'Your presence hurts me,' Richard admitted, 'but do not forget me.'

Lionel was waiting at her apartment, but he was cold. Inside, he made disparaging remarks about all the 'tasteless' furniture and expensive artefacts Richard had bought for her. Lionel then produced the pièce de résistance in the form of an emerald-and-diamond set of jewellery, including a bracelet, a brooch, earrings and rings. He had paid his Royal Palais jeweller 40,000 francs for the set, double the amount he had offered her as a parting settlement before. But this was now an enticement to come back, and in particular to return with him again to his Berry estate.

In the euphoria and romance of the moment, she accepted without reflecting on the sluggish life (compared to her high-kicking Paris life) she had endured the last time. There was always the hope that things would improve. But they did not. Lionel hunted more boar than ever, and she became more bored than ever. He was slipping into debt again and as ever this offended her somewhat hypocritical sensibilities. Predictably, she and Lionel were heading for a big argument. It was precipitated by him coming home without shooting a boar. He was grumpy over what he considered a defeat.

Céleste took the moment to go on the attack.

'This chateau is bad luck,' she said. 'Your gardener has lost his two daughters to The Fever in less than a month. The little girl after whom I named my daughter has lost her mother. There's rabies in your kennels. All I hear is howls at night. Each day one or two of those wonderful hounds I practically raised must be hanged.'

Lionel's face was expressing a kaleidoscope of emotions, most of them dark. His face puffed up red.

'You spend money madly and this household is ruining you!' Céleste continued. 'You made me an accomplice in your follies by giving me those magnificent jewels.'

'They made you happy!' he exclaimed.

'Happy? I shall tell you what I need to be happy near you: I need to see you curtail your expenses! I would be delighted to stay cooped up here if I encouraged you to straighten out your fortune.'

Céleste was hitting home more than she knew. A few days later Lionel lost an 'important' amount on the stock market, not necessarily due to his poor judgement. He could not be blamed for the vicissitudes of his stocks and the market. But it exemplified his less-than-golden touch. Nothing he did in business or with money, at least in Céleste's experience, seemed to be sound. He was a loser at the Bourse or roulette, in investments or even in his choice of agents and managers. The volatility of politics and the markets at the time damaged his luck, and his dwindling, credit-driven fortune.

Lionel no longer mentioned his quests for a rich partner anymore, but Céleste's deep love for him made her sensitive to every nuance of his emotions, perhaps even his deeper thoughts. Failure to shoot a boar only exacerbated his more important preoccupations. She sensed that he was yet again considering the prospect of a more suitable, wealthy wife.

'When you are jealous,' she would later write, 'you look for the truth until you find it. Then you are ten times more miserable.'

'Since you care so much for the chateau,' she said, pushing him, 'go ahead. Accept a marriage that will make you twice a millionaire.'

She half expected the bluff would not work this time. He admitted that a marvellous proposition had been offered.

'I turned it down because of you,' he said with a measure of regret.

He suggested she return to Paris, which she did.

CHAPTER 23

Actress

This time the split changed her thinking. She had forsaken Richard, although she hoped he would remain a friend. This meant she could not rely on him to prop up her finances. She was approaching twenty-five years of age and she had Solange to provide for. Like all the demimonde habitués, Céleste realised that the brainless party life could not go on forever. She either had to find a man to support her in marriage or somehow obtain a job that would deliver security. And since she believed she would never find another man she truly loved while Lionel was alive, she had to seek a trade or profession that would sustain her. Her mind ran over several options. But after her exposure to fame at Bal Mabille and the Hippodrome, which had been only two years before, she could not really countenance another dress or fashion shop, or any mundane retail job for that matter.

Her mind turned to her deepest passion: the theatre.

She did not regard her former flirtation with the stage as a serious, planned and organised effort at acting. But having attained the status of a top courtesan, there was only one level above in her world that enjoyed more fame, rather than notoriety, and was more acceptable in French society, and that was being an actress. Céleste decided that this was the moment to try for this profession and follow her youthful dreams. She had been forced into risk-taking and now it was part of her way of life. She did not wish to die wondering whether or not she had what it took to be a success on the stage. She needed the adrenaline rush that she had had at Bal Mabille, the Hippodrome and her few previous dance performances. The fame and the thought of being loved and even more recognised were also important to her. There was always the hope that an elevated position in society might help erase the past and assist her in her fervent desire to be removed from the prostitutes' registry. If she maintained her reputation as a courtesan, the police prefecture and courts would always regard her as a prostitute, albeit one of high class.

Céleste at first fumbled around the theatre world. From a series of rejections she learned that she must try to present herself to Monsieur Mourier, director of the Théâtre des Folies-Dramatiques. He had a reputation for being fierce and direct and the best theatre administrator in Paris. Céleste liked the fact that he paid his actors well, and had still accumulated a fortune for himself. She asked actors about him and always received the same positive response. Céleste thought it better to write to him, which would display her ever-improving command of French. She had been barely literate as a teenager, but reading as a hobby and writing a diary had developed her confidence in the written word. She expressed herself well and with more than a dash of panache.

Mourier was impressed. Like everyone in the Parisian theatre world and most of the city's inhabitants, he knew of Céleste. He invited her to meet. She entered his office, its walls adorned with colourful posters of his countless successful stage productions. He was at his desk, writing. He did not get up, but let her stand in front of it. Perhaps he was judging her composure under pressure. Maybe he was just rude and impolite and this was part of his 'blunt' image. He looked sideways at her and asked, 'Have you ever acted?'

'Yes, Monsieur, but very little and not well,' Céleste replied. 'I was in a play at Beaumarchais and one at Delassement.'

'And so you would like to be here?' he asked, taking off his glasses and running a weary hand over his bald pate.

Céleste nodded firmly.

'I must warn you that you'll have to work and be on time,' he said, scrutinising her now.

'If you wish me to try out, you don't have to pay me to start.'

That seemed to touch a nerve, perhaps his pride. He got out of his chair. 'Mademoiselle, I don't hire for nothing! I pay the people who serve me.'

He reached for a script on his desk.

'Someone has sent me a parody called *The Wandering Jew*,' he said, putting on his glasses and examining the front cover. 'There's a part for a bacchanalian queen.' He looked over his glasses at her and asked, 'Will that do?'

The director may have been making a cynical choice, given that bacchanalian festivals were riotous affairs ending in orgiastic rites. But Céleste did not care. It was a break. She asked about the play.

'The Wandering Jew, as a twelfth-century legend has it,' the director replied, 'was the fellow who would not let Jesus Christ, carrying the heavy wooden cross to his own crucifixion, rest in front of his house. God allegedly told this mean yet unfortunate chap that he would have "to wander the earth until I come".'[1]

'Nicely set up for a parody,' Céleste said, accepting the part.

Céleste was elated. She felt like shouting to passers-by in the street about her breakthrough. She happened to be in Boulevard Saint-Denis, where Richard lived. He was surprised to see her. He listened to her enthusiastic babble about the contract she had just won. He was 'cold'. He inquired about the relationship with Lionel and was told about yet another split. Richard was naturally sceptical. The off-again, on-again affair was well known in the demimonde. Céleste judged that the meeting was hurting Richard, who dampened her enthusiasm for the theatre contract by saying it was a wrong move.

'You'll end up spending more than you earn,' he said. He would be threatened by any success she had because he feared that even if Lionel was removed from the scene, she would be desired by more rivals than ever, which would once more make her inaccessible. Nevertheless, Céleste's charm had thawed him by the time she left. She had dangled hope, just enough to kindle his interest again. Soon afterwards, with the euphoria of her new stage deal, their affair was reignited. Richard, however, would never feel secure knowing that her real passion was still for someone else.

Céleste brought all her wit and charm to the Folies-Dramatiques but found it wasn't enough in this rarefied world of massive egos, extreme narcissism and perpetual insecurity. It was not unlike her early days at the brothel. The female performers wanted to know why Mourier had dared to hire the notorious Mogador. They whispered that her main claim to public interest was being a chariot rider. They were not quite mollified by being told she would boost ticket sales. The older performers felt alarmed; the younger ones threatened by her looks and reputation.

The male performers were a different proposition.

'They were all very charming with me,' Céleste wrote, 'and fought over the pleasure of giving me the advice I so desperately needed.'

She prepared with some of the biggest names of the day, including the famous Jacques Odry, who was sixty-eight, a bit doddery and prone to forgetting lines and missing cues. She found the talented, popular Alphonse Lassagne too cocky for her liking. He played tricks on her on stage.

'He would add [lines] to his part,' she recalled, 'and I would miss my cue and not know what to do.'

Mourier stepped in angrily at these moments and Lassagne would be threatened with fines, but it did not stop him tormenting the new girl. However, Céleste was not put off by the stunts. It toughened her. Yet she did not make an impact on the stage and struggled to be thrown bit parts that neither satisfied her nor the audiences. The critics sneered and jeered.

Meanwhile, there were more dramas in her private life. Lionel kept reappearing from the country and went to extreme lengths to woo her back by mortgaging his lands and giving her ever more expensive gifts. The peak of this was his buying, rather than renting, her an 'adorable little surrey drawn by a pretty bay horse'. The carriage was bright blue. The silk interior was lined in the same colour. Céleste's name was on the harness. A small, painted garland on the door panel held the words 'Forget me not' alongside her initials. She was overwhelmed.

'I walked around it ten times,' she wrote in her memoir. 'I touched the ivory ornaments; I opened and closed the windows. I looked at the passers-by with pride.'

She rushed inside her apartment to put on a green dress, red shawl and yellow hat. 'I must have looked like a parrot,' she wrote. Dressed in all this finery, she went on a two-hour ride around the Bois de Boulogne. 'Everyone let out an "oh" and "ooh" when they saw me.'

Céleste felt she had reached the pinnacle of her life as a courtesan. She was part of the continuous procession of sparkling, ornate carriages trotting around the Bois. It was where the top women of the demimonde promenaded in the mid-afternoon for eager spectators who lined the path on either side from the Grande Cascade to the middle of the Place de la Concorde.

She found it difficult to leave on that first exalted day. On the way home, she spotted Richard, and in a moment of vanity signalled for him to come closer. But he walked away without a friendly gesture. He was not, at that moment, an enchanted admirer. But his aloofness did not last long.

That encounter led to Richard sending her a note at the theatre urging her to see him. She obliged and visited his apartment. He appeared tired but what he had to say was new. He proposed marriage.

'I'm offering you a happy, honourable future,' he said, taking her hands in his. 'It will help you forget a past I shall never again mention.'

Céleste was dumbfounded.

'I shall give you 40,000 francs,' he added. Seeing she had not rejected him, he said, 'We shall immediately leave for England where I shall marry you without difficulty. I'm English and have no parents.'

She buried her face in her hands. 'But it's impossible!' she cried.

Richard was furious. She calmed him by saying that she had no idea this was coming. He had caught her off guard. She said she felt faint, but to mollify and stall him, she suggested he go to London to see if it really could be arranged the way he was proposing. She would write to him in a few days' time, which would be the signal for him to return to Paris and then take her back to London. Richard was defensive. He didn't believe she would write. But once reassured, he agreed.

The stakes were now higher than ever before. She wished to see Lionel's reaction before doing anything so precipitative with Richard. She got in touch. Lionel invited her to dine at his apartment, but in the presence of a male friend. Midway through the meal, she was in two minds about bringing up Richard's proposal. Then Lionel started a quarrel, 'as usual, for no reason'.

'Once and for all,' she demanded, 'why do you reproach me?'

'Because you have poisoned my heart!' he replied.

The argument built. Céleste finally revealed her secret offer.

'I wish I didn't have to tell you,' she said, 'but this life is hell! It would be better to leave you for good.'

'Bravo!' he said and laughed. 'What great acting. What imaginative blackmail. You only told me this to force me to match the offer. Well, I urge you to accept.'

Céleste was exasperated. She left, vowing never to see him again. It was a vow they both made to each other regularly but never kept. However, she was determined to go to London to be with Richard. She got leave from Mourier. When she arrived home there was a letter waiting for her from Lionel.

'The heart of a girl like you is like a disreputable inn,' he wrote. 'The honest wayfarer who inadvertently enters, endures the sneers of the regular guests.' He said his love for her was real, whereas her fake love 'began with a caress and ended with a price. I am not rich enough. You are free.'

Richard received a letter from her and returned to Paris. They decided to leave the next night for their marriage in London. Céleste had to get her mother's consent. He also wished to deposit the 40,000 francs in her bank account. Céleste refused to take it.

'It will help your little girl,' Richard said, insisting she take it. 'The money is yours, whatever happens.'

Céleste began to regret her move the moment the train left Paris. It was the whistle, the yell of the guard for 'all aboard!' and then the steady shunt of the carriages away from the station that symbolised her leaving Lionel. It was an emotional moment. Richard comforted her, and may have guessed her misgivings.

Her impression of London did not help her mood. The fog blocking the daylight was bad enough. When it cleared it released a black snow, a consequence of the industrial revolution's factories belching out smoke and waste. It stained her white hat and spotted her face.

'I looked like a chimney sweep!' she wrote in her diary, disgusted. After cleansing her face with cold cream, she only went out by carriage to visit the British monuments. She was not impressed to have to pay entrance fees, especially to see 'a few jewels in a glass case'.

Richard fussed about, arranging nights at the opera, theatre and clubs. He remained most concerned that Céleste might leave because of nerves brought on by boredom. He prepared everything for the wedding. Her resolve wavered. It was not improved by a letter from Lionel at the post office. He had contacted Céleste's maid and bribed her into revealing where Céleste had gone. His communication was mostly negative and a squeak of the heart, rather than a cry. It spoke of his perpetual suffering because of her, but said the marriage would be 'sheer madness'.

'Once the whim has passed,' he told her, 'all you have left are regrets and bitterness.'

Céleste, in her own dramatic and perverse way, seemed to thrive on these moments. She cried and declared to her diary that she believed this letter proved Lionel still loved her. The pressure was truly on—it was just hours until the wedding began. Richard had even gone to the trouble, a dangerous one for a man, of choosing her entire wedding outfit: a pearl-grey brocade dress, a black lace shawl and a white hat. The veil was 'fit for a queen'. It may have been wiser to consult the bride.

'This outfit,' she told him, 'is terribly gloomy.'

As effete as Richard appeared, he didn't quite have a woman's touch. The carriage arrived at their Knightsbridge hotel and they headed off towards a small church in Sydney Street, Chelsea. Céleste remained silent. Whatever niceties he offered her, and no matter how many times he told her she looked 'ravishing' and 'angelic', she hardly looked at him or reacted. When they were on the King's Road and in sight of the church, Céleste panicked.

'No, no!' she instructed the coachman as they reached the church's entrance. 'Keep going! Don't stop!'

The coachman turned a querulous face to Richard.

'Richard,' she said, 'tell him to go past this door! I must speak to you!'

Céleste sat back in the carriage, gripping a cushion. Richard ordered the coachman to drive back the mile or so to the hotel. Once inside their suite, he asked her sweetly what she had to say to him. His gentle manner made it tough for her to tell him what was on her mind. Her body shook.

'Richard, you should have nothing but contempt for me!' she wailed. 'I'm not worthy of a love like yours. Send me away. I'm a wretch!'

She may have spoken his mind. He had just been jilted, not too far from the altar, and by an unseen rival. Richard was suddenly very angry, but in keeping with his controlled gentlemanly nature, all he could utter was, 'How you must love this man!'

They returned by train to Paris the next day with hardly a word exchanged between them.

CHAPTER 24

A Platonic Solution

'I have just been at the Count de Chabrillan's house, Mademoiselle,' a doctor informed her on her return to Paris. 'I've seen him four times since 6 p.m. yesterday. I've bled him twice. Blood is choking him and he's delirious. He has twenty times asked that you be brought before him.'

Céleste rushed to the house with the doctor and they arrived just as Lionel was having a seizure. The doctor attended to him. Hours later, when he was fully conscious, he recognised Céleste.

'Come closer,' he said, 'so I can see what a woman who can cause such pain looks like. What magic did you use to seduce me, daughter of Satan!'

He haemorrhaged again. The doctor bled him a fifth time and gave instructions to Céleste to stay with the patient. She obliged willingly and spent a week with him. In that time she wrote to Richard, who despite the humiliation in London was still keen to see her. She told him of Lionel's illness and that she was caring for him.

'Forget me,' she said. 'A bit of courage will spare you a life of regrets. Forgive me.'

Richard could not quite take the advice, but in order to preserve his sanity he left Paris to stay with relatives in the country. Lionel began recovering and Céleste left his apartment but kept seeing him over the next three months until he was fully recuperated. In that time, his elder brother, the 'fat, jolly' Marquis Marie-Olivier, came to see her. His message from the family was that she was 'sending Lionel broke, like an idiot!'

Céleste was nervous at her first meeting with the head of the family, but his attitude incensed her. She stayed calm. The marquis, who did not care for Lionel, added, 'Tell him he should get married. What will you do with him when he has not a single farthing left?'

She felt like saying she would love him even more, but the brother's attitude reflected that of the family, who hated her and her influence on Lionel. She again said nothing. Instead, she reported the discussion to Lionel that evening. It was a useful pretext for considering his future. Although she discounted the marquis as a man and a messenger, his approach made her realise that the family would never let Lionel marry her. Quite simply, her reputation and background were unacceptable to such an aristocratic clan.

Lionel's severe illness had shaken Céleste and she seemed sincere in telling him that if he wished to marry, 'I would not be angry with you'. If she was in the way, she would leave Paris. 'We would go from this great love to friendship that always endures.'

Lionel saw the wisdom in this and suggested a halfway house of sorts. He would set her up in a modest house in Berry near the estate so that he could continue to see her. They would be friends. On the surface this may have seemed a fair solution, given that breaking up had never worked. But Céleste was oblivious to the possibility that she would soon become bored with such an arrangement, which might see her even more isolated from the Paris she loved. Besides that, she still had high hopes for her acting career, which was going through a lull at the Folies-Dramatiques. Nevertheless, if it were to be simply a retreat, where they both saw each other from time to time, then it just might work. They went ahead with this new plan. A 'darling little house' opposite a forest was found in nearby Poinçonnet, and she moved in, while not giving up her Paris apartment.

Around this time her mother came to see her, needing help. Céleste said she would set her up in a tobacco shop, if she swore she would not see Vincent anymore. Céleste did as she said she would, and also acquired a suite for Anne-Victoire at a hotel on Rue de Cléry. A short while later, she went to see her mother at the tobacco shop, which had an apartment above it.

'Her brightest idea had been to rent the apartment to M. Vincent,' she wrote with contempt in her diary. She was so angered by this that she evicted them both and sold the shop. She made it clearer than ever that she could forgive her mother, but never Vincent.

The 'friendship' arrangement between Lionel and Céleste worked well enough for several months, with Céleste staying occasionally at her country retreat. But it enchanted her less and less, and she and Lionel were spending more time in Paris, although not together. The arrangement became unmanageable when Richard Maylam returned to Paris after 'recovering his equilibrium' in the country.

Céleste had invited a female friend to dine at her place, and a table for two was set by the maid. Back from his country sojourn, Richard arrived unannounced. Then the doorbell rang a second time. Céleste asked Richard to answer the door. Instead of her friend, Richard found himself facing Lionel, who entered the apartment. Noticing her table set for two he said, 'Fine, I know what I wanted to know.' He then addressed Richard. 'You wanted to marry this girl; you can have her. She's yours.'

'I thank you for your advice, Monsieur,' Richard replied. 'You've known her for four years. Four years from now, I shall give you an answer.'

Duels were fought with pistols at dawn over lesser incidents during this era, but Lionel left after directing a look of loathing at Céleste. Distressed, she asked Richard to leave, too. Then her guest arrived and spent the rest of the evening consoling Céleste over her moment of melodramatic farce. But it was more than that and threatened to revive the triangle of dysfunction that had prevailed before.

Lionel reacted by taking another mistress, Charlotte Odene, an attractive, auburn-haired twenty-year-old from Montpellier in France's south, whom another man had brought to Paris for 10,000 francs. Lionel doubled the offer and Charlotte accepted when he swore to her that his well-publicised, now long-term rough ride with the formidable Mogador was over. He then put his newly purchased mistress in his apartment. Céleste heard rumours of this development and was unhappy. She tried to convince herself that had Lionel taken a richer, aristocratic partner and married her, she would not have stood in his way. But taking another, younger version of herself—a *lorette* or courtesan on the make—was not what Céleste had envisaged. Lionel's excuse was that he had failed to reach any agreement with the numerous suitable but wary young women. The possible countesses had not been so concerned with his looming poverty or even the likelihood that he would have to mortgage his lands and eventually sell them. Most would have put up with that. The big problem was his never-ending affair with the prostitute/dancer/chariot rider/actress Mogador. How could any self-respecting wife of the Parisian elite deal with having to foot the bills for his ongoing dalliance with and generosity towards such a woman? The families rejected this even if the smitten young beauties of France's highest circles did not. In turn, Lionel's passion for Céleste was so deep that it showed. Subconsciously or otherwise, he was putting off every prospective wife. A newly ensconced concubine amounted to him avoiding everything except anaesthetising himself with a flurry of sex, drinking and more gambling.

Despite the haze of the decadent high life, he still wanted some connection with Céleste. He wrote to her demanding she come to see him. Richard told her Lionel was boasting that she would 'go to his house any time he wanted'.

This prompted her to reject his invitation. Lionel then wrote a pitiable letter saying he only wished to see her 'to wallow in the misery of hatred you have left in me'.

'I want to end up between the bottle that supplies the drunkenness it promises,' he wrote, 'and a pistol that will grant me forgetfulness.'

The letter unsettled Céleste. It sounded like a suicide threat.

CHAPTER 25

Crime of Passion

Richard invited Céleste to a benefit dance performance at Paris's Cirque. Despite the vivid lighting and costumes, she found it all too dreary. That changed, hideously, when she spotted Lionel with his new mistress. Charlotte began to behave in a coquettish manner, more for Céleste's benefit than Lionel's. Out of the corner of her eye, Céleste saw Charlotte touching his arm, then his hand. The bold Charlotte even leaned up to kiss him several times. It was too much for Céleste, who asked Richard to take her home. He pleaded with her not to go or make a scene for once, for his sake.

'Today, in front of all these people who are observing us,' he said, 'make the effort, for one hour.'

In these moments of almost uncontrolled feelings she had often behaved as if all men were Vincent. She would either walk away or make them pay, at least emotionally. This time, she acquiesced, writing that she felt 'like a child'. In other words, it was very much against instinct. Richard dropped her off at her apartment and she went to bed. But the whole experience of seeing Lionel at play with this younger, sexually inviting mistress built to a rage. She got up, dressed and at 1 a.m. made her way on foot to Lionel's place. Céleste woke the porter, persuaded him to let her in and hurried upstairs to the second floor.

'I rang [the bell],' she recalled, 'powerfully enough to make the house shake.' Lionel answered the door holding a candle.

'You here!' he said. 'What do you want from me now?'

She thrust his letter at him as she pushed past. 'I'm here because you wrote to me yesterday!'

Lionel laughed and then implied that the letter was written in a state of alcohol-induced melancholy. 'So I did, after lunch.'

'You mentioned killing yourself!'

'You only came because you saw me with another woman … She's here and can hear everything,' he said and then taunted, 'I love her! She's beautiful; as beautiful as you are ugly!'

Céleste was fuming. 'I would be married if it weren't for your letter to me in London.'

She turned to go, but Lionel blocked her exit. He wanted to insult her in front of his one-person audience.

'I despise you,' he said, 'you miserable wretch, whom I picked up out of the mud! In gratitude you have defiled me!'

Céleste tried to push past him, but he thrust the candle at her.

'You used me as a ladder,' he continued. 'You placed yourself on the auction block and sold yourself to the highest bidder!'

Céleste picked up a knife from a sideboard and threatened him.

'Finally.' Lionel laughed. 'I see you're suffering.'

'Banish this woman,' she said, 'or I shall kill you!'

Lionel shrugged and still blocked her way.

Céleste pushed the knife at her chest. It was not an overly vigorous act, but Lionel now moved to take the knife from her. She attempted to stab him in the right arm and only succeeded in opening the skin on his bicep. Blood smeared his shirt. Moments later, Céleste collapsed.

Céleste awoke the next morning in a four-poster bed, still at Lionel's. She heard him speaking to someone, saying that her wounds and his were superficial. The horror of the night came back to Céleste. She examined her chest and saw a small bandage where she had cut herself. It had been dressed by a doctor who had been and gone while she slept. She began crying. Lionel entered the room, torn between care for her condition and contempt for her behaviour.

'You're feeling better?' he asked. 'My word, you are insane! You knew what you were doing when you left me. I really do wish to be free from you.'

Charlotte came into the room and spoke to Lionel in a strong provincial accent. Céleste asked her to leave so she could dress. Charlotte obliged, leaving the room with a scornful laugh after first embracing Lionel. Céleste expected at least a handshake from him as she left, but there was no effort to do so.

It was 6 a.m. Humiliated, Céleste wandered the deserted streets back to her apartment. Her tempestuous relationship had reached its lowest point and was just short of a crime of passion—and any wounds deeper than the ones she had inflicted would have caused that. She turned, as ever in the last year, to Richard for solace, and learned that he, too, had given up on her and taken another woman.

Lionel's financial position, meanwhile, became even more dire as creditors moved in. He sold all his possessions, but could not raise nearly enough to meet his debts. Lionel's jeweller, who drained a small fortune from him by offering him credit on usurious terms of up to thirty per cent, turned on Céleste and held her responsible for the count's failure to pay up. She received demands for bills of 46,000 francs. This was a desperate move, for under the law, only the payer for the goods, not the receiver, could be held accountable unless unlawfully obtained. Yet still it hurt Céleste. Lionel's extravagance had collapsed on her as well, and it promised to bite her financially. The house in Berry, along with all the furniture in it, had been seized by creditors. Creditors were also going to dispute her loan to Lionel of 20,000 francs, which stood as a mortgage. If successful, they would receive the sale proceeds that again, under the law, were due to her.

As Céleste's slide from grace accelerated, she received a note to visit Denise, the woman who had drawn her into prostitution. She was dying in abject poverty. Céleste was kind and not judgemental, realising that at the time, Denise believed she was helping her waif-like but wilful new friend. The experience of seeing Denise during her final days, at just twenty-eight years of age, made Céleste reflect more on her own life. She sifted back through her diaries, which had begun soon after the attempted rape by Vincent. In their pages she could trace the trajectory of her unusually eventful years and how episodic and startling they had been.

Céleste was still in her mid-twenties and facing a tragic end like Denise if she did not reassess her own existence. She was aware that she could not forever rely on her fame/notoriety as a former Hippodrome star and courtesan. She needed a more solid and steady source of income. Given that she never expected to marry, especially with her dedication to the increasingly desiccated Lionel, she would have to create her own destiny. At first she considered success in the theatre, which had so far evaded her. She'd had more dramatic follies in her private life than with the Folies-Dramatiques. Mourier had not quite given her the big roles she wanted and there were many lulls without income between shows. He felt she was a better dancer than she was an actress, and even she admitted this was probably right. It may have been because Céleste's real life was one of considerable drama. She was a figure of substance, however she was viewed. Audiences would always see her as Mogador playing somebody else of lesser interest. Very little invented by playwrights for characters on the stage could match her own experiences.

With this in mind, she joined forces with a pretty and charming young dancer, Adele Page, for a revue at the Théâtre des Variétés in a dance called 'Le Pas de l'Imperiale'. It was an attempt to regenerate her flagging career on the boards.

Power peak. Céleste, age 30, photographed around the time she married Count Lionel de Chabrillan. She had achieved fame in Paris as a celebrated courtesan and chariot-rider at the Hippodrome. Her published *Mémoires* enhanced her notoriety in the mid 1850s.

The poet, the artist and the courtesan. In 1833, aristocrat Alfred de Musset (below) wrote his most renowned poem, *Rolla*, about a prostitute in the high-class brothel he patronised. Six years later, 16-year-old Céleste was his partner of choice at the same place. Decades afterwards, artist Henri Gervex depicted the pair with his painting, also entitled *Rolla*. (Gervex had read Céleste's memoirs and knew her well.) The man shown in the painting is de Musset, the young woman is Céleste.

Waltzing the era away. Parisians waltzing at the Bal Mabille in Faubourg Saint-Honoré, Paris. The most popular dance step in the mid-nineteenth century, Céleste caused a sensation with her livelier version.

The cancan's precursor. Céleste was a star of the Paris dance halls, where she improvised with the waltz, performing a high-kicking adaptation, which emerged decades later as the cancan. This poster was designed by Henri de Toulouse-Lautrec towards the end of the century.

Haute couture. Céleste was the muse for French painter Thomas Couture's *Romans During the Decadence* (1847). She is depicted as the naked fair-haired woman in the centre of the scene.

Program
Prix 10 Centimes
July 15 1889
Programme
HIPPODROME
TOUS LES SOIRS
Representation à 8h½
LES DIMANCHES, JEUDIS & FÊTES
Matinée à 2 heures ½
PRIX DES PLACES
LOGES 5 Fr. _En Location 7 Fr.
PREMIÈRES 3f50 _En Location 4f50
DEUXIÈMES 2 Fr. _En Location 2f50
TROISIÈMES 1f25 _Sans Location
BUREAU DE LOCATION 3, Avenue de l'Alma
Ouvert de 11 h. du matin à 6 h. du soir

Alexandre Dumas Sr. World-famous author Alexandre Dumas Sr was Céleste's greatest inspiration. They had an affair before she met Count Lionel, but their friendship never waned. He suggested she work at her fiction, instructing her on an approach, and did much to help her realise her books as plays, thus adding other dimensions to a brilliant career.

The chariot-rider. Already well known as a dancer and courtesan, in 1845 Céleste joined the Hippodrome as an equestrienne. She became a daring Paris superstar, performing as a courageous chariot-rider for several seasons, until she nearly lost her leg in a race.

Carmen's inspiration. Historians claim composer Georges Bizet (above) used his close friend Céleste as the basis for the feisty, independent main character in *Carmen*, his most-celebrated opera. Céleste encouraged and patronised Bizet through his lean years and asserted that their relationship was platonic – she was 15 years his senior.

ROSABEL MORRISON IN
THE KISS
CARMEN
UNDER THE MANAGEMENT OF
Liebler & Maass

The Count of true love. A portrait of Count Lionel de Chabrillan. He was a classic ne'er-do-well aristocrat until he married Céleste. Two days after marrying, they set sail for Australia, where he did sterling work as Melbourne's first French Consul, from 1854-1858.

MARKET SQUARE, MELBOURNE, FRC

Melbourne, circa 1855. Living in Melbourne in the mid 1850s allowed the couple to develop a relationship without the strains of class divide, his disapproving family and Parisian society. It also gave Céleste the opportunity to observe a very different environment and the time to develop her writing skills.

VAULES OF THE YARRA-YARRA.

Lola Montez, heartbreaker. Renowned Irish exotic dancer and courtesan Lola Montez is depicted leaving Europe on a swan as a group of sad high-society paramours wave her farewell. Arriving in Australia in 1855, Lola toured around the country, shocking some observers with her spectacular *Spider's Dance*, and she developed a friendship with Céleste.

The professional creative. Taken by famous French photographer Nadar Atelier in 1869, this portrait shows Céleste, age 44, when she was at the height of her creative output of books, plays and operas.

Pose for posterity. Céleste on a bridge over the Seine, age 70. She was a restless creative, who continued to write into her 80s, despite being seen by the press as a curio from France's Libertine Period, a time of great hedonism, before the Franco-Prussian War of 1870.

CHAPTER 26

The Lawyer's Incentive

The love–hate, on-again, off-again relationship with Lionel continued into the 1850s, when he finally proposed marriage.

'Your count's crown would be my crown of thorns,' Céleste said in her written response. 'I could never again face those poor lost souls who were part of my life, and I'd never have the right to face a decent woman.'

Céleste ended her rejection letter with: 'There are two paths, yours and mine. I shall remain Mogador and you Count Lionel de Chabrillan.'

This was hard for her to write. In her naivety, when they had first met that night at the Café Anglais back in the mid-1840s, she had wondered about the possibility of becoming a countess. It had seemed to her at the time to be a title that would not quite erase her past, but at least be an antidote to it. However, the reality of the class divide and Lionel's degrading fall from grace seemed to make this impossible.

In desperation he made the drastic decision to quit France and try to restore his lost fortune in remote goldmining areas overseas. At first he considered Africa. But after reading about the French explorers' commentaries on Australia, the huge island in the Pacific with a land-mass larger than China, he decided to chance his luck there, especially as gold had been discovered in a couple of places in the British Colony of New South Wales and the Colony of Victoria, newly formed in 1851.

This was the equivalent to exile for Lionel. Not only would the culture be foreign, but only the Antarctic ice circle was further away on the map of the globe. Australia had been, until recently, a dumping ground for British convicts, although free settlers were rapidly out numbering the criminals as the ancient land offered the promise of a new life for those disenchanted by an over-crowded, under-nourished Europe. The discovery of gold precipitated a gold rush. The population of Victoria grew from 21,000 to more than 330,000 in just four years, making it the second biggest colony in Australia. New South Wales's population had nearly doubled to 378,000 due to gold being found near Bathurst.

Lionel would be a real foreigner in this British-held territory, although there was a small population of French who had also read the papers and travelled in rickety tubs for four months to join the get-rich-quick goldminers. Somehow, he believed his connections would allow him to deal rather than dig his way to a restored fortune, as if it were always his destiny to have money. However, he did declare he would buy tools for the mines once he reached Australia, just in case he got lucky.

Céleste was struggling as much as he was. She had Solange to provide for and the mess that Lionel had left her in to sort out, including four law suits against her. On Lionel's recommendation she secured a good lawyer, Maitre Desmarest, who was well connected in the arts. On hearing parts of Céleste's life from dealing with the cases, he asked if she had kept any written records.

'I always kept a record of my ideas,' she told him. 'It's a kind of diary in which I put on paper the unhappy or pleasant feelings I had known.'

'Could I read them?' Desmarest asked.

'You cannot be interested in a life such as mine.'

'Mademoiselle, on the contrary, an unusual life like yours is of interest to many,' he told her. 'It may well help me in the cases we're fighting, and I have contacts in the publishing world.'

'What?'

'Mademoiselle, you said yourself that you would struggle to pay those bringing these cases against you, let alone me. A book of your life may well be a bestseller and generate enough funds to cover all your needs, including your lawyer's fees.'

Céleste was suddenly alerted to a way out of her financial and professional predicaments.

'Two new feelings came to give me some happiness,' she would recall in her memoir. 'The first was that I might be able to please apart from the pleasure of the senses. The second was that my fate would perhaps gain some degree of interest in view of the events that so constantly overwhelmed me.'

But she had reservations. 'Some memories are so terrible that it's difficult to confess them,' she told Desmarest.

'You mean your time in the brothel?'

'I'd prefer not to have to write about this part of my life.'

'Have you notes on it?'

'I have, some.'

'Then let a publisher be the ultimate judge.'

'I'm not interested in writing something pornographic.'

'An honest memoir would not be viewed that way. I've dealt with publishers enough to know there are discreet ways of handling such issues.'

'I can tell you I lived in vice but loved virtue.'

'Knowing you as I do now, I'm sure this is true.'

Céleste pondered for a moment.

'I shall try to describe as chastely as possible,' she said, 'the most unchaste life in this world.'

Céleste spent four months in 1851 editing and putting together her handwritten memoirs and diaries. Desmarest read them and was more than impressed with her literary skills, from describing her tough family life and the ugly Saint-Lazare prison to Lionel's castle and the illegal gambling dens of Paris. He was taken also by her dry wit, which was neither black humour nor knock-about belly laughs. She had her own grey style of observation, born of experience and an at times world-weary view, which had developed a controlled cynicism with an acerbic edge. Céleste saw much love in the world but recognised and analysed more than most its concurrent cruelty and unfairness. Desmarest, patronisingly yet helpfully, gave her suggestions for the manuscript, especially grammatical corrections, which Céleste did not hesitate to act on.

He showed the manuscript to Delphine de Girardin, a notable French writer known as 'France's muse'; to her husband, Émile de Girardin, Paris's leading book editor and a prominent politician; to writer Camille Doucet; and to a few other big-name authors, such as Alexandre Dumas Sr. They were unanimous in judging her work as first class. Comparisons were made to French philosopher Jean-Jacques Rousseau's book, *Confession*, an autobiographical work that showed how society distorted man's natural goodness.[1]

They all told Desmarest that her memoirs should be published. They were 'hot' for the time, although not salacious.

On Desmarest's advice, she referred to most of the men with whom she had been involved only by their initials. This might avoid further lawsuits unless the lover involved was prepared to step forward and deny a relationship. Count Lionel was called

'Robert', and wisely, there was no direct mention of the fiercely private and well-placed Chabrillans. But the memoirs—written as five short volumes—were frank and revealing. They had a rather valedictory title for an author still a few years short of thirty: *Adieux au Monde: Mémoires de Céleste Mogador*, which translated as *Farewell to the World*: *The Memoirs of Céleste Mogador.* But she may well have been thinking of Lionel when she came up with it. He was going to the ends of the earth, and her world at that moment had all but collapsed with his proposed departure.

CHAPTER 27

Dalliance with Dumas Sr

Desmarest arranged an introduction to the big-hearted Alexandre Dumas Sr, forty-nine, who was then a world-famous author, having published two outstanding and widely translated bestsellers in 1844: *The Three Musketeers* and *The Count of Monte Cristo*. Dumas had been astonished to read the memoirs and it was he who initiated the meeting with Céleste. He was a celebrated—especially by himself—womaniser, who newspapers claimed had slept with more than forty women.

'Slept?' he had responded when asked about it. 'I never allow them to even doze when they are with me!' He also commented that the figure of forty was 'insulting, defamatory and preposterous! It has to be more like four hundred and forty!'

The two authors greeted each other like two long-lost friends. The fuzzy-Afro-headed, roly-poly author sported a moustache and goatee beard, which only managed to cover one of his chins. His round face was one continual beam as he ushered Céleste into the studio. Most men were dazzled by Céleste and her reputation, yet she held double the attraction for him because she could write. Not only was she physically desirable, she was bright and intelligent, with gifts with the quill that Dumas, despite his popular success, marvelled at, especially her wit and character observations. He also admired her courage, first at the Hippodrome, and second in her writing.

Céleste was just as enchanted to meet Dumas. He was everything she now wished to be: a successful author. But it was more than that. She wanted to maintain her name but turn it from notoriety into genuine fame. Céleste desired respectability after a life that had defined her in part as disreputable. She also wished to stretch her brain, which she was now beginning to appreciate.

Dumas, who prided himself as being a chef among many other things, had prepared a lunch, but apart from the wine and champagne it was hardly touched. Within an hour of meeting, Dumas had puffed his way up the ladder to his bedroom, Céleste willingly following. On the surface it may have appeared an odd attraction. He was fat, not good-looking and short. She had a perfect figure, was half his age and three times as attractive. But it was what they offered each other at that particular moment that counted. Dumas could not now afford to keep a courtesan of her standing, but the lure had not been transactional for either of them. He admitted that he had fancied her very much ever since he had witnessed her near-fatal chariot crash at the Hippodrome. He said he had always been jealous of Count Lionel but that he was thrilled that her new interest in books had drawn them together.

After the roll in the loft, they devoured exquisite Belgian chocolates and sipped coffee.

'You should write fiction, my dear,' Dumas told her. 'I've worked as a journalist and travel writer, but I found the fiction form to be much easier and far more lucrative. I've made a vast fortune and then lost it. You've seen for yourself the way rich men throw away their fortunes. That would make grand, tragic fiction.'

Lionel's woes were well known in Parisian circles. But she had no wish to tackle a topic so sensitive to him.

She turned the subject to books.

Dumas's son, also named Alexandre, had been an inspiration with his book, *Les Dames aux Camelias*, which was based on the life of his former lover, Marie Duplessis, whose career as one of Paris's adored courtesans ended abruptly with her death from consumption in 1847. Duplessis had been dead just eighteen months before she re-emerged as a fictional character in Dumas Jr's novel.[1]

This, and Henri Murger's *Scènes de la Vie de Bohème*, had encouraged Céleste to give her real-life account of a courtesan's existence. Now Alexandre Dumas Sr was going to give her advice about writing and fiction, and also promote her memoirs.

'I want to review your book in *Le Mousquetaire*,' he explained speaking of the paper he published and edited. 'Do not worry, my dear, I will only give my heartfelt opinion of your memoirs, which is how wonderful I think they are.'

True to his word, he crafted an article that was sure to attract attention without giving anything away. The day after it appeared in print, Monsieur Bourdilliat at publisher Librairie Nouvelle offered Céleste a contract. She accepted without question. She needed the advanced funds. She wrote in her diary that she signed the contract 'because I could not bring myself to burn the pages I had taken so much trouble to write'.

But there was more to it than her creativity. She had sold off most of her furniture and jewellery to meet creditors' demands and fight the legal cases. Creditors had taken her apartment on Rue Joubert and her carriages on Rue de la Chaussée-d'Antin and had set their sights on the house at Poinçonnet in Berry. There was ongoing opposition from the Chabrillan family and creditors over the mortgage Lionel had given her to cover the

20,000 francs she had lent him. On top of that she still needed some funds for Solange to be looked after.

The publishing deal promised some respite. But there was no date set down for publication. Céleste did not consider herself a writer yet. It was still only a dream inflated by the praise of Dumas and others.

'I studied the legal code,' she wrote. 'I spent my time in lawyers' and magistrates' offices, I haunted the Courts of Justice. When all my cases were in hand, I worked seriously in the theatre.'

Céleste saw her three roles simultaneously as 'a courtesan, an actress and a plaintiff … I ran from the Law Court to the Variétés.'

After two months she won a case over her possessions, mainly furniture at her former apartment at Rue Joubert. This boosted her confidence, on top of the enormous lift she had received from the publishing deal.

'The more I thought things over,' she reflected, 'the more I regretted not to have owed to my intelligence what I had gained by my beauty.'

Alexandre Dumas's worst fears for the political situation in France—and himself—came to fruition when his enemy Louis Bonaparte organised a coup d'état in December 1851 in order to remain president. Previously, a president could not run for a second term, but Bonaparte changed the constitution. Dumas and others who had campaigned against him were now in trouble. The celebrated author fled to Brussels, in Belgium. However, the consolidation of the Bonaparte family in power worked in Céleste's favour. One of her main aims in life was still to have her name erased from the dreaded prostitutes' registry. By April 1852, it had been there for many humiliating years. Now with a restored financial position and an invigorated sense of self, she wished to clear her name from the ignominy attached to the registry.

Dumas had suggested she approach Prince Napoleon, or Plon-Plon as he was nicknamed, a cousin of President Louis-Napoleon. Céleste knew both to be supreme womanisers.[2]

Céleste was two years younger than Prince Napoleon and had first met him at parties when she was at the Hippodrome. He had flirted with her on numerous occasions, and that had led to a short affair. Céleste managed to avoid becoming one of the charming, tubby prince's long-term mistresses and adroitly kept him as a friend and contact. The pudgy-faced, big-nosed Plon-Plon was a close adviser to his cousin, and an influential government member, who used his position and power more freely than most. So much so, that there were rumours he might even stage a coup d'état himself to oust his cousin. This resulted in Louis-Napoleon being wary of leaving Paris in case someone, possibly Plon-Plon, moved against him.

When Céleste approached Plon-Plon, he was delighted to help, but at a small price. And so after an evening out at the Café Anglais with several of his friends—as a cover should anyone guess their reason for being seen together—she accompanied him to his grand apartment for the night. Plon-Plon was discreet. Like her, he did not wish his friend Count Lionel to know of the assignation, even though the prince believed that the affair between the two was over.

Céleste left him after breakfast the next morning with a big smile on her face. The conceited prince believed it was as a result of his powers in the boudoir. But Céleste, the expert courtesan who knew how to please any partner, had used all her imaginative skills to extract a promise from him that he would act quickly to have her name struck from the book of shame, *tout suite.*

A week later, on 27 April 1852, the Fifth Bureau of the Paris Police Prefecture recorded that 'Vénard, Élizabeth-Céleste is no longer on the list of public prostitutes'.

It was a profound moment for a sophisticated and talented woman, who had once been trapped unwittingly as a naive and abused young girl into a life she never desired.

CHAPTER 28

Lionel's Voyage of Discovery

Céleste's easy intimacy with Dumas and Prince Napoleon was because she finally did believe that her relationship with Lionel was irretrievable. As his lands were sold off he became an inconsolable wreck and insulted her in between moments of reprieve and occasionally spending time with her. Céleste did not make any effort to stop him sailing for Sydney, Australia, in May 1852. She believed the parting would allow them both a chance at a new life. But Lionel was still in her head, if not her presence. He began writing copious letters that became more observational and interesting as he distanced himself from Europe. He continued with his insults, baleful outpourings and bleatings about their relationship. But they were becoming fewer with each communication.

Lionel reached Sydney in mid-September and announced that he had bought a horse and would be riding for the mines in Bathurst, 210 kilometres west. He calculated it would take him eleven to fifteen days to cover the distance. He had decided on Bathurst, rather than travelling on to Melbourne and the Victorian goldfields. The New South Wales Government had been encouraging arrivals to its goldfields, after the gold rushes to California in the United States and to Victoria had begun to drain the Sydney population.

Lionel had read about the rivers around Bathurst containing gold. The area's geological features of quartz outcrops and gullies seemed similar to those of California. The fact that finally swayed him was that 880,000 ounces (24.5 tonnes) of gold had been discovered around Bathurst during 1852. The Great Western Road from Sydney to Bathurst was now clogged with miners and the shortest route to his dreams and hopes.

Lionel could not resist a double-edged comment to Céleste before heading west when he wrote, 'It seems that my love for you has increased in [inverse] proportion to the pain you have caused me.'

Lionel ended this letter with, 'I love you as I have always loved you.'

CHAPTER 29

Céleste's Haut Couture

After dealing with Céleste for some time, her advocate Desmarest fell under her spell and they began an affair, with her reminding him, as she had Richard Maylam, that she would never care for another as much as she did Lionel. The lawyer, like those before him, would happily forgo any declaration of love if they could have regular sex. Bedding Mogador was hardly a national sport, but those who accomplished it would be hard-pressed not to boast of their achievement. Desmarest also sensed that her creative skills beyond the mattress might make her famous in another career. He did his best to help her to this end, acting as her literary adviser and editor, and in the process fell in love with her. Céleste paid him for his legal services in kind, which had him wanting to win the cases for her more than ever.

Some of the cases Desmarest worked on were against the powerful Chabrillan family. Desmarest found that he had inherited a more-than-competent, quick-learning, even brilliant assistant in Céleste. She had been on a self-education reading binge for seven years. Now she was studying legal books, attending trials and keeping track of legal procedures. She even began pointing out mistakes in the cases backed by the Chabrillans, particularly where they objected to Lionel's decision to make Céleste his proxy when he sailed for Australia. The Chabrillans viewed this as a deliberate and wily attempt by Céleste to entangle her assets with Lionel's. She was able to show this was a fabrication in the family's sloppily researched and arrogant court declarations.

This helped Desmarest in the second of four cases brought against her, which concerned the cottage. The proceedings were pleaded in a Châteauroux courthouse and Céleste had to make the trip back to Poinçonnet, in Berry, again. She was shocked to find the cottage had been seized legally. It was guarded and she was not allowed to enter at first. A few days later five agents working for the plaintiffs forced their way into the cottage and sifted through Lionel's papers in the hope of discovering that Céleste was not his proxy. They only found evidence that backed her claim.

Céleste complained to the public prosecutor. It ended with the Châteauroux court sentencing the bailiff, who had accompanied the plantiffs' agents, to one month's suspension and court costs.

This was more than simply a legal win for Céleste. It was a victory against the Chabrillans and the creditors. The strong-arm tactics and overbearing approach from the plaintiffs had proved counterproductive. Desmarest, who joined Céleste at Châteauroux, had shrewdly made sure that the case was contested where Count Lionel de Chabrillan was most popular with everyone.

The judge did not present his summary and verdict for several months, but when it came in June 1852 it was in Céleste's favour and she was delighted. It was an even sweeter victory than the furniture at Rue Joubert. Céleste had shown the family she was no pushover. She was a fighter. She received 40,000 francs in compensation and all expenses, and another 45,000 for the furniture from the first case, which she sold. Desmarest warned her that the plaintiffs would appeal and choose a more propitious court for them at Bourges, the main city of the Berry region, where they had all the right connections.

But Céleste didn't care. That would take months, perhaps more than a year to be heard. In the meantime she could afford to buy a more modest apartment on Avenue de Saint-Cloud. It had a garden for Solange to play in when she was brought for a visit. Céleste celebrated her victories in the courts with a party in March 1853. It was attended by many Paris celebrities, including Plon-Plon and another luminary of the demimonde, the lean, dark-haired and good-looking Thomas Couture, thirty-eight, whom she had met recently after one of her shows at the Théâtre des Variétés. He was a painter and history teacher, who instructed Édouard Manet, among others. He had offered to draw Céleste, like the sketches he had done of George Sand and Pierre-Jean de Béranger, a poet and writer of popular and patriotic songs. Couture followed through.

'Because it is signed by a great artist,' Céleste said of the drawing, 'it is probably the only thing of me that will endure.'

Enchanted, and her vanity flattered by his artistic attention, she displayed the portrait drawing at the party. Couture received many compliments for it.

Another of her guests was young writer Alexandre Dumas Jr, so-called to distinguish him from his illustrious father. He impressed Céleste, who may have had an eye to making him a conquest, just for the sake of having had her only father-and-son combination.

'He was distant and had a sceptical, discerning mind,' she noted. 'He could be mean, but if he paid you a compliment, you could believe it. He never gave them readily.'

Dumas Jr had been at the premiere of the Variétés stage show *The 1852 Revue*, in which Céleste starred. He remarked in a critique that 'She sang, played and recited divinely; if she is willing to work, she will have a true talent.'[1]

CHAPTER 30

The Near Gatecrasher

Céleste, very much in a festive mood because of the court-case windfalls, held a dinner party for six friends, a week later. It began at 7 p.m. The main course had been served and desserts were on the table when her maid rushed into the room looking shaken, followed by the hand-wringing concierge.

'The Count de Chabrillan is in Paris, Madame!' she said.

'What?!'

'*Oui*, Madame. Since he was told you had guests, he did not wish to come up. He's in the Passage du Havre.'

She left the maid to explain the situation to the guests and hurried from the building to locate the count. She found him lurking in the Passage du Havre. He had a beard like a bushranger. His face was thin and his skin tanned; his eyes were lifeless. She saw 'pain written all over him'.

Céleste moved to kiss him but he stopped her with a look.

'You're entertaining,' he said, 'I have disturbed you.'

'Just a few friends for dinner ...'

'I have no right to ask you who is at your house.'

'Oh, there was—'

'Do you want to come to my hotel?' he interrupted her. 'We need to talk business.' It was his way of speaking about everything *except* business.

Céleste followed without saying a word. Her manner of immediate compliance would have been obvious to him. Her feelings had not changed in the six years they had known each other.

'Here, these are my special present for you,' he said at the hotel as he uncovered a cage to reveal small, colourful birds. 'I smuggled them back. They all lived!'

'They're all darlings!' Céleste exclaimed as she took one from the cage and fondled it. She began to cry. Lionel did not move to comfort her. She noticed long scars on his hands.

'How did you get those?' she asked, attempting to touch him. He pulled away, rolled up his sleeve and showed her a tattoo.

'That's you,' he said, 'in case you don't recognise yourself. I had it done on the trip. Here see, the date …'

Céleste embraced him. Lionel hardly responded and it was clear to her that the hardships in the New South Wales bush had squeezed all the passion and much of the life out of him. But he had returned and that was all that mattered to her. Without hesitation Céleste wanted to renew their relationship.

'I want you to move into my apartment, right away,' she said, holding him.

'No, I can't pay the rent. I will not be a burden to you.'

They spent the night together, and then Céleste moved quickly to make living arrangements that would not offend Lionel's sensibilities. With her usual resourcefulness, she passed her lease on to a new tenant and 'sent everything (including cashmere shawls and jewellery) to be sold off'. The proceeds helped as she rushed about Paris buying back everything that Lionel's creditors had put up for sale, especially paintings and pistols that were dear to him. She also paid off all his debts.

Once more, without hesitation, she was uprooting her existence for Lionel, but this time going down-market to a 1000-francs-a-year ground-floor apartment on Rue de Navarin, which had a small yard for Solange's visits. Lionel rented a small room in Rue Laffitte, but spent his days with Céleste. To her delight, she found he had mellowed. Gone were the slights and verbal abuse directed so monotonously at her. The harshness of his experiences in Australia had had a positive impact on his mind, not initially obvious from his weather-beaten and downtrodden appearance. As he regained his strength and dignity, he had the odd grumble about her performing at the theatre. But Céleste assessed this in a good light. He was snobbish about it and not a little jealous of her popularity and of who might be attracted to her before and after the shows.

As expected, the appeal by the Chabrillan family and Lionel's creditors against the ruling over the cottage was heard at Bourges. Céleste applied herself with her usual diligence and summarised her case for the court. Lionel wrote a strong note in support of her case but did not appear. It was embarrassing enough that he was supporting his partner in a legal fight against his own family. Had he appeared, there would have been massive press interest. As it was, Mogador's involvement caused more of a stir over the three days 'than if the case had been that of a notorious criminal'. But Lionel's written assistance boosted Céleste's confidence in the change in him. Until his trip, he had been bullied by his elder brother the marquis, and dominated by his sister the countess. Now he was showing the moral courage Céleste had always believed was in him.

Two weeks later the Bourges case again went in her favour, despite the expected home-town advantage.

'This was a great day for me,' she wrote in her memoirs, 'and created much confusion among my adversaries.'

It was a significant victory in her war with the Chabrillans. However, it was just one battle in an ongoing conflict.

'I'm not done with Australia,' Lionel said a month after returning.

'But it nearly killed you!' Céleste exclaimed.

'What doesn't kill you makes you stronger. I grew up a lot in the bush. It was a great leveller. I will go back, but on my terms.'

'But how?'

'I've had some business meetings and have found a prominent merchant, Monsieur Jacques Bertrand. He's willing to assist.'

'What about me?' Céleste asked, fearing the worst.

'I won't go without you, I can assure you.'

'What about your family? If you take me with you, there will be even greater disapproval of you. Your siblings will be aghast.'

'My courage is you,' he said. 'My country will be where you will be.' Then he uttered the words Céleste never really thought she would hear.

'Will you marry me, please, and come with me?'

She had seen this coming with his fresh declarations of love, but she was still speechless. But she prevaricated, bringing up again the problem with the Chabrillans.

'What do I care for the opinion of my relatives? I'm glad of this rejection. It sets me free.'

This articulation of his thoughts was as sweet to her as the proposal. But Céleste had to think hard. Her career in the theatre was steady, though without rave notices. She had re-established her finances by solid work in the courts and shrewd management of her assets. Still not thirty, she was able to perform her duties, if necessary, as a top courtesan. Céleste had a large and growing number of friends and admirers of both sexes. She would be leaving all that for struggle and hardship a world away from Gay Paris and the good life she had established. It was a real sacrifice and gamble on a man who *appeared* to have changed for the better.

'What if Lionel became bad-tempered as in the past?' she asked herself.

'I am afraid of going so far away from my country, my beauty, my youth,' she wrote with a perspicacious, gloomy interpretation of what it meant to her. 'Soon they will all be just a memory.'

'Only virtue and goodness can be loved for a long time,' she noted in a moment of introspection and doubt. Would Lionel love her as she matured? Would he respect her? In the end she gave him the benefit of her love, placing only one provision on marrying him and sailing to Australia: they had to take Solange. His reply was to kiss the child twice on the cheeks.

Lionel had told his sister and brother that he was intent on returning to Australia without letting them know that he was taking Céleste, let alone that she would be his bride. They readily agreed to help with their excellent diplomatic contacts, believing that his removal from France for an extended stay would end the affair with his *scarlet woman*. They secured him a position as the first French Consul to Melbourne in the Victorian Colony. It was a new position and there were few places held in less regard by the diplomatic service, although Melbourne had rapidly become one of the world's richest cities. But this modest role and the merchant's support meant he would go with at least some financial backing, and to a fresh frontier in the free-settled colony.

'I only accepted the consular role so that I can speculate on stocks and commodities,' Lionel told Céleste to ease her fears about how long they would be away. 'I want to make a lot of money in a short time … Love me as I love you and when you are my wife, the future will be my responsibility.'

Céleste had one pressing issue she wished to resolve before setting sail: to stop the publication of her memoirs. Now that she was back with Lionel she was distressed at what he would think of the book. Would he see it as a betrayal? She could not ask Desmarest to get the rights back or prevent the book going public. They were still connected, but he had been cast off now that Lionel was back on the scene, and Céleste judged he would not work quite as assiduously as before for her. Instead, she chose Émile de Girardin, the brilliant 47-year-old political journalist and polemicist, and founder of *La Presse*. He had changed the nature of journalism in France by lowering the price of newspapers and boosting the role of advertising. But he found dealing with the two principals at the publisher Librairie Nouvelle, Messrs Jocottet and Bourdilliat, a tough task.

De Girardin and Céleste pored over a copy of the contract. She would receive no advance against the rights, but she would take half the profits after all printing costs were paid. It was a typical deal for the time, but a good one originally negotiated by Desmarest. The contract was watertight.

'I was left with no transaction or repurchase rights, even judicially,' she noted in her diary.

The publishers would not countenance giving up the publication. Céleste tried to play down the value of her work, but the publishers insisted the book was bestseller material.

Bourdilliat saw it as 'the love story of the century'. Céleste feared it would destroy her hard-won relationship with Lionel.

Céleste, as usual, would not give up. She went to see her good friend Alexandre Dumas, who was secretly back in Paris plotting against the French president, Louis-Napoleon. Just as she was about to leave, a servant announced that 'His Highness Prince Napoleon' (Plon-Plon) had arrived. Dumas suggested she enlist his help in preventing the publication. Céleste had no idea that Plon-Plon was considering ways to wrest the throne from his cousin, and that he and Dumas were about to have a clandestine meeting concerning it.

These two lovers of hers delayed their talk of overthrow and listened to her pleas about her memoirs. She was surprised to learn that Plon-Plon knew about the problem.

'There's simply nothing I can do,' Plon-Plon said. 'It's a business matter and the publishers are within their rights.'

'But, Your Highness,' she said, 'I'm about to be married!'

'And that's another act of folly!' Plon-Plon said. 'I have said so to your Lionel, whom I've seen several times since his return from Australia. But he will go on with it, unless you're more sensible than he is.'[1]

Plon-Plon's forthrightness dismayed Céleste, who looked at Dumas.

'Folly or not,' the ever-generous Dumas said in her defence, 'they've known each other for years. Their love has stood the test of time. That's a mutual guarantee for the future.'

Plon-Plon was about to comment, but Dumas added, 'Lionel is handsome, noble and brave. Céleste is intelligent and courageous. I can guarantee that she will prove herself worthy of him. But these wretched memoirs must be withdrawn. Everything depends on that.'

'Are they likely to create a scandal?' Plon-Plon asked Dumas. 'Have you read them?'

'Yes, in manuscript. They're a kind of confession. Quite captivating! And they can hurt no one but herself.'

'Well, then,' Plon-Plon said, turning to Céleste, 'let matters take their course. We shall review the situation after your departure.'[2]

Prince Napoleon's decision not to help meant that Céleste was forced to give up the fight. She consoled herself that she and Lionel would be almost in Australia before the book was in Paris stores. She refused to help in any way with the promotion. There would be no comment from her at all to journalists. She believed that only a few friends would bother to read it. Critics would either refuse to review it or ignore it altogether. It would be forgotten by the time she and Lionel returned to France in a few years' time, if all went according to plan.

Lionel demonstrated his commitment to their relationship by engaging a top specialist in family law to draw up a marriage contract. He decided on separate ownership of property in case of any future divorce settlement, which would favour Céleste in their current circumstances. He also decided to pay her an annual allowance of 6000 francs if they separated. This was again generous, but his financial position at that moment could not justify such a figure. Yet if nothing else it was a significant gesture of his dedication to her.

This act encouraged Céleste to buy a prefabricated gable house in Bordeaux, which she would have shipped to Melbourne. Under the terms of the proposed marriage contract, it would be solely hers once she bought land on which to erect it.

The thought of being a landed property owner in her own right, even if it were in a remote country, thrilled her.

CHAPTER 31

Courtesan Countess

Lionel's first act was to have the wedding banns made public in London while organising their marriage there before they took a boat to Australia. Using England was a smart move, as it avoided any action by his brother, in his powerful role as a member of the Council of State, to stop the union. Lionel's sisters had joined the Chabrillan chorus of voices attempting to stop him from any further liaison with the hated Mogador.

By contrast, Céleste's mother was joyous about the proposed union. She could not wait to sign the document authorising the marriage of her daughter. On 3 January 1854, Céleste, Solange, another maid named Marie, a peasant girl from Berry and Céleste's two small dogs crossed the Channel in atrocious weather and arrived in freezing London. Snow had fallen like a thick white blanket over the city. Lionel, swathed in furs and 'looking like a bear', met them at a South Kensington hotel.

When the others were in bed, Céleste sat with her husband-to-be in front of a fire in their room. Demonstrating more managerial skills than she had witnessed before, he outlined the schedule for their wedding the next morning, 4 January, as if it were an order of battle.

'Get everything ready this evening,' he said. 'We have to be at the registry office at ten a.m., the church at eleven and the Chancellery of France at noon.'

All locations were within the City of London, and through the haze of the moment, which, like the weather, had numbed her mind, she did not really absorb the 'campaign' and the reasons for each move. He smoked a cigar and she nervously dragged on three successive cigarettes as he spoke. Lionel missed no detail in ensuring the marriage would be judged valid everywhere. He feared that the British ceremony would not be recognised in French courts. Shrewdly, he organised the marriage registration on French soil at the French embassy in London. This would counter any move by Marie-Olivier or his sisters, now or at any future time, to stop or annul their wedding contract. Lionel was well aware that the women in his family would rage at the thought of his wife—this wife—carrying the title of countess.

They slept the sleep of lovers, together, and then dressed in separate rooms; he in a black suit and white cravat, she all in white—hat, veil, long dress, gloves and cashmere shawl.

'Lionel looks superbly elegant and distinguished,' she wrote in her diary. 'He is rather pale, but his lips are red and his eyes are shining. He seems to be very happy.'

They rode in a smart carriage to the registry office. Céleste felt surprisingly calm and recalled that the wedding ceremony went well. Witnesses reported that the English magistrate made a fulsome speech about her, although she did not understand a word. She left the building surprised that she had held up well and had not broken down in tears. Step one in the consolidation of their marriage was over. She was officially Countess de Chabrillan, although not yet in the eyes of the Church. She had two steps to go and they were more challenging. It helped that Lionel said he had forgiven her, which meant more than any holy man in a foreign land. He had also gone to the trouble of preparing the frocked clergyman, and had given him a generous tip to facilitate his understanding and kindness.

They approached the confessional where the priest was waiting with a beatific smile. It was just another ceremony for him, but to Céleste it was the second-last hurdle in a race through a maze that until this moment had led nowhere. She hesitated. Her nerve failed her. All her Catholic upbringing about guilt and sins revisited her. She had stood up to all sorts of abuse in her life from those close and others remote. Her strength of character had brushed it aside. But now before her god she nearly collapsed. This omnipotent voyeur from heaven would know about her work at a brothel and how she had used men to her ends.

'Please let's go,' Céleste whispered in Lionel's ear. 'We're married enough!'

Lionel steadied her. She fell to her knees before the priest.

'Father, I have sinned!' she repeated several times. The priest helped her through the self-imposed ordeal by asking the questions he needed to and answering them as well.

'Come, my child, show yourself equal to the duties that lie ahead,' he said, leaning towards her. 'Only remember the past to let you lead a better life in the future.'

This was sound, unthreatening and nebulous enough to help her towards the end of the ceremony. Lionel knelt beside her and Céleste was certain he was praying for her. The confessional torment over, they walked to the Saint-Paul Chapel at the other end of the church. Lionel had invited a handful of London-based French witnesses for the exchange of vows. According to French writer Françoise Moser, there was one secret witness who would have caused a stir had she been recognised outside the chapel.[1] Queen Victoria, a good friend of Napoleon III and Empress Eugénie, had heard much about Céleste, and it was whispered, with some glee, that the famous courtesan and equestrienne was about to marry into the French aristocracy and one of France's most notable families. The tittle-tattle would have reached Victoria via Prince Napoleon. Victoria was intrigued to see her. It was reported back to Prince Napoleon and later, Lionel, that Victoria had confided she thought Céleste even more beautiful than Eugénie.

'Never take it off,' Lionel said to her as he slipped the ring on her finger. 'If one of us passes, the one who survives will wear it.'

The priest pronounced them man and wife. Céleste was now a countess.

They climbed into the carriage a third time and trotted off to the French Consulate. Snow was falling. The houses were covered and it was a foot deep in the street. They waited an hour before the French consular official, gold-rimmed glasses perched on his nose, summoned Lionel to his office.

'You wish to register here the marriage you have just entered into, witnessed by the English authorities,' he said and paused to glance unfavourably at his new wife through the door, 'with this young lady, Céleste?'

'Yes, sir.'

'Think for a moment,' the official said, removing his glasses and standing. He moved close to Lionel and lowered his voice. 'You will perhaps regret having carried out this formality. Your family—'

Lionel cut the official off before he further overstepped his authority.

'I am thirty-two years old,' Lionel snapped, bringing to the fore the full weight of his aristocratic background, 'and quite old enough to understand the importance of the agreements I enter into.'

The bureaucrat hesitated, went back to his desk with a disgruntled look and wrote out a document. He handed it to Lionel. A moment later, Lionel passed it to Céleste, saying, 'If I were to die, no one would be able to cause you trouble over the name I am giving you.'

CHAPTER 32

Croesus *Crossing*

Lionel continued to be refreshingly assertive on board the sturdy 2500-tonne boat, the *Croesus*, as it prepared to sail from Southampton carrying 500 people and a farm's worth of livestock on the journey of several months to Melbourne. Céleste complained about the puny size of the first-class cabins, necessitating her precious books to be stored in the hold. She threatened to leave even before they sailed.

'That time is past, my dear Céleste, and will never come again,' Lionel said. 'I'm your lord and master in the name of the law.'

This may have been uttered tongue-in-cheek, but Céleste bowed to his judgement on the trip. He had sailed to and from their destination and his confidence buoyed her. But she was cautious.

'I have the impression that after this voyage,' she said, 'I will only like ships in paintings.'

Céleste and Lionel wandered up on deck, which was a hive of activity. Céleste was appalled at the drunken sailors, perhaps unaware of their time-honoured exuberant excesses before they sailed. Some had to be dragged on board by police after a night of drinking and brawling in the local inns and taverns.

'You don't expect to see those poor devils do their manoeuvres in white gloves and patent-leather boots, do you?' Lionel said with characteristic brusqueness. 'You'll see how splendid they are in times of danger.'

As the boat slipped its mooring, there were tears and cheers from the pier as relatives and friends waved their goodbyes.

'They invariably express their emotions by frantic cheering,' she later wrote. 'Their row was enough to wake the dead.'

Lionel urged her to learn English on board, hoping it would change her parochial attitudes, or at least make them better informed. Céleste saw the wisdom in this and did apply herself to the task of learning, under tuition, thirty words a day, and the grammar.

The family of four—Lionel, Céleste, Solange and Marie—endured the first terrible day of sea sickness in fearsome weather as the *Croesus* ploughed through a sea of what seemed like tidal waves, heading for Lisbon, Portugal. It had to pick up the despatches left there by the last mail boat, which had lost its mast off the Portuguese coast and was under repair for half a year.

Lionel, Solange and Marie 'looked like corpses fished from the sea', Céleste observed, and she was not faring much better herself. One of the few laughs during this testing initiation to life at sea was courtesy of a parakeet, a gift from her friend Adele Page. It recognised Céleste and no matter what the time of day or how ill she looked, it squawked, '*Cocotte est belle!* Have you had your lunch today, my *cocotte*?'

But her tiny dogs were less cheerful and remained curled up as if dead. All the others on board, including the other animals, hardly fared better.

At the end of the first day, a wave hit the ship like a clap of thunder and smashed in windows. Water rushed in through the holes, flooding the lounge. There was panic. The captain jumped over tables; passengers climbed onto seats to stop themselves being swept down passageways. Sailors frantically blocked the openings with mattresses. Wasting no time, carpenters began making wooden window frames and fitting new glass panels.

The next morning the weather had calmed. Most of the passengers were on deck breathing the fresh air 'like carp opening their mouths on breaking the water's surface'.

At lunch, Céleste sat between Lionel and the ship's English captain. She observed that 'the other diners don't eat, they devour', after the frightful night of buffeting and flooding. Relief that the ship hadn't sunk caused everyone to exhibit an exaggerated bonhomie and many were soon drunk. The captain remained sober and was enamoured with Céleste. He was about fifty-five years of age, and had been sailing for forty of them. She noted, 'He is ugly, he has thinning hair, his teeth are black and his complexion is gingerbread yellow.' But she forgave him because he spoke French, and was well educated and courteous. Céleste was in full charm mode and he responded by taking her and Lionel to his cabin to smoke cigars.

Céleste said she would love to have a geographical map so she could plot the ship's position each day. The captain said he would oblige and offered to plot each day's course with her.

'If you will allow it, sir,' the captain said tactfully to Lionel. 'I shall have great pleasure in being the countess's tutor.'

Lionel laughed. 'If you give in to her every whim this way,' he said phlegmatically, 'I warn you that you'll have your work cut out.'

But the captain was captivated and very happy to surrender to her wishes.

When the couple left the captain Céleste noticed that Lionel was smoking his cigar furiously. She said nothing at first but after a while commented, 'Be careful, you'll burn your moustache!'

'Céleste, my dear,' Lionel began. 'I don't want to start off by making unpleasant comments …'

'But?'

'You have an unyielding, uncompromising character, which is not becoming in a woman when her husband is with her.'

'Must she bow to his better judgement, keep quiet or say amen to every remark, like an idiot or a schoolgirl?'

Lionel was chomping even harder on the cigar when Céleste added, 'You can really be unfair in a way that's quite peculiar to you. Just pointing out that you're wrong is enough to annoy you.'

'You show surprise and astonishment at everything,' he countered, 'which makes you seem ignorant.' This was the old Lionel surfacing.

'When one wants to learn,' Céleste replied, keeping her cool and a measure of humility, 'one must admit to knowing nothing.'

They were interrupted by an acquaintance, which kept a lid on their first heated discussion in a long time. Later, Lionel occupied himself by playing with Solange, which was his way of being contrite over his demeaning comment. The couple kissed and made up. At least, Céleste thought, his remarks were less acidic than before. He was quicker to see the unfairness of the comment, which in reality was more a defensive position. Before his own 'education' in humanity and survival in Australia, his caustic observations were due to a false sense of superiority and a lack of respect. But the experience in the bush and the sea voyages were great levellers where true character could emerge.

CHAPTER 33

Distractions and Dangers

Lionel's work as consul began on the ship when Madame Weber, a Frenchwoman who was travelling to Melbourne, told him that she would be searching for her lost music-master husband in the Victorian Colony. They had moved to England but struggled as music teachers. Her husband had decided to go on ahead to Australia in the hope of making a living for them and their two children, who were with Madame Weber. The consul was compassionate and helpful, saying he would take care of her when they arrived. In gratitude, the woman put on a superb performance at the piano in the first-class lounge. Then the captain cajoled Lionel into playing a few polkas that Lionel had composed himself. Céleste was proud of her man daring to follow such a grand show, and noted: 'Energy replaces charm, the pride of the performer replaces the performer's technique, and he comes out of it very well.'

Honours, she judged, were shared.

It was a sad case of triumph to tragedy for Madame Weber. The next day the *Croesus* nosed into the Port of Lisbon, but no one was allowed to disembark. Instead, local authorities came on board and quarantined the ship. A man in third class had died; Madame Weber's son, just six months old, was extremely ill in second class. Céleste went to see her and found the child close to death, perhaps from a health condition he suffered from or from a disease more threatening to everyone on board, such as cholera.

Madame Weber was distressed.

'My poor husband,' she cried. 'He would have been so happy to have a son! He'll learn of his birth and his death at the same time.'

Céleste told her not to give up hope. But the ship's doctor did not instil confidence.

The child died. Céleste fell short of blaming the doctor for the boy's demise. Madame Weber was inconsolable.

The first day in port ended in sadness, while everyone on board wondering how long they would be kept ashore. As night took hold, Lisbon lit up and music could be heard, it helped relieve the gloom of the preceding hours. The next day, 15 November, the quarantine was lifted, but the gloom remained with the death of Portuguese Queen Maria II. The streets were empty, with the occasional knot of people dressed in black.

'The town looks like a cemetery on All-Saints' Day,' Lionel said. He hired a carriage and took Céleste on a visit to the countryside. They returned to the city and the ship for a second night.

The crew mutinied the next morning just before the ship was due to sail. They said that there were not enough men on board to manoeuvre the *Croesus*. The mutineers' leaders said they would not allow the boat to leave port without another fifteen crew members, who could be hired in Lisbon. It put the captain in a quandary. He did not disagree with the need for extra hands, but he was not authorised by the ship's owners to do this. The mutineers ganged together menacingly. Many were armed. In response, the ship's officers formed a phalanx around the captain. Passengers panicked. A battle seemed likely. Lionel involved himself in discussions and then, grim-faced, ushered Céleste to their cabin.

'Why doesn't the captain give in?' she asked.

'Because he wants it noted that they're using force against him.'

'Will they fight?'

'No. The numbers are too unequal. The captain can't send them to prison or put them in the hold. There would be no crew.'

Céleste stayed close to Lionel as he took part in the heated discussions between the two warring parties. The issue was finally resolved the next day, when the captain agreed to take on the extra sailors, which was inevitable.

Céleste and Lionel believed the *Croesus* was ailing in some way. In fact everyone seemed to be at one in saying that the engine was too strong for the hull. The hold appeared to be splitting under the strain.

Céleste and Lionel were happy about one effect of the contretemps and subsequent delay. It allowed them another night in Lisbon.

The next major event on board the ailing *Croesus* was the ceremony to mark the crossing of the equator. Most passengers and crew wanted it and the captain was forced to comply, although he was uncomfortable. Traditionally, the captain and officers surrendered their power and authority to the drunken sailors for a day as the ship was made ready. The main focus was on creating a makeshift pool by filling a sail with water. All the crew members wore fancy dress, most of it hideous, and danced around a barrel of brandy, which would be consumed during the evening's 'fun and festivity'.

They forced the novice sailors into a humiliating baptism ceremony, throwing them in the pool where six men (called Tritons) all but drowned them by forcing them to swallow as much salt water as possible. One sixteen-year-old recruit, whose parents had pushed him against his will into life as a sailor, was so terrified that he hid in a cabin. He hated the sea and sailing, and could not swim. He was dragged kicking, screaming and crying to the pool of terror, where he received the roughest treatment of all.

'You have to stop this!' Lionel told the captain.

'I can't do anything before sunset,' he replied helplessly, 'otherwise they'll give me the same treatment.'

The teenager was carried semi-conscious from the brutal ordeal to a cabin. Later in the evening he developed a fever. He wandered to the deck in a delirious state, intending to throw himself overboard. One of the former Tritons spotted him perched on a railing about to leap and rushed forward to pull him back. The boy was locked in a cabin and put under guard until he recovered.

CHAPTER 34

Watertight

All concerns were soon swamped by a huge problem for everyone on board. The heat was oppressive and the *Croesus* had not made much progress for a week. The captain had turned off the engine and proceeded under sail with the aid of a strong breeze. But when the wind died the engine was not stoked up again. Passengers wanted to know why. A four-man delegation, including Lionel, was sent to inquire. After a long meeting, Céleste cornered her husband and demanded answers.

The issue of the silent engine would have to wait. There was a more pressing problem. Pale and near tears, Lionel broke the news to her, 'There's no more drinking water.'

He explained that a window had not been shut in time during a swell. Waves had swamped the main tank, ruining the fresh water supply. On top of that, machines that could condense steam and create a large supply of fresh water daily were broken. Thc alternatives in the oppressive heat were to drink the copious amounts of alcohol on board, which the crew was intent on doing, or soda water. Lionel bought bottles of the latter, but Céleste was wary.

'This effervescent water can cause dysentery,' she warned, 'an illness which in the tropics is similar to cholera. You can die from it in a few hours.'

On day three of the water crisis they were forced to consume beer and undiluted wine that 'burnt out stomachs without quenching our thirsts'.

They prayed for rain, but the blue sky was clear, the azure water calm, and there was not the slightest breeze. In this situation no movement was much worse than a storm. They drifted towards their now hoped-for destination, the Cape of Good Hope on the coast of South Africa. The working crew, drinking alcohol, suffered most from dehydration. Engineers, stokers and carpenters worked in the hold while sailors and officers manned the pumps day and night. But every passenger felt the pressure. The livestock began to die of thirst and were heaved overboard.

On the fourth day of misery, Lionel and Céleste were sitting on deck under a window, which was open on the captain's cabin. Unseen by those inside, they could hear the conversation between the captain, an officer and the first mate.

'If God doesn't help us, we're finished,' the first mate said.

'What about the repairs?' the captain asked, subdued.

'Hopeless! As soon as we seal up one leak, a large one develops alongside.'

Céleste and Lionel looked at each other in dismay. After a few seconds, the first mate said, 'The hull isn't strong enough to cope with the propeller's motion. This is causing all the planks at the stern to move apart. The water keeps coming in. It would take four hours or more at the pumps just to empty out the water we've taken on in an hour.'

Lionel admitted to Céleste that he had known about the problem for some time. He held her in his arms and wept, not for himself but for her and Solange. Céleste told him not to cry. She was stoic and fatalistic.

They then heard the captain say they would take three days to reach the Cape of Good Hope. But the officer was adamant they would not make it. He wanted the crew to prepare lifeboats and order the second-class passengers to stay on deck for the night. The captain refused, saying that would alarm all the passengers.

Most passengers chose to sleep on the deck anyway. The next day a light breeze raised hopes. The stricken boat began to move towards the Cape but now with an alarming roll from side to side, and it sat three metres deeper in the water than when they had first set sail. In other words, the vessel was sinking, slowly and imperceptibly. Ballast and provisions were dumped to reduce the forty-tonne load.

A boat was spotted on the horizon but did not come to their rescue, despite frantic signalling. Lionel was almost suicidal with despair for having invited Céleste and Solange to come with him. He'd known the risks, he said, but his feelings had overridden his good sense. Céleste remained brave as women cried and men quarrelled.

'They all lost their heads,' she recalled.

When the situation seemed hopeless, it was announced that the engine was repaired. The captain consulted the four men representing the passengers, who reported that the passengers wanted him to take the gamble and use the engine. He then made a hard-headed decision to use steam, knowing that the force and thump of the propeller would separate any loose planks with each jolt. More water would seep in and the *Croesus* would sink further.

The engines were stoked up. They had to work harder than ever to slug through the water, but progress was made.

The captain told Lionel in confidence that it would be touch and go to make the Cape, as the ship ground and groaned its way through the night. Dawn brought cheering as the Cape could be seen. They reached it an estimated six hours before the boat would have sunk, justifying the captain's decision to gamble and use the engines.

The damaged *Croesus* had to be put in dry dock for repairs that would take an unspecified time. It was an enforced, unwanted vacation for the passengers, who after two, at times agonising, months at sea were keen to reach their destination.

After several weeks' repairs in Cape Town, the boat struggled for another six weeks across the Indian Ocean and round the south coast of Australia to the colony port of Melbourne. At one point when everyone on board was straining to see landmarks, a flock of small birds flew to meet the ship and perched in the rigging. This mass landing signalled that the boat was close to land. The passengers cheered. After four gruelling, dangerous, intoxicating months, mostly at sea, they were close to their final destination.

The captain took no chances. He sent for a pilot boat and relied on sail, rather than the problematic engine, to slip through the heads of the horseshoe-shaped Port Phillip Bay, where Melbourne was sited. It was mid-morning on 15 April 1854.

Céleste noted that Solange, Marie and most of all Lionel were happy. She was both nostalgic and depressed at arriving at a place of exile, halfway around the world from her beloved Paris. Yet she was optimistic. The journey had drawn her closer to Lionel. Amid the stress, strains and extreme challenges of the trip she had seen more of the man from the Café Anglais, who had been so gallant in the first hour they'd met. If this was the real Lionel after all, then she had hope that she could overcome all the future tests and trials that were sure to come in this wildest of frontiers.

CHAPTER 35

Trials in a Wild Southern Town

Ten other boats arrived from Europe before the month-delayed *Croesus,* and one of them held a small crate of Céleste's *Mémoires.* The book had been a controversial hit in France, rising quickly to the top of the bestseller list. The crate of ten books would remain in a local Melbourne publisher's warehouse, their contents in French and unlikely to be translated into English.[1]

The Chabrillans were oblivious to all this as the *Croesus,* surrounded by a score of craft, drifted into the Bay under sail. On dropping anchor off Sandridge (later Port Melbourne), Céleste said her goodbyes to many passengers. While she was a little sad to see them go after sharing so many memories and experiences, more bad than good, her regrets were few now that the ordeal was over. Lionel went off alone in search of accommodation. He had been in Melbourne briefly before returning to Paris and thought it would be wiser to go alone around the town, much of it trudging on foot in the mud.

As the passengers disembarked, Céleste was alarmed to see a contingent of port guards and soldiers man the boat. The authorities feared the crew members would try to jump ship, as many others had, to join the gold rush to the north in the towns of Ballarat and Bendigo.[2]

A brawl broke out. Shots were fired and police reinforcements aided the guards and soldiers. Many sailors were put in irons and ferried to prison ships, at least for the two-week duration of the *Croesus*'s stop in Melbourne before its onward journey to Sydney.

The ferry services in the Bay finished at 8 p.m. and Céleste retired to their cabin for the night, realising that Lionel would not reappear until the next day. Céleste had trouble sleeping. She had just drifted off when she was awoken by loud hammering. Incensed, she dressed and climbed on deck to protest only to be shocked to see a coffin maker at work. A body draped in a British flag was lying on the deck. The coffin maker lifted the flag for her. She was deeply saddened to see the boat's 'boy', the lad who had been so terrified by the crossing-of-the-equator 'baptism' that he had tried to jump overboard. Céleste was speechless and did not inquire how his end came. She would never know if he had succeeded in a second suicide attempt or had been stricken by illness. His demise was a reminder, not that she needed one, of the perils of being at sea for so long.

'I can't believe the changes in Melbourne,' Lionel said when he returned in the morning. 'It's only been a year, but prices have doubled everywhere. Carriage rides are exorbitant. Café food is ridiculously priced and rents are ruinous.'

He looked disturbed. Céleste asked, 'What's the matter, darling? What else is bothering you?'

'You know me too well.' He sighed. 'An old friend from Berry, the Duke d'Esclignac, died in July of last year in the direst poverty. He's been buried in an unmarked grave in the main cemetery. It's gone unrecorded. I tried to find it, but it's impossible.'

'We can create a memorial for him …'

'More than that. We'll have a ceremony befitting his status.'

Marie imagined Australia to be a land where everyone was carried about on palanquins.[3] Instead, they took a slow steamer up the Yarra Yarra River to a makeshift quay at the Melbourne Terminus, which was under construction (and would later be known as Flinders Street Station).[4] The previous month of March had been unusually wet, and from the *Croesus* Melbourne had looked lush and green. But close up the fields by the Yarra were uncultivated. Céleste noted 'scraggy, sickly livestock, some of them dead and left to rot in the sun … the few trees are misshapen … lined up in battle formation like a regiment of hunchbacks'.

Her feelings were not helped by the way they were treated at the terminus. The porter fees for their considerable luggage were high, and finding someone willing to take it all on a handcart was difficult.

'We followed behind, paddling through the mud like poodles. The roads had potholes … Lionel helped push the cart.'

After an hour and a half they stopped at an eating house, which was not quite the Café Anglais. 'The bread, butter, eggs, ham, sauerkraut, beer and even the coffee seemed off,' Céleste noted. 'The cost of sixty-eight shillings was far too high for this feast that was inadequate in every way!'

The group set off again. Céleste carried Solange, who carried their talking parrot, which fell silent as they trudged onward. Marie, no longer dreaming of palanquins, straggled on with a dog under each arm. They crossed Melbourne's central street, which looked like a fairground.

'The shopkeepers were not dealing in gingerbread,' Céleste noted, 'but in gold.' They were gesticulating wildly to attract miners wishing to sell their nuggets, large and small.

'There is movement everywhere,' she wrote. 'Everyone yells; it's exactly like the Paris money markets.'

Along the main street were shops that sold everything, forerunners to general stores and, much later, the shopping emporiums. Dresses, York hams, hats, miners' boots, candles, perfumes, pickaxes, children's toys and a thousand other items could be bought by the discerning and undiscerning newly gold-rich miners. Then they would go to the hotels to unload their surplus money on beer, whisky and rum.

Beyond this frenzied circus of eager transactions were some brick houses, huts and tents.

Céleste was most unimpressed with what she observed of her new home city. Paris, with its boulevards, dance halls, castles and grand homes, seemed a painful distance away. She also abhorred the local manners. People pushed every which way and were most reluctant to stop and give directions. As a result they took the wrong tracks and were soon lost in woods.

'I'm not going on!' the carter said finally.

'Oh, yes you are, my friend,' Lionel said.

'Bugger you, cobber! We've been up hill and down dale, and along wrong tracks. I've done twice as much as I should for the payment!'

Lionel was seething. He stared at the carter, who began to wander off.

'Hey!' Lionel yelled. 'Stop there!' He pulled out his pistol and pointed it at the carter's head.

'No!' Céleste said. 'Lionel, please ...'

Marie started crying.

The women's reaction gave the carter pause. He walked back to the cart and began hauling it again.

He pushed on, grumbling, for another hour until they reached some huts in the middle of a forest. The two-level house was poorly constructed, but none of them cared. It was late; they had somewhere to sleep that night.

Céleste was alarmed to learn the next day that they were in an area called Collingwood and its isolation made it a favourite haunt of Melbourne's worst criminals. She imagined that everyone in the area looked like a 'veritable bandit'. Lionel, cool-headed and stronger than she had ever seen him, was less perturbed, even though everyone was armed. He settled Céleste's mind a little by saying that the weapons were for defence rather than attack. Road repairs were going on nearby and Céleste noted that the workers were shackled 'like horses in a field'. The guards carried muskets. Some of these men had been shipped from the Sydney penal settlement; others were local miscreants.

Lionel wasted no time in opening the consulate, using a room in the house as his office. Within a day there was a stream of clients wanting assistance. Most had stories about confidence tricks, theft and daylight robbery. Many wanted repatriation to France and soon it was like a combined doctor's surgery and solicitor's office, with never-ending tales of woe, some of them atrocious. At the end of day three, a 26-year-old Frenchman, Louis-Édouard Manceau, came with perhaps the worst experience short of death. He had been ambushed by six thugs in Collingwood, who broke his arm and shot him in the leg. He ended up in the Royal Melbourne Hospital for three months and had only been out for two days. Manceau had no money and no food. Lionel felt sorry for him but explained he did not have the authority to ship him back to France at the government's expense. Instead, he gave him some money from his own pocket and said he would be his guarantor if he could raise funds for himself. Manceau was consoled by Lionel's idea that the man's mother might meet the cost of the trip back to France.

Hearing this conversation from the other side of the thin partition, Marie commented that if the count continued to be that generous they would not have the money to buy the not-so-pure water, which was dearer than wine, from the over-used Yarra, which doubled as a sewer. Yet Lionel could not deny his own heart, which went out to those suffering and less well off in the new territory. He could not resist the plight of a stonemason father of three from Berry, whose wife was ill in hospital. In a moment of inspiration, Lionel bought a tombstone for twelve pounds, the equivalent of 300 francs, and paid the man to engrave something for the unfortunate Duke d'Esclignac's grave. He and Céleste went to the Melbourne Cemetery but could not find the grave in the large area set aside for paupers. They ended up leaving the stone by the entry wall.

'Lionel's good intentions were not really wasted,' Céleste noted cryptically. 'The stonemason profited from them. But we are poor enough already without wasting 300 francs.'

May brought torrential rain. It swamped their unstable dwelling and Lionel had to work under an umbrella. The southern winter had come early and the Chabrillans experienced cold they normally associated with January in France. Wood was also expensive, but at least it burned long and economically.

Céleste felt uncomfortable in dangerous Collingwood and could not sleep. She was also bothered by rats that were 'fighting each other to eat my shoe'. When an Irishman was murdered for his tools just a hundred metres from their home, they decided to move to a small four-roomed brick house in Victoria Heights, located between Melbourne and Port Melbourne, with a view of the Yarra and Richmond village. The rent was high at ten pounds (250 francs) a month, which was not much less than Lionel's salary.

In the following months Céleste turned her idle time to writing in French and learning English. She was unsettled in her new life, but it had given her a fresh start with Lionel, despite the hardships. She observed, sometimes acutely, the rapid growth of a new city and a population of mainly immigrants, some of whom coped and some of whom did not. She was damning of the farmers and stockbreeders, the real pioneers who had arrived in the decades before the gold rush in 1851. Some had acquired vast tracts of land and made it tough for newer immigrant farmers to establish themselves. The available fertile land, it seemed, had all gone. Céleste foresaw a problem when the gold dried up and miners would be forced back into Melbourne to look for scarce work.

On the positive side she noted the beautiful Botanic Gardens south of the Yarra, where she took carriage rides with Marie and Solange. She visited the university, founded only a year earlier, to see if there might be a course for her. But her English was still poor, and besides, she had responsibilities as the consul's wife, Solange to look after and a household to run. Yet still she hankered to learn and write, and saw this as her calling now, rather than the theatre. Her stage career was slipping away like a nostalgic dream.

Social life existed, too, not with the flair of Paris, but with the excitement of new openings in 1854. The count and countess were invited to the completion of the Melbourne Terminus; the first steam-train ride from the terminus to Sandridge; the Melbourne Exhibition; the State Library opening; the celebration of the first telegraph service to Williamstown across the Bay; and the completion of the first town hall. It was all very uplifting for the locals, and even the sophisticated Chabrillans could not help but be swept along with the rapid development of a village into a city backed by extraordinary wealth.

Still there was a sense of isolation. Céleste had dealt with this before at Berry. She could not help dreaming of Paris and the high life, but with new challenges and projects arising constantly, she put it to the back of her mind. A return to France was not contemplated and could not be for some time, or at least not until Lionel had made his hoped-for speculative fortune. Besides, she was preoccupied with buying land in the village of St Kilda about three kilometres from the centre of Melbourne. This would be the place where she would erect the gabled house she had bought in Bordeaux.

The sound of a cannon firing, which heralded the arrival of a boat in the colony and the possibility of letters from home, would trigger a reminder of France and cause Céleste to be 'overcome with excitement'.

'It is the only emotion I feel in this country,' she wrote. 'A letter addressed to you, even if it is from a creditor, gives immense pleasure.' She always hoped for mail, even if it wasn't due.

'At midday,' she said, 'you see the postman in his red uniform approaching in the distance, you run to meet him.'

If he had no letters, she felt downcast. He would not return for a month.

After four months—on 18 August—she was elated to hear the cannon boom announce the arrival of *The Great Britain*, carrying her furniture and her prefabricated house. It had taken

120 days to travel from Le Havre, and her prayers that it arrive undamaged were answered.

Six weeks later it was erected on Céleste's land in St Kilda, a few hundred yards from the edge of the Bay.

'Here I am, a landowner in Australia,' she wrote with joy. 'A weatherboard gable with a forest view. I no longer fear anything but fire and water.'

CHAPTER 36

Memoirs of Another Life

The consul's office received a twenty-kilogram bundle of French papers and letters, which carried only disturbing or irritating news and information. Céleste was depressed by some of the reviews and comments about her book.

'I'm sorry about this,' she told Lionel.

'I knew about the *Mémoires*,' Lionel said. 'My friends, including Prince Napoleon, forewarned me. I can't say I'm happy, but what's done is done. We move on.' He paused, and nodding to the papers, asked, 'And what do these reviews say?'

'Listen to this,' Céleste said, '"Her self-deprecation and expressions of God-fearing guilt give balance to her memoirs. The authenticity is between the lines. It is an honest rendition of a not always honest life."'

'That's fine. People will buy it.'

'And this,' she said, ignoring him. '"She shows intellectual skills in her humour and observational capacities. Mogador is clearly intelligent and sharp in analysis of people. Pity that her writing does not match these qualities."'

'That is a silly review,' Lionel said. 'You show all those qualities in your writing but it's not up to standard. That's contradictory.'

'Some are personal. They dredge up the past.'

'But it's top of the bestseller list in France …'

'Does that worry you?'

'Not from this distance,' he said, trying to sound cheerful.

'You haven't read the book, have you?'

'No, and I won't.' He paused and added, 'Oh, I might, sometime in the future. I am curious, of course.'

'The sales mean one good thing,' she said. 'We'll have income to supplement your salary here.'

Lionel comforted her further by appealing to her vengeful streak. 'When I'm rich I shall settle my score with all those individuals', referring to those who had attacked her in print. He embraced her. 'Just think of me, the one who loves you. My love will last longer than the petty spite of the gossips.'

'Lionel is suffering,' she observed in her diary, 'but only on my behalf. He is the one who restores my strength by being especially considerate and loving.'

It secretly thrilled her to receive such supportive and flattering comments.

Céleste's mother, living at Céleste's property at Poinçonnet, wrote a plaintive, miserable letter, for which her daughter had only thinly veiled contempt. There was no mention of the detested Vincent, but her negativity made Céleste shudder. It reinforced her decision to distance herself from Anne-Victoire, who was a universe away from her daughter in temperament and experience. Céleste decided she could not care less whether Anne-Victoire was with Vincent or not.

More encouraging was a letter from Ernest Baroche, a friend and previous paramour of Céleste, who was the son of an important conservative Minister of State under Napoleon III. Baroche, who had the reputation of a playboy, was working in a government ministry at the time. His views and those of other friends such as Alexandre Dumas Sr and Jr, who were opposed to the incumbent emperor, meant that Céleste could gauge a wide spectrum of views on everything, from the general political climate in France to the attitude to her personal image.

Baroche wrote to introduce a good friend, who was coming to Melbourne. Baroche had read in the Paris papers a false report that the *Croesus* had sunk with all on board lost at sea.

'All those who know you and love you,' he wrote, 'you know that I am among them, were greatly grieved. We very often speak of you as an author. You have your supporters and enemies. Don't distress about anything. In my opinion, to be talked about gives us proof that we have a relative value …'

It indicated to her that she was being gossiped about in Parisian circles, but this was nothing new.[1]

Céleste occupied herself by furnishing her new home while Marie did the shopping and amused everyone with her straightforward manner.

'She comes back from the market,' Céleste recalled, 'and goes into Lionel's office, and whether there are people there or not, she adds up the cost of every item from water to cauliflower, and groans at the expense.'

Marie also complained about the number of carriages and horses that crammed Melbourne streets and the crowded omnibuses, which cost one shilling (three francs) a ride. They were clear signs of the ongoing, gold-generated boom, as were the numbers of carpenters, builders, locksmiths and painters that jostled for space on the ride. The demand for tradesmen was out-stripping supply and they were charging two pounds (fifty francs) a day, which was as much and more than professionals such as some doctors or lawyers were earning. Lionel went on with his 'surgery', dealing with cases large and small. A French mechanical engineer, Jacques Mureut, had been on board the 220-tonne *Tayleur* that left Liverpool on 19 January 1854. It was shipwrecked off the coast of Ireland. Two hundred and fifty of the 705 people on board survived. Mureut's wife and child were lost. He was picked up by a passing boat that took him to Melbourne. Now he wished to be repatriated to France to be with his mother and sister.

Lionel gave him some of his own money and took Céleste to see the captain of the French ship, *Hirondelle*, who piped them aboard with full ceremonial honours. Lionel, showing some finesse, flattered and cajoled the captain into taking on Mureut as an engineer for the trip back to France.

On the way back to port in a small boat they saw a British ship, the *Onyx*, with its flag at half-mast. It had sailed from Hong Kong on 3 May 1854 with 214 Chinese passengers, all bound for the goldfields. Later it was discovered that many on board had suffered a food-poisoning calamity, or a bad case of scurvy. Their diet of rice, water and inedible fish had not been supplemented by citrus fruits, which would ward off the scurvy. Twenty-four died on board. The other 190 were quarantined in an area north of the Princes Bridge and the Yarra, in what was already becoming a Chinatown. More than forty more died there within twelve days of landing on 22 August.

After such a sobering, tiring day, Lionel had some light relief the next morning from a 'jolly, fat English laundress' who had been deserted by her French husband. She complained about 'these rogues of Frenchmen', and 'what liars they are'. The woman also claimed that he would kick her. Lionel discovered that she was pregnant.

He took down the Frenchman's particulars.

'I shall return your husband to you,' Lionel said, with a serious expression. 'It will be punishment for insulting my compatriots!'

CHAPTER 37

A Hanging and Miner Rebellion

Céleste reflected on the success of her memoirs and was encouraged to continue writing in her diary about the boat trip and life in Australia.[1] But fermenting in her fertile, ambitious and creative mind late in 1854 were the ideas for a novel. Her fervent dislike for the Australian environment and some of the people there was a driving force. And she didn't have to look or read far to find riveting material. Emerging now in her thoughts was Alexandre Dumas's advice to try fiction; to note everything around her and to sketch mini-biographies on any real *characters* she came across. Dumas had made her realise that the people who revolted her most, the individuals she had no intention of wasting her intellectual energy on, were the ones she should definitely write about. It was the despised types, even more than the ones she admired, that would draw out the real writer in her.

With this in mind she organised Lionel to take her on an official French Consulate tour of Ballarat, the goldmining district seventy miles north-west of Melbourne. But instead of hiring a carriage the adventurous Chabrillans, wishing to save on costs, decided to go on horseback over two days, stopping first near a Chinese tent village. At first the inhabitants were hostile to them.

'They were exasperated after being treated like animals by the British,' Céleste wrote. Through an interpreter, the couple made it clear that they were French and had sympathy with them. A Chinese senior then presented Céleste with 'some very pretty handcrafts'.

The next day they trotted on to Ballarat, population 20,000, which frightened Céleste on first sighting.

'It was like a huge cemetery,' she noted, 'where each person digs their own grave.'

The miner representatives gave them a respectful reception, assuming, correctly, that anyone representing the French would not necessarily be supportive of the British-run Victorian Government's policies. There was simmering dislike for the colonial administrators, now headed by Governor Charles Hotham. He had arrived a few months earlier in June, to the alarming news that his coffers were almost bare from the cost of policing and running the goldfields. Miners had to pay a pound a month, or twelve pounds a year, for a licence. This was a heavy imposition for most of them, and many avoided paying the licence fee. Hotham ordered the police to redouble their efforts to collect the fees, and this was when tensions—colonial masters versus miners—began to increase.

The Chabrillans picked up on this sensitivity. Lionel, representing several hundred Frenchmen in the area, listened to their grievances; Céleste, not understanding much of the discussions, learned by watching the miners' agitated faces and body language.

After the initial political chat, Céleste was asked if she would care to go down a mine shaft. She had no wish to go, but in front of her husband and so many eager watchers, she relented and switched to 'show time' in an instant. Céleste looked her ravishing best in long dress, bonnet and with a colourful parasol. She smiled her regal smile, waved to two photographers present and stepped with fashion-model elegance into the mine trolley to the applause of a hundred onlookers. She was given a lantern and lowered carefully into the pit.

'I am plunged about eighty feet,' she wrote in her diary, 'and arrive at the bottom feeling very apprehensive.'

A miner showed her around the cramped underground passage. He gave her a pick and invited her to dig. Céleste scratched around, and with the miner's help 'discovered' a few small grains of gold, which had been secretly placed at her feet.

Lionel embraced her on her return to the surface, where she was cheered again.[2]

Dumas's comment about revulsion being a spur for characters and incident in fiction and non-fiction was tested when, much against her instincts, Céleste decided to attend the trial of an alleged serial killer in the Melbourne Supreme Court. The man accused was John Hughes. There was a wealth of evidence that said he had slain at least fifteen people, and perhaps double that number. Hughes was already branded as Australia's worst mass murderer. The courtroom was crowded. A mob of hundreds more waited for the verdict outside. Chances were that in the small colony, there were many who knew someone who had been killed by this alleged monster.

Céleste better understood Dumas's advice. She found the insouciant Hughes an 'interesting' character, mainly because of his behaviour at the trial, which began on 19 September. On day three the jury broke to deliberate for an hour. When the trial resumed Hughes said to the judge, 'You're in too much of a hurry to find me guilty.'

The judge glared but said nothing. This only encouraged the accused to add, 'It's six o'clock. You're thinking of the dinner that's waiting for you.' Some in the audience giggled nervously at the outburst. 'Come on, hurry up, or the pudding will get cold.'

It seemed as if Hughes may have been correct. A minute later the judge read the sentence to him, 'The accused has been found guilty and is condemned to death by hanging, in three days.'

Hughes, now sounding on the verge of hysteria, gesticulated at the judge and repeated the sentence. 'I wish you *bon appétit*! Drink my health with a glass of sherry before I die!'

Over the next two day gallows scaffolding was erected in the forecourt of the courthouse. On 22 September a big crowd gathered on high ground in Victoria Parade to witness the event. Céleste had been intrigued by the trial. Now she wished to follow it through to a conclusion by viewing the actual execution. A doctor friend offered her a place at a window in his house, which looked over Victoria Parade. It was a scene reminiscent of the glory days of the guillotine in Paris only a few decades earlier, but without women knitting. There was a similar bloodlust and desire to see a humiliating state-determined end to a human being.

'I accepted despite my repugnance for this kind of spectacle,' Céleste said, but she was thinking of Dumas's advice to experience such incidents so she could write about them later with the authority of a first-hand witness. 'I want to familiarise myself with all life's atrocities,' she added. 'It will make me philosophical.' Seeing such a grotesque demise, she felt, would focus her mind on the more important issues in life and help her 'rise above the petty afflictions that beset me constantly'.

This was at odds with others, who wanted revenge for the many people slaughtered by Hughes, and still others who were there for the thrill.

The condemned man arrived, shackled and flanked by four burly policemen.

'The crowd is suddenly full of movement like an ants' nest that has just been run over by a carriage wheel,' Céleste observed in her diary. Hughes looked scornfully at the inquisitive throng, 'all riveted and open-mouthed'. He put on a bold front as he was escorted up the steps to the platform. Once there, he bent his head forward towards the executioner, 'smiling as if he were only going to try on a cravat'.

Hughes's careless, almost carefree attitude incensed many onlookers. They wanted him to suffer indignity, fear and pain, but he was denying them that pleasure. Hughes, hands tied behind his back, was not allowed the right to say some last words, usually a chance to repent. But knowing he would never do this, the executioner steadied him in position over a trap door, stepped to one side and pulled a metre-long lever. The trap door fell open, sending Hughes into space and eternity. There were gasps as his body twisted and his neck muscles fought a losing battle against strangulation.

'His eyes become bloodshot,' Céleste noted with a writer's eye for detail and drama, 'the veins on his forehead and temple swell fit to burst. His mouth gapes open, showing his swollen, distended tongue, as big as an ox's. Soon all that can be seen is a featureless purple, round mass.'

Lionel was alert to the unrest at Ballarat. He had direct involvement with French miners there and it was a talking point every night at dinner. Deep unrest was sparked on 7 October 1854 when Scottish miner James Scobie was murdered at the Eureka Hotel, Ballarat. The proprietor, James Bentley, was charged with murder but acquitted on 17 October. Several thousand miners gathered at the hotel to protest, and this forced Bentley and his wife to flee the area. The miners rioted and burned down the hotel, despite the efforts to stop them by a small contingent of soldiers. Two miners were arrested and charged for lighting the fire. This provoked 4000 miners to hold a meeting, and they resolved to establish a Diggers' Rights Society. Seven more miners were arrested over the hotel fire, which led to a second meeting of miners at Bakery Hill. A third meeting on 11 November saw about 10,000 miners attend and the Ballarat Reform League was created with John Humffray as chairman. He had been in the Chartist Movement in England, which fought for political reforms such as the vote for all males. He and other former Chartists were turning miner unrest over licence fees into a more fundamental force for change. This was all in defiance of the goldfields commissioner, Robert Rede, the British son of a naval officer. Rede had lost control of the situation and swore revenge against the miners.

Lionel was forced to return to Ballarat, where he met with the French miners again and warned them not to get involved in the movement. The count knew from his contacts in the colonial government that there would be swift and tough action if matters in Ballarat looked to be getting out of hand. He warned his compatriots they could expect immediate deportation if they were found to be active in any serious protest against the British colonial rulers.

The Reform League put forward a resolution, based on the UK Chartist Movement, which said, 'That it is the inalienable right of every citizen to have a voice in making laws he is called on to obey; that taxation without representation is tyranny.' This was compelling enough for most miners, but it was a further resolution that excited many of the French miners: 'The League will secede from the United Kingdom if the current situation does not improve.'

Lionel warned his compatriots that this would not happen and to not take part in any resultant action. He went further and published a proclamation to all French expatriates residing in Victoria, advising them to dissociate themselves from the agitation at the Ballarat goldfields.[3]

Céleste observed that the governor, Sir Charles Hotham, whom she described 'as a man of the highest breeding and most amiable', was caught in a dilemma. He needed to police the area and he would lose his job if there was a serious move to secede by part of the colony. He was trying the middle ground by courting the miners, but they saw weakness and pushed harder for their additional demands as well as dropping the licence fee. Hotham became more authoritarian. At the same time, he declared his support for 'democratic principles' in spite of objections from the propertied and official classes who formed the Executive Council that ran the colony. Hotham took the time-honoured stalling route of appointing a Royal Commission on goldfield problems and grievances.

But Rede was the man in charge of operations on the goldfields. Backed by military reinforcements, he stepped up the hunt for miners who hadn't paid their licence fees, resulting in more confrontation with the miners, despite Hotham directing that he proceed cautiously and legally. More soldiers sent from Melbourne on 28 November were attacked by an angry mob of miners. There were injuries but no deaths, although there were rumours that a drummer boy had died.[4] The next day 12,000 miners met and the Reform League delegation reported it had failed in negotiations with the authorities, dominated by Rede, with Hotham in contact by cypher (a forerunner to the telegraph). The miners resolved to burn their licences.

On 30 November, Rede responded by ordering police to conduct a licence search. Eight 'burners' or licence defaulters were arrested. In turn, the miners rioted again. Soldiers had to extricate police before a possible lynching. This provided Rede with his excuse for his tough methods, which he believed were further justified when the miners, led by Peter Lalor, held a provocative meeting. At this meeting, a white-and-blue Australian Flag of Independence, bearing only the Southern Cross and no British symbols, was consecrated. Miners swore an oath to it: 'We swear by the Southern Cross to stand truly by each other and fight to defend our rights and liberties.'

A crude Eureka Stockade was built from timber and overturned carts. Armed miners took up the barricades. In response at mid-afternoon on 3 December, a contingent of 276 police and soldiers approached the Stockade. A battle ensued and the miners were routed in ten minutes. Twenty-two Irishmen (fourteen at the time, and eight dying later) were killed, and another twelve were injured. Six soldiers and police were killed in the battle. Martial law was imposed and the miner resistance collapsed much faster than it had formed.

Lionel had opened an office in Collins Street, in Melbourne, to cope better with the crisis, and he feared an international incident. He hurried to Ballarat and was relieved to find that no French miner had been involved in the Stockade battle. His compatriot miners had been in sympathy with the rebels, but obeyed Lionel's proclamation that they should stay out of the confrontation.

CHAPTER 38

Whatever Lola Wants ...

The Chabrillans experienced their own form of siege in Melbourne in the last weeks of 1854—a most eventful year—and into 1855. Céleste was snubbed by elements of Melbourne society, who'd learned, second-hand and from rumour, a little about her past.

'I have been the victim of a kind of persecution,' she noted, but 'I had to be seen, nevertheless.' Yet some 'braver and kinder' society matrons called on her in St Kilda to invite her to visit them. Despite this she remained suspicious of their advances.

'I was not sufficiently well brought up to sustain a long conversation with well-bred people,' she said in a frank self-analysis. But her attitude began to change when she accepted invitations to events where some people showed respect for her as a countess by bowing.

External pressures continued. Ernest Baroche wrote from Paris again, warning that the sustained sales success of her *Mémoires* had created rumblings about the suitability of her carrying the countess title. Her marriage was under scrutiny, and Céleste and Lionel suspected his family was behind the outcry. There were calls from some quarters for the French Foreign Ministry to recall the count from Melbourne. But Baroche was quick to reassure the couple that nothing would be done without Emperor Napoleon III's authority—and he had more on his mind than worrying about his consular officials. Céleste wrote to all her high-level contacts, including Prince Napoleon, in an effort to bolster support for Lionel and her.

This news gave the count's get-rich-quick schemes greater urgency. Prime among these was to import flour, which two compatriots had convinced him was in short supply. They wanted him to put up guarantees to charter two ships to bring flour supplies from Chile. They reckoned they could buy it in Chile for 200 pounds and resell it in Melbourne for a thousand.

Lionel tried to justify the deal on moral grounds by saying the flour would help stop immigrants from dying of starvation. Céleste remained unconvinced, knowing that Lionel, while well-meaning, was not an experienced businessman. He had shown a high level of incompetence in money matters, and she had been the one to drive their return to solvency with her courage and intelligence. Céleste was sceptical about the flour deal. The partners alleged they did not have much money. They wanted to raise funds by securing Lionel's personal guarantees.

'One is the son of a shipowner from Bordeaux,' Lionel said. 'The other is from Toulouse and a real braggart … but is so industrious he succeeds in everything he does.'

Céleste quizzed him. 'How much would you make out of it?'

'A million francs', or about 40,000 pounds.

'And how much do you stand to lose?'

'From fifteen to twenty thousand francs each shipment.'

'And if the flour arrived in bad condition?'

'We can insure against that.'

Céleste learned more. The ships were ready just as soon as Lionel gave the word. One of the French merchants involved was on one of the ships to make sure they bought the right amount of the commodity.

'You'd better think it over carefully first,' she advised.

'To gain all,' he told her, 'one must risk all. Don't worry, I'm doing this for your sake, and I shall be careful.'

Céleste remained cautious, although she conceded that the best way to create real wealth away from the goldfields was to deal in commodities, particularly foodstuffs.

'All the grocers made their fortunes very quickly,' she noted in a prosaic, hopeful observation. 'Fat candles are being sold for five francs [4 shillings] apiece.'

Governor Hotham, ill from the stress of crushing the miners' rebellion, put on a ball. He invited Lionel, who was obliged to go without his wife. It irked them both.

'One-third of the invitees are ex-convicts,' Céleste exaggerated in her diary, 'and some are even escaped prisoners from the Sydney penal settlement.' She had great delight in reporting that the ball was a flop. The food was ridiculed in the papers and offended her French sensibilities. The buffet consisted of nothing but cold meats and hams. The only drink was beer in barrels.

Another contact from Paris's demimonde was the adventurous Antoine Fauchery, a well-known writer, artist and photographer, who spent two years in the goldfields, with the usual experience of failing to make the hoped-for fortune. In 1854 he founded the Café Estaminet Francais in Melbourne's Little Bourke Street, which featured a billiards table, a rarity in

Australia at the time. The café was patronised by Europeans and French exiles who longed for the boulevards of Paris and the bohemian life there. When Fauchery's café began to struggle, Lionel suggested he set up a photographic studio in Melbourne. But by 1855 his rent debts to the landlord had mounted and Fauchery left the café, making sure to hide his precious billiards table. He was pursued in the courts by the landlord. Lionel's private, rather than consular, advice was to return to Paris and come back to Australia when he could pay his debts, then set up the studio (which he did with French girlfriend, later wife, Louise Josephine Gatineau).[1]

Céleste's competitive, conquistadorial and creative spirit was inspired by the arrival of the sparkling and sensual Irish-born Lola Montez, formerly Marie Gilbert. She was thirty-six when she arrived in Melbourne with a dance troupe in 1855. She had trained as a dancer in Spain and was famous/notorious for her erotic performance in Europe. Like Céleste, she had not made it as an actress, and her singing was not a box-office puller. Again like the countess, she had cut a swathe through the bedrooms of the rich and/or famous of Europe, including that of renowned Hungarian composer/pianist Franz Liszt. The affair with Liszt placed her high on the scandal register when it caused a split between him and his beautiful aristocratic mistress, the Countess Marie d'Agoult, with whom he had three children. But he soon regretted the Lola encounter. She was given to histrionics on and off the stage, and was a publicity seeker, which irked the studious Liszt. She was a supreme tantrum thrower, and when she took one temperamental fit too far in Dresden, Germany, he locked her in their hotel bedroom and fled. Shrewd and tidy, Liszt paid the hotel in advance for Lola's anticipated destruction of everything not bolted down.

Her penchant and capacity for seducing those at the pinnacle of society was matched only by Céleste, and they had more than a few belt notches in common in France, including Alexandre Dumas Sr.

Céleste was a better dancer, but even she bowed to the grand gimmick of Lola's 'Spider Dance'. This had shocked critics in Europe, ensuring good theatre ticket sales for several years wherever she performed. Warned that puritanical Melbourne society might be scandalised by her hip-and-pelvic gyrations, Lola advertised the dance in a way to arouse curiosity rather than censorship.

'A young Spanish girl, when amusing herself while dancing, is stung by a spider or tarantula,' she told the press. 'It fastens itself upon her person. As the poison gradually disperses itself through her frame, she becomes faint and exhausted, falls on the stage, or reels off distracted.'

In the show, she added a final, dramatic and amusing twist by finding the spider and stomping on it in triumph.

Lola had performed in Sydney before her Melbourne debut, and Céleste was intrigued by the *Sydney Morning Herald*'s review, which called it 'the most libertinish and indelicate performance that could ever be given on the public stage'.

Lola ignored that comment, saying that the reviewer had clearly never lived outside Australia, but she did embrace a review in the magazine *Bell's Life in Sydney* that found 'nothing in her beautiful saltation [leaping about] beyond descriptive, coquettish eccentricities'.

Céleste went to a five-act performance, *My History*, which was very loosely based on Lola's time in Bavaria with the king. At the end of act four she claimed to have only two things left in life, her conscience and her virtue, which Céleste laughed at as cheekily self-serving. Yet Lola confounded the audience in the last act by making a speech. She wanted everyone's support and 'protection'. They could prove their goodwill by coming to her plays every day. She blew kisses to many patrons.

'Reduce the price of the seats!' an Irishman called. Lola answered by arguing that they were worth 'every penny'. Some in the audience agreed, others weren't so sure, and a strident debate flowed back and forth with Lola holding her positions on all points. Others called out questions.

'She replied with remarkable presence of mind,' Céleste noted. 'She speaks English very well. They clap and they whistle. There is an infernal din.'

The Spider Dance followed the play. Céleste called it 'ballet'. 'It consists of moving about a lot,' she said, 'while frantically shaking the folds of an extremely short gauze skirt.'

This exposed Lola's long, slim legs and other tantalising glimpses, at least for the men.

'All the women walked out before the end of the ballet,' Céleste observed, 'although there is nothing improper in it.'

The police did not agree. They banned a second Spider Dance show.

A day later, Lola made a point of coming to Céleste's St Kilda home for tea.

'People say she is mad,' Céleste reported, 'but she is simply very excitable.' Céleste could not understand her rapid-fire Irish accent but did ascertain that Lola was hoping to make her fortune entertaining on the goldfields. Céleste wished her luck but did not think she would make her fortune in a place that was so rough and challenging.

Lola was part of the drive for more and more entertainment in Victoria. Bars, cafés, concerts and dances burgeoned to soak up the hard-earned money of miners and others in the increasingly wealthy environment, especially Melbourne, which was fast becoming a very rich city. It was this burst of new entertainment and eating venues that first gave rise to the expression *Melbournians would go to the opening of an envelope*. It may have been said first by a visiting Sydneysider, but it was true.

The Chabrillans were no longer disregarded. Invitations poured in. By mid-1855 they had become an essential item at openings, which obliged them to invite others to their own official events, such as the Bastille Day Ball.

Once irritated by being ostracised, Céleste now resented the social whirl interfering with their private hours, and her chance to have time with the growing Solange. Céleste taught her everything from arithmetic to reading; but the little girl, now five, seemed difficult to inspire intellectually. Her limited desire for knowledge of any kind frustrated Céleste, who designated her as 'thick-skulled' and felt like giving up. The only consolation was having more time for her first attempt at a novel.

Céleste, however, did lap up the newfound respect for her, and enjoyed all the attention after the earlier snub by the governor at his less-than-spectacular ball. She was especially gratified by the Freemasons Ball held in the aid of Allied Wounded. Melbourne Mayor John Thomas Smith organised the show, featuring a flower display in honour of Queen Victoria and Napoleon III. Smith was forty-nine, many times mayor, a publican and conservative politician and he had an affection for the Chabrillans. When he entered the ballroom of his own creation—the Queen's Theatre Royal—it was to the strains of 'Leaving for Syria', which was France's official march for public ceremonies during the Second Empire (from 1810). The mayor's gesture was a tribute to France and their representatives in Melbourne, the Chabrillans.

Smith then asked the countess to dance with him. Céleste was intimidated by the honour. She looked to Lionel, hoping he would indicate she should decline, but he knew the protocol and encouraged her to do it. She felt it did her 'too much honour', and thought she might faint. Smith bolstered her by whispering in her ear that he was demonstrating to the inhabitants of Melbourne his respect for the Chabrillans. Lionel and Céleste went home happier than at any other time in the colony to that point. They would never be completely comfortable with life in Melbourne, but this accolade did much for their morale, as did a remark by Lady Hotham late in 1855. Her husband had just died of either cholera, the official version, or distress and depression after he was blackguarded in many quarters, particularly by the press, following the miners' rebellion and the disaster of the Eureka Stockade.

'The English are quite savage when it comes to making fun of people,' Céleste noted. 'They don't even stop out of respect for the dead.'

Lionel travelled to the governor's mansion in South Yarra to pay his respects. The sad Lady Hotham apologised for the way she had treated him and Céleste.

Lionel, ever the gentleman, was genuinely sorry for her especially given the trying time that she continued to have with the press.

CHAPTER 39

Counted Out

Céleste's prediction that Lola Montez would not find success on the goldfields did not prove correct at first. The miners loved this exotic and erotic Spanish (Irish) show-woman. They all turned out to be arachnophiles, at least when she performed her revealing sensual/sexual, 'ballet'. The miners gave Lola the greatest reception of her life throughout February 1856. But in Ballarat, she was heavily criticised as much for her reputation as her stage show and Spider Dance. She was furious, claiming that the attacks were because she had refused to pay for promotional articles and favourable reviews. In what was seen as a Spanish tradition, she marched, horsewhip in hand, around to the *Ballarat Times* accompanied by Sally Bell, the wife of the impresario who had organised the trip around the goldfield towns. Bell thought the whip was simply part of Lola's ongoing theatrics when she demanded to see the editor/owner Harry Seckamp. At first Lola verballed him for his 'libellous' remarks. Halfway through the tirade on the doorstep of the paper, her histrionics turned hysterical. She lashed him with the whip several times. When she could not be restrained, Bell, a friend of Seekamp's, stepped in and punched Lola in the face.

This incident happened at the end of her goldfields tour. Unrepentant and despite two black eyes, she returned to Melbourne for more performances, this time in a big, improvised circus tent. Her fury from Ballarat spilled into this performance and was not helped by her audience being made up in part of vocal, drunken miners on leave from the diggings. Her 'intercourse' with the audience, which had worked before, now became a harangue at heckling patrons. She was booed and abused. The next morning's newspaper reviews ridiculed her. She responded by having notices of complaint pinned in Melbourne's main streets.

Lionel became concerned when he heard rumours that she would be dragged out of her hotel—the Grand Imperial—and horsewhipped in a city square. He hurried to see her and was alarmed to find protesters already gathering outside the hotel at the corner of Elizabeth and Little Collins Streets. Lionel tried to talk her into leaving Melbourne right away. Her stubborn streak surfaced. She refused. He took her to the window and pointed out the growing mob. Lola still resisted, saying she'd rather fight them. Lionel finally made her see reason and secreted her out of the hotel. They took a carriage to St Kilda, where she stayed with the Chabrillans for two days before he could arrange her 'escape' on a ship to Sydney. From there she planned a further tour, this time to America, with the good money she had made in the goldfields.

Lionel let government officials and newspaper editors know his feelings about the way Lola had been treated, and also the manner in which Céleste had been smeared by association. Defending people who had on occasions offended prudish Victorian sensibilities did not endear him to some. The

Chabrillans began to lose the goodwill that had built up around them in recent months.

Lionel and Fauchery, who had become best friends, sought out the detractors of Lola and Céleste. By coincidence two other Frenchmen were about to settle a dispute in the time-honoured but crude method of a duel, with pistols at dawn, in Alma Road, St Kilda. A policeman intervened and arrested one of the combatants. Lionel waved the French flag, literally, in the police court in an attempt to stop the second combatant from also being taken into custody, but to no avail.

The newspapers attacked Lionel for his impetuous act and accused him of not understanding the limits of his power and duties as a consul. Lionel was unhappy with this reportage and with caricatures of him, Céleste and Lola that appeared in some papers. Urged on by the meddling Fauchery, Lionel, in a fit of pique, challenged a reporter to a duel.

'Laugh at me, write anything you please,' he wrote in a note to the allegedly offending reporter, 'but I forbid you to have anything to do with my private life … You don't know how to handle a sword, and I cannot box. I shall therefore be forced to put a bullet in your head. I mean what I say, and I swear to you I will do what I say.'

The Argus on 15 March 1856, in an article headed 'Consular Dignity', accused the count of displaying 'a morbid idiosyncrasy'. It exposed his folly in the court in attempting to protect the French duellists from arrest and revealed and rubbished his rash threat to kill the journalist.

Céleste eventually calmed him down. But his behaviour bothered her. She knew her man better than he knew himself in certain circumstances and she believed something else, something more fundamental, was causing these outbursts. She became ill with liver complaints, which may well have been brought on by stress.

By April 1856, around the time Lionel started showing signs of renewed strain and odd behaviour, Céleste had been working secretly for more than a year on a novel, *The Gold Thieves*.

'I have revised it a dozen times,' she wrote in her diary. 'I don't know where to hide it in case Lionel finds it. Perhaps he would laugh at me, and anyway he would scold me.'

She found the painstaking work affected her health, but on the other hand she discovered the writing helped her forget her troubles. The act of living in a parallel world of fiction was cathartic, creative and liberating. She reckoned the odds were heavily against success, yet she was spurred on by the sales of her memoirs, which had been on the bestseller list in France for more than a year. The publisher was thinking of another edition. Even so, she was uncertain, realistic and hopeful rather than delusional about a follow-up big seller in another, more demanding form of writing.

'I know it's ridiculous,' she wrote, 'but I fancy that if misfortune strikes, I could manage to earn some money.'

Céleste knew that the harsh, different, more demanding life she had experienced in Australia was as valuable from a creative and observational point of view as any inert gold nugget she and Lionel could ever have stumbled across in the goldfields. It depended on her writing a good book. No local had succeeded, despite plenty of scribblers trying something. She had perspective on this brash new country that was fresh and honest, at least in her opinion, as depicted through her characters and narrative. Her source material was vast. While Lionel toiled at his city office, she had plenty of time on her hands to take notes and reflect. Her English was now strong enough that she could read the papers, which served drama up daily and in stimulating variety. Céleste drew on all her experiences at sea, and in St Kilda, Ballarat and Melbourne. As she wrote the book, she included everything from hangings to hurricanes and from street fights to bushfires.

Not only was there the heartbeat of the gold industry and all the wealth it was generating, along with the greed, court action, thieving, murdering and city development evident on the skyline; there was also the micro-drama, mainly tragedy, told to Lionel every day by his French compatriot victims of misfortune, as well as by others—British, Scandinavian, American, German, Dutch, Chinese and Indigenous Australians, who were being swept, often mercilessly, from their own lands.

Everyone coming to Australia had a story to tell. No one travelling halfway round the world to take a chance at a completely new and pioneering life, in the cities and on the often hostile land beset by floods and fire, could claim to have had a dull, uneventful existence.

All these tales touched Céleste and she wove some of them into her narrative.

Her attitude to the huge, clandestine effort behind *The Gold Thieves* perhaps reflected her strength of character, drive and ambition more than anything else.

'I would rather lose everything,' she noted, 'than one day [have to] say to myself, "If only I had persevered more, perhaps I could have achieved something."'

But she remained humble when she added, 'Who knows, in a few years' time, Lionel might be forgiven for having married me.'

She did not stop at one novel. Over the two years spent in Melbourne she made time to produce several fictional works. Though she never revealed it in her diaries and memoirs, she was giving everything she had to succeed in this creative area. It was her biggest secret.

Céleste was alone at the French Chancellery in May 1856 when she discovered the reason behind Lionel's precipitous acts and moods. Reading his private business files, she learned that his representative handling the flour shipments had gone bankrupt and fled with the 40,000 francs he owed the Chabrillans. The flour in Melbourne arrived by ship from Chile, but only after many other shipments of the same commodity had already arrived. Consequently, the bottom had dropped out of the market. The flour had to be sold at a massive loss.

The bad luck that Céleste feared had struck.

'Lionel has once again been taken by being too trusting,' she wrote in her diary. 'The business partners have nothing associated to their names but debts. He is left solely responsible.'

The Count de Chabrillan was on his way to bankruptcy. While he was at his Melbourne office, a sheriff came to the St Kilda house to seize it and any personal effects of any value. Céleste owned the house and it was in her name. She could have resisted the seizure, and would have been within her rights under the terms of her marriage contract. Instead, she signed over all her possessions to make sure the situation did not lead to her husband ending up in court.

Lionel was furious when he discovered her actions.

'I owe much more than the house is worth,' he said. 'Now we shall have debts and nowhere to live. It's an act of absolute madness!'

Céleste was angry at his insensitive and ungrateful reaction to her attempt to extricate him from yet another major financial mess.

'We had a very heated argument for the first time in our marriage,' she said, 'but he admitted he had been wrong. He kissed me and begged forgiveness. We both cried and made up.'

The law moved fast. The house was put up for sale, but there were no initial buyers. Lionel now hoped he could raise enough money so the debts would be mostly paid off, which would mean that the deeds to the property would revert to his wife.

But he would not be allowed to leave Victoria until his finances were stabilised, one way or the other. Céleste could travel if she wished. Once more the resilient Countess de Chabrillan knew she had to show her ingenuity and come up with something that might just save her husband.

CHAPTER 40

Solvency Solutions

'I think I have a solution to our financial situation,' Céleste said one morning. 'Your cousin owes 40,000 francs for jewels I sold him. That would clear our debts.' This cousin was also Count de Chabrillan.

'But you sued him for the capital and interest, and it failed.'

'Because we're so far away. If I confront him in France, he'll pay up.'

'I'm not letting you travel back. You're still not well enough. Besides, I can't go with you.' He looked away and added, 'I don't wish to be left alone.'

'It's the only solution we have, darling,' she said. 'A little bit of hardship on the trip will be worth it.'

She sold all her best dresses and remaining jewels to raise funds for the boat trip for her, Solange and Marie. Then she went to the trouble of having a senior government official intervene with Lionel's creditors so that he would be given time—six months—to pay back the money owing. This influenced Lionel to at least consider allowing her to make the voyage. Yet in another moment of weakness, more symptomatic of the old pre-marriage, pre-Australia Lionel, he said, 'I'll die worrying about you. If they make life too hard for me here, I'll put a bullet through my brain!'

Céleste would have none of this talk, which she viewed as self-indulgent. But she also knew that he was capable of killing himself in a moment of discouragement. The easy access to weapons and the fact that most people in Victoria carried arms also bothered her.

'If I were strong enough,' she told him, 'I would beat you for saying such a thing! Your life is no longer your own. It belongs to me, and I value it more than my own. In time everything can be arranged.'

'Your liver won't stand the trip. You know that.'

'It's true, I'm not well, and nor is Solange. But our doctor says we're more likely to die if we stay in Australia. Something about the climate. We haven't adjusted as well as you.'

This swayed Lionel slightly. He became convinced when Fauchery told him he feared for his own wife's life because of a sudden sickness. Madame Fauchery wanted to go back to France to heal or die but had been ordered by her medico not to attempt the arduous trip.

Céleste did not show it, but she worried about this 'very big step' of leaving Lionel and even 'the wretched country of Australia'. Yet she felt it was her destiny to go. In the back of her mind, she would take the opportunity to sell her novels, which Lionel had no idea she had written.

She was struck by a surprising bout of nostalgia for Australia after having complained endlessly to friends in France and bitched to compatriots in the privacy of her own home.

'I felt myself loving that hard Australian soil,' she recalled. 'The plants, the trees, my own loneliness—I was going to regret [leaving] them all.'

Céleste, Solange and Marie were set to sail on board an American ship—the *James Baines*—when Lionel turned up to spend one last night with her. He risked a treacherous trip by boat in a squall on Port Phillip Bay to give her his most treasured heirloom, a small ivory figure of Jesus Christ on an ebony cross, which he had inherited from his mother. It was the only item of his mother's that he possessed.

'Keep it with you always, do you understand?' he said through chattering teeth after his mid-winter ordeal in rough seas. 'It's the last sacrifice I can make for you, the last proof of love I can give you.'

Céleste was more touched than she had ever been, especially when he added, 'I have no regrets, and if you were not my wife, I would still marry you.'

'That's the sweetest thing anyone has ever said to me,' she said, tears welling.

'My only regret is that I have involved you in my failed business affairs.'

'You should not feel remorse. I don't. We're a team; all marriages are in themselves business relationships. We share the same problems and successes. That's marriage. That's married life.'

The night was spent exchanging promises and when day broke they had hardly slept. Céleste awoke with less courage for her plans than when she had fallen asleep.

'I want you to stow away with me,' she whispered, trembling. 'I don't think I can stand to be away from you.'

'Céleste, please don't talk like that. I gave my word to the Victorian authorities that I wouldn't attempt to escape the colony.'

Her plea, however, played on his conscience. He stayed in the cabin until well after the time visitors were supposed to leave, almost as if he was planning to sail away by 'mistake'.

After he left, sorrow, fatigue and emotion overtook Céleste and she collapsed in her cabin. When she came to, the ship was eighty kilometres from Melbourne. Céleste climbed on deck, but all she could see was the 'huge, sad, green expanse that often makes us believe in the end of the world'.

Céleste kept a diary for the hundred-day journey. As with all long ocean trips of the era, death stalked the *James Baines*. But Céleste hung on to life, her duties and ambitions. She was driven by her responsibilities to Solange and her husband, and the grand prospect of seeing the boulevards of her beloved Paris again. At last in late November 1856, after more than two and a half years away, they arrived home.

Céleste wasted no time in taking a modest apartment at 11 Rue d'Alger and wrote to her mother, inviting her to visit. Anne-Victoire came and was saddened to see her daughter's appearance. The harsh Australian sun and conditions had hardened her looks, and she seemed to have aged beyond her thirty-one years. But Céleste was unperturbed by her reaction.

On the fifth day of her return, she met with her ex-lover and lawyer, Maitre Desmarest, in her battle to recover money from Lionel's cousin.

'I want to sue him again,' she said, 'but this time we'll really put the pressure on.'

'There's no guarantee we would win at the second attempt,' Desmarest said.

'Typical lawyer's attitude!'

'Yes, and we deal in realities.'

'Without imagination. The family hates publicity. If they thought the legal battle would be in the papers …'

'The case could take six months.'

'No. Lionel would be bankrupt in Melbourne by that time.'

'Is there any way he could be brought to Paris?' Desmarest asked. 'That would put pressure on the cousin. Lionel would add a certain level of integrity to the claim that you sold the jewellery to him. I would imagine that this could swing the dispute your way.'

'Then I must find a way to get him back. Under the colony's legal restrictions, he must stay there until his financial situation is cleared up, one way or another.' Céleste paused to consider another problem. 'Under the terms of his contract as consul he can't leave until 1859.'

'Again, too late!' Desmarest said.

In less than a fortnight, she had fulfilled Lionel's wish to place Solange in a convent at Ardentes, near Châteauroux. Now she felt free to turn her mind to how she might make some money to live. Top of her list was an attempt to sell her novels. It was her deepest desire.

While making inquiries on where she might sell *The Gold Thieves*, Céleste was surprised to see how well her memoirs were thought of in Paris literary circles. But she was less than pleased to learn that the publisher was about to issue another edition. She once more sent Desmarest into the legal fray in an attempt to stop publication. He failed, but Céleste again called on Prince Napoleon for assistance and he managed to get a temporary annulment of the contract for the memoirs after the fifth volume had been published. A further three volumes would sit in limbo until a court case sorted out the dispute.

A friend at *La Presse*, Charles Edmond, was now in charge of magazine serialisations, which were all the reading rage in France and England. He said he had too many serials piled up to fit her book in, but suggested she see another publisher, Michel Lévy.

Edmond's recommendation was so glowing that, with the promise that Céleste had more novels on the way, Lévy bought *The Gold Thieves*. Céleste was ecstatic. It gave her even more joy than when she had found a publisher for *Mémoires*. She felt that her gifts lay in fiction—in character depiction drama, plot and narrative.

'It *had* to be a success,' she wrote in her diary, 'so that Lionel would not scold me for having gone into this new venture into the public arena without telling him about it; a venture that could do me so much harm.'

An advance from Lévy and more proceeds from *Mémoires* meant that Céleste could send some much-needed funds to Lionel, who had borrowed privately himself. Collectively, they had enough to pay off his debts. Ownership of the St Kilda house reverted to Céleste, which was a turn in their fortunes because property prices were rising fast. Under the colony's laws, Lionel was also free to leave Victoria if he wished. But his first tour as consul ran for five years and he could not request leave before that time was up in 1859.

Lionel was distressed at Céleste being away and feared she might not return. In a letter he said:

> *I reproach myself for letting you go. This life at the other end of the earth, which pleases me because you seem to belong to me more truly and completely here, may not be enough to make you happy. I have broken the vow I made to God and to myself not to part from you for a single day of my life. Everything makes me anxious, even my dreams!*
>
> *On the 4th of January [1857] at midday, send me a loving thought: it's our wedding anniversary. At the same*

time here, I shall send you all my wishes, all my desires, and all my thoughts. Don't forget from 11 a.m. to midday to shut yourself off alone for an hour to think of me. Our thoughts are sure to cross.

Yours until my dying day.

Céleste was so moved by the last lines that she wished to 'fly' to him immediately, leaving all the court cases, publishing deals and other obligations unfinished.

'On reflection,' she said, 'it would be folly to have made such a long and arduous journey only to be faced with the same problems again.'

However, she could not resign herself to being separated from him for any longer. She called on the distinguished Ferdinand-Marie Viscount de Lesseps, the minister handling diplomatic appointments, and an influential member of the French Academy. She begged him to consider giving Lionel leave after three years, which would be up soon, rather than the regulation five.

'You're making a very difficult request,' the viscount said, wilting a fraction.

'But it's not impossible?' Céleste pressed.

'I shall see what I can do.'

Céleste was pleased that she had made an impression without resorting, as she had on occasions in the past, to her seductive powers to achieve her aims. She mused that perhaps her *new* reputation as an author was taking over her old one as a sex symbol.

Her charm and strong character won through. Three days later she received a letter containing the notification that Lionel's leave could start immediately. She was overjoyed and wrote a long letter to Lionel, closing with, 'Come to me! First of all I need you, and then so do our affairs. I shall be very happy to go back with you.'

Lionel was on his way back to France by late January 1857 and so was unaware that on 1 February, his beloved sister and favourite sibling Louise, the Marquise de Chabrillan, had died. Céleste shed a tear for Lionel, who would not learn of this until he reached France. But she had no love for her sister-in-law. They had not met, but Louise had never forgiven her brother for 'besmirching the family name by marrying that whore'. She made her attitude reach beyond the grave by cutting Lionel out of her substantial will.

CHAPTER 41

The Battle for Mémoires

Despite the ongoing success of *Mémoires*, Céleste continued with her efforts to have its publication stopped. Desmarest advised her to engage the celebrity president of the French Bar Association, Maitre Liouville, whose mere presence in court as her barrister would, he was convinced, mean she would win—probably. But he seemed to be resting on decades of laurels. Céleste was amazed at Liouville's lack of interest in the case, but Desmarest maintained he would deliver a grand performance when it was required in court. Desmarest explained it was 'all about form' in front of a judge on the day. She was less and less swayed with every meeting. She began to worry that 'age, fatigue and pain had worn out Liouville's faculties'.

Céleste would arrive at his home and stand in front of his study desk, pleading her case against the Librairie Nouvelle to him. Liouville would go through a ritual of having his dressing gown, slippers and Greek cap brought to him by a maid. Then he would sip a warm saucepan of milk. After that he would invite her to sit, not having absorbed a word of her explanation. She was so discouraged that she complained to Desmarest.

'He doesn't listen to me,' she said.

'He hears everything,' Desmarest assured her.

'He doesn't even respond to me.'

'He's saving his words for your case.'

'If he does speak, he's always hoarse.'

'No matter,' Desmarest said with undiminished confidence. 'People listen to him with such attention. He's a great man, I tell you.'

'Scarcely five feet tall!'

'Do you think that genius is measured in feet and inches?'

'I don't wish to appear disagreeable about your president of the Bar, but you exaggerate his worth. He has Maitre Senard against him.'

'Oh, you're acting like a typical woman!'

'Why?'

'Appearances are everything to you. You have no conception of what a fine mind he has.'

'As far as I'm concerned, it's imperceptible.'

'You need someone delivering fine phrases; high hopes.'

'I don't deny it. They help you be patient … You should get me another barrister.'

'You can't be serious. Take a file away from Liouville? You might as well take it away from the emperor himself!'

'But would you do it for me?'

Desmarest refused. The case was heard a week later. Liouville, all theatrics and little substance, didn't help his cause in front of the judge by sipping alternatively from two flasks of whisky and brandy in his pocket. Then he pleaded, Céleste said, 'the very opposite case to the one he should have'.

Senard won the case. She was forced to hand over the rest of the *Mémoires* manuscript, volumes six, seven and eight, to the publisher, who now wanted to bring out a second edition of eight volumes. Desmarest was obliged to agree with Céleste that Liouville's capacities as a barrister had declined. He was on the verge of senility.

'Liouville was very pleased with himself,' Céleste wrote later. 'He received his cheque with the aplomb of a man sure that it was well earned.'

Céleste was now compelled to allow her complete memoirs to be printed in a second edition. The publisher had the delicate task of asking her if she would like to make additions to it. At first she refused to have anything to do with it, but on reflection she decided that since the book was coming out anyway, she would improve it by updating the story with twenty extra chapters. They included her life with Lionel before their marriage and the letters he wrote to her on his first trip to Australia in 1852. She justified the book by adding a preface claiming that she wished to stop innocent girls falling into prostitution. It was an afterthought and a bit lame given she had not mentioned this in the first edition. But it may have been a reminder to the publisher that she had not wanted her memoirs made public. Now that they had to come out again, she wished to have this 'warning' label in the book.

It was a draining experience and it spurred Céleste on to work harder, despite her illnesses, when she really needed complete rest. She measured her lack of wellbeing by the increased number of visitors, who made her feel as if she did not have long to live. They included a priest, Father Mullois, who made frequent visits. He mentioned a passage in her memoirs concerning reformatories for children. Céleste had claimed that these places, and especially the agricultural institution at Mettray for juvenile offenders, only increased delinquency. The priest told Céleste that Napoleon III, the moral guardian of all France's reformatories, had read everything she had written about them with great interest. Céleste was surprised but flattered that the nation's most powerful individual had read her memoirs, and it lifted her flagging spirits. The priest, concerned with her illness, promised to return, which only served to deflate her again. He was also concerned about some passages in her book and recommended, as she later recalled, 'some changes regarding certain admissions that I should only have made to my confessor'.

Céleste listened attentively but would make no deletions of future editions. She didn't want the more juicy elements to be read or heard only by Father Mullois.

'I no longer count my existence in years or months,' the 32-year-old told her diary. 'I live from day to day. Let us hope that Lionel does not linger too long!'

This was not simply melodrama. She was too ill to be doing anything other than convalescing, but she continued to work feverishly, up to fifteen hours a day, writing and rewriting as she attempted to polish the books that she hoped would follow *The Gold Thieves*. She was pushing her limits and the work made her 'delirious'.

'It was passion!' she wrote. 'Like love, drink, gambling, and it got worse and worse.'

Céleste worked through most of the night, losing sleep, appetite and strength, and could only revive herself with black coffee.

'My mind overheated my blood,' she observed, 'but Lionel would be arriving soon. I needed fame, money and heavens knows what else. I was mad!'

Céleste wrote three short novels and six 'bad' plays in a manic creative assault. Her sudden rising star upset some fellow authors, such as Henri Murger, who complained to their mutual publisher, Lévy, that Céleste was being paid more than he, a more experienced author.[1] But there were others who gave unqualified support, such as Alexandre Dumas Sr. He restored her 'faith' in herself, and her 'energy and zeal'.

During this frenetic burst of creativity, a letter of reconciliation from the solicitor representing Lionel's difficult cousin arrived. Her pressure, coupled with the fact she'd let it be known that Lionel was returning and would be prepared to act as a witness in court, had won the day. Céleste's celebrity was taking on more substance because of her writing and the news snippets about expectations for *The Gold Thieves*. The family had influence, but in the fluid world of personality and celebrity in the post-revolutionary era, the famous and their connections had intrinsic if intangible power. There would be big press coverage for whatever she did now. For a proud, patrician family this would be a horrendous development, best avoided.

The cousin's solicitor brought with him a cheque for 40,000 francs, plus interest and costs, for an out-of-court settlement. This was not quite the moment of ecstasy Céleste had experienced when Lévy said 'yes' to her novel. It was more like relief, followed by delight. Céleste paid off Lionel's debts for the failed flour-import operation, then got rid of the mortgage on her house at Châteauroux. This left her with just 6000 francs, but she was debt-free.

Once more she had saved herself, Lionel and their relationship.

CHAPTER 42

Golden Moments; Lionel Returns

The Gold Thieves proved to be another literary success for Céleste, whose title as the Countess de Chabrillan, author, was usurping her sobriquet of Mogador, heroine of the Hippodrome and courtesan. It was what she wanted, especially with Lionel's imminent return. The book was published in May 1857 to a string of good and even rave reviews. There was a degree of surprise, some had patronising comments, but for most critics it was Céleste's skills and freshness that lit up the literary scene with her coverage of a new world.

The novel was a roller-coaster rather than a rollicking yarn that included unrequited love, violence, a rape, a hanging, two births, three natural deaths, three weddings and a dozen murders. This meant twenty-two scenes of emotional pull that ensured it was a page-turner. Though the book was fiction, there was integrity to the tale. It had an authentic feel of Melbourne and the goldfields, having often drawn on her diary or memoir entries exactly as she'd written them.

Nestor Roqueplan, a humorous observer of the time, would not erase her past, even if it displeased Céleste, but nevertheless praised her.

'Those who have not read Céleste Mogador's very unusual memoirs, and who do not know the author, will read the whole of *The Gold Thieves* with unflagging curiosity,' he wrote in *La Presse.* 'They should be doubly satisfied with the book itself and with the worthy aims of the author ... Australia is a land where poverty struggles, angry and disillusioned, against uncontrolled and insatiable wealth; where the fierce energy of murder is pitted against the heroism of noble sentiments ... The style is simple and elegant, the narrative is fast-moving and the dialogue lively. There is no sentimentality, no recourse to that romantic flirtatiousness that is a weakness of so many works written by women. Madame de Chabrillan has lived in contact with this civilisation that has its beginnings in greed and violence ... She has sought two titles: that of countess and that of writer. She has won them both.'

Alexandre Dumas Sr paid her a grand compliment by reviewing her in his *Monte Cristo* in the same column as the outstanding French writer of the era, Gustave Flaubert, who had just produced his most popular book, *Madame Bovary.* After dealing favourably with Flaubert, Dumas wrote:

> *Another work of a quite opposite kind, but most extraordinary, has been published by the same firm ... Madame de Chabrillan is a courageous soul, one of those creatures that God has destined for dedication and struggle ...*

Dumas said that he saw the dawn come in the two nights he read *The Gold Thieves.* He went on to compare her work with that of the very popular adventure writer, Gabriel Ferry, saying she had the 'same energy in the characterisation, the same life in the characters, the same feverish activity in the plot. Both writers have been eye witnesses, and being able to see is a tremendous thing when one is a gifted observer.'

The reviewer for *Revue de Paris*, Léon Laurent-Pichat, said 'there is in this novel an intelligence, or rather a quite perfect conception of dramatic motivation'.

Céleste loved and was humbled by these reviews, but the remarks by Jules Janin, the finest French literary critic of the era, moved her most. They touched the integrity of her transformation without patronising her:

> *This is a real book … Only a very gifted and intelligent woman can transform herself, redeem herself by intelligence, give up the free and easy life and win an honourable place among the distinguished women and good writers of her time.*

Céleste backed it up by selling a second novel, *Sapho*, to Lévy. This had a French setting and drew on her youthful experiences. Lévy wasted no time in getting another publication by the countess into the market. Inspired by this confidence in her skills, she laboured on two more novels on Australia, *The Emigrants* and *Miss Pewell*. The latter centred on an anti-heroine, a gossipy, spiteful, snobby and vindictive spinster.

Early in June 1857, Céleste received a telegram from Marseilles:

'I have arrived from Australia,' Lionel wrote. 'I will be in Paris at seven tomorrow evening.'

'Feverish impatience was followed by convulsive nervous trembling,' she recalled. Her prolonged illness could hardly take such excitement. She felt faint and could 'scarcely think'.

She arrived at the station three hours before the train was due. Lionel stepped off the train and ran towards her, arms open.

'My beautiful darling Céleste!' he said, hugging her and almost in tears. 'You look so thin.'

'I've been very ill. I didn't want to tell you. I knew you'd worry yourself into a state if you knew.'

'At least we're together again. These breaks are too long. They're bad for both of us.'

'I promise to get better now you're here.'

At that moment Lionel was not so sure.

In the carriage en route to their apartment (at Rue de Ventadour) Lionel asked, 'Have you heard from dear sister Louise?' Before she could answer, he added lightheartedly, 'I don't expect her to rush to me with open arms. She really objected, even more than my brother, to us getting married.'

'Lionel,' Céleste said, taking both his hands, 'she died.'

'No! When?' he asked in anguish.

'The first of February.'

He began to cry.

'I'm so sorry. We had no way of letting you know.'

Lionel was devastated.

'My Louise is dead,' he wailed, 'without forgiving me. It's not possible!'

Again, after all the time and everything they'd been through since the worst pressure from his family, Lionel's feelings and allegiances reverted to them first, ahead of the love of his life.

That night in bed, 'he turned away from my caresses and perhaps regretted having loved me', she noted. She had not seen him for half a year and his rejection was nearly impossible to take, especially as she had worked herself into such poor health that it was now threatening her life. Seeing the unnecessary pain he had inflicted, he apologised. But 'it was too late', she wrote. 'It hurt me dreadfully.'

To make her point, she gave him a full accounting of receipts, bills and everything that was evidence of how she had turned their financial affairs around, even to the point of them now having a modest bank account in the black. Lionel was more contrite and tried to counter by informing her of his 'success' in selling their St Kilda house. But that was due to simple market forces and property prices rising, rather than any cleverness or good management on his part.

'I've paid off everything back there,' he told her. 'I'm no longer in anyone's debt, except yours.'

He promised that one day he would pay her back for everything. But at that moment, Céleste only wanted his declaration of continued love for her. There was just a little reserve on his part and Céleste thought she found the reason when she discovered two of her books in the bottom of his trunk. He had bought *The Gold Thieves* and *Sapho* in Marseilles and had devoured them on the trip to Paris. Yet he had not mentioned them. Perhaps he had mixed feelings. He should have been proud of her, but her freedom, acceptance and success in France may have threatened his security. He would have realised that his wife had more fame, earning power and independence than he would ever have.

Céleste sent for Solange in an effort to restore the nuclear family, which was a sensible move.

'They greeted each other so affectionately,' she wrote later, 'and exchanged so many hugs and kisses that I was almost jealous.'

Solange was taken from her boarding school to be with them for a month.

Emotions settled down and the Chabrillans resumed married life, for the first time ever in Paris. Céleste should have been hospitalised or convalescing, but instead she went out with Lionel to the races, dinner parties and balls, where she, not the count, was feted and congratulated. Despite her delight, her health deteriorated further.

Lionel, still seeking redemption or forgiveness or some sign of humanity from his relatives regarding his marriage, wrote to the younger of his two sisters, the Countess de Motholon-Sémoulville. He asked for permission to see her. She wrote back, 'I can forgive you, but I do not wish to see you ever again. I no longer know you.'

Céleste intercepted the letter and kept it from Lionel. But this unkindest cut from the family to date affected her deeply. If the sister had meant to ruin her brother's happiness and relationship, she would have been pleased with the initial reaction. Céleste, with acute bronchitis, a liver complaint, heart inflammation and other problems, was left prostrate with grief and sadness. She called for her family doctor.

'If she does not die soon,' he told Lionel frankly, 'she will be ill for a long time.'

Lionel, abandoned by the only member of the family that he cared for, was shaken. Only one love, Céleste, was left. He did not believe he would survive without her.

'If I lost you,' he told her, 'I would kill myself.' He urged her to fight against the illnesses. 'Your life is my life.'

Doctors went to work. They 'tattooed my chest and shoulders with vesicatories [substances that created blisters], frictions and castor oil' for two months. That treatment did not work. The next prescription was 'a change of scene'. She was taken to Berry, but was soon so bad that the doctors, and she, believed she had only a short time to live. Céleste made her 'confessions' not to a priest just yet, but to her husband.

'Please, Lionel,' she begged, 'if your family curses my name, you will not banish me from your heart and mind.'

'I promise you that no matter what happens I shall always, always stand up for you.'

Not too long after this, she decided to give him Louise's hurtful letter in which his sister said she could never forgive him for 'besmirching the family name by marrying that whore'.

Lionel screwed up the letter and cried. Holding Céleste close, he said, 'I have absolutely no regrets. The fact that I've been disinherited gives me a kind of secret joy. Acceptance of it is just another sacrifice I can make for you.'

Céleste felt as if she were in her own funeral procession when she was taken to Châteauroux and her Poinçonnet home in a wagon with a bed made up in it.

'The local people took their hats off [as if in] the presence of death, and crossed themselves at the sight of this shadow of my former self going by.'

Some people cried.

'I realised I was finished,' she noted, 'or at least terminally ill.'

The parish priest arrived and prepared her 'imminent departure'. Her Paris doctor was summoned, only to discover her face was covered in big yellow blotches. He gave her three consecutive applications of fifty leeches each time, but her condition remained dire. Lionel stayed by her bedside and prayed incessantly for her. He wouldn't eat and only took some nourishment when Anne-Victoire cajoled him into it.

After a few days Céleste stopped vomiting. After a week, her facial discolouration disappeared. In another week, she seemed to have recovered somewhat. Lionel, believing in his prayer rather than the leeching, decamped to Paris to try for another consular posting in Europe, realising that Céleste would never again be able to make the long, arduous trip to Melbourne. But by early January 1858, he had failed to secure a position closer to home or even an extension of his leave so he could stay longer with Céleste. She was in no mental state to digest the news, but Lionel returned to Châteauroux and finally got around to telling her he would have to return to Melbourne.

'If I don't go,' he told her, 'I'll have nothing at all. As this post is our only resource from now on, I cannot let it go.'

He explained that while on leave, he was only on half-pay and that was not enough to cover her medical costs. He would take a boat back to Australia in July.

'The very name of Melbourne made me shudder,' she noted. 'I was haunted by the idea that one of us would never leave there.'

Céleste pleaded with him not to return.

'How would we live?' he asked her. 'It's not in my nature to retire here in the country. I adore you, Céleste, but I like excitement, travel. Besides, here we would be nothing, but over there we are something.'

Bedridden, Céleste was too weak to argue. If she'd been well, she would have convinced him that her burgeoning career, which was generating income from royalties, would be a base. But Lionel might have hated the idea of her being the breadwinner, and especially the fame and public exposure that her books brought.

CHAPTER 43

Lionel Departs; Dumas Inspires

At the end of June a determined Céleste managed to stagger from one piece of furniture to another. Lionel laughed at her and said she had not got her 'sea legs', which was a way of telling her yet again that she could not return to the other side of the world with him. He took her into the garden and with the aid of Anne-Victoire walked her around. In an attempt to giver her a boost, he said she was prettier than ever before.

'I was white as a sheet and nothing but skin and bone,' she wrote later, feeling despondent as they congratulated her on managing a few steps.

She urged Lionel to take her with him, but he reiterated that she needed a long recovery time and that any relapse would be fatal.

'I don't want to kill you,' he said. 'After all, I went through so much to save you.'

Céleste was grateful for those moments together as the day of his departure, 12 July 1858, loomed. When he finally set off from Poinçonnet she was left with a fatalistic belief that she would never see him again. Through their tearful last night, they made plans for her return to Melbourne and what they would do together, but Céleste was too depressed to believe that anything other than death would intervene.

She had Solange and her mother's support, but Anne-Victoire was no help in the circumstances. She was fond of Lionel but most relieved that Céleste had not left with him. Anne-Victoire became 'obsessed' with stopping Céleste from leaving.

Tension built between mother and daughter. Many of the old issues between them resurfaced. Céleste wanted nothing more than to leave as soon as possible.

'I was bored to death,' she noted. 'If I have to die, I prefer to be with him.'

Céleste felt inspired when Alexandre Dumas Sr, visiting his daughter in Berry, called on her. Céleste was embarrassed when Anne-Victoire, in her haste to greet him, knocked over a basket of embroidery wool she had been using in a tapestry. Dumas bent over to help Anne-Victoire pick up the balls of wool, and said with a laugh, 'Ah, Madame, you did a better job the day you produced your daughter.'

Céleste took him for a walk around the property.

'I hope you're not going to bury yourself here,' he said, no pun intended. 'Our Berry is about as lively as the catacombs.' After a moment of silence, he went on, 'You are such an attractive woman in every way. It is a pity I did not know you earlier in my life. I wonder if we would have loved each other?'

Céleste deflected the comment with a smile in this opportunistic effort to bed her, now that her husband had left France.

'Ah, my dear, your greatness as a writer would always widen the gulf between us,' she said, 'and I could never compete with so many of your wonderful conquests.'

It was Dumas's turn to be flattered. Seeing his acceptance of the situation, Céleste added, 'You're a danger to all women, my great friend; you're capricious, changeable. Many loves have come and gone without making a deep impression on your generous heart. Constant work has been the reason for it. And it's very fortunate for our dear France, as you are one of her greatest glories. For you, loving means nothing, and being loved very little more. You change mistresses, or deceive them with a facility that proves you really don't care … the conquests provide you with subjects for your conversation and your novels. You think aloud, which makes you dangerously indiscreet for anyone who loves you.'

Dumas listened. Her analysis meant something, and it demonstrated a clear judgement of character on her behalf. And her subject was his favourite.

Céleste claimed she wanted him as a 'demigod', and under no circumstances did she want to see her 'idol in nightcap and underwear'.

Dumas expressed a certain insecurity about his looks and sex appeal, which was something that drove him to prove himself with woman after woman. He remarked that Céleste simply saw him as 'unattractive to the point of repugnance'.

Céleste countered with an explanation to which even this master of expression could not respond. She claimed she would be hurt if he treated her like all his other women friends, which was with fickle disregard. She told him she was 'exceedingly' proud of his friendship.

'I want people to know that it's honest and disinterested,' she told him. 'Then I shall be able to receive you and visit you without being taken for a sultana in your ever-changing little harem.'

Céleste was no doubt sincere in her rejection. She was a married woman. Furthermore, to be seen as Dumas's lover would have restored the image of Mogador the courtesan, when she was now the countess author. Being seen with the famous Dumas as a friend would help her new reputation as an accomplished writer, accepted by the literary elite.

Dumas saw her declarations as a challenge. He wished to conquer the now famous writer, but Céleste had all the answers.

'I shall see a procession of all your former favourites,' Céleste told him, 'and I shall say to myself: "my reign has been less brilliant but it will last longer." I shall do my utmost to make it sustain the test of time. Does that suit you?'

Never one to quit, Dumas responded, 'Yes, and if I stray from this plan of action, you must not hold it against me. I'm so used to courting women out of politeness.'

He was trying to keep a foot in the door; Céleste slammed it shut.

'Rest assured,' she said, 'I shall call you to order.'

Dumas stayed for dinner. Anne-Victoire remained dumbstruck as they discussed Lionel, travel, literature and theatre.

His surprise visit lifted Céleste's spirits. Dumas's confidence in her recovery and their chat about the future gave her hope.

CHAPTER 44

The Long Farewell

Céleste kept writing, novel after novel, as she slowly recovered, while Lionel's boat chugged on towards Melbourne. She waited eagerly for the postman to deliver her husband's letters and took time to respond immediately and at length, knowing that apart from the first few, he would not read them until he arrived at his destination and her mail caught up with him. She was pleased that he seemed content and well, and to help maintain this, she only gave him good news about her condition.

But now, not alarmingly at first, concern turned to Lionel's health. After leaving Aden (a port in what is now known as Yemen), he began to experience stomach cramps. This was usual rather than unusual on voyages of that era. Almost everyone had them during a trip. It was either seasickness or some form of diarrhoea, or something more or less serious. But on 16 August, thirty-five days into the trip, he was writing to Céleste when the pain became so severe he fainted. He was carried to the bed in his cabin. He remained there for another two days until the boat reached Trincomalee, Ceylon (now Sri

Lanka). He went ashore, feeling a fraction better, and glad for the break on land. But a week later he was again laid up in bed on the boat. The pain had exhausted him, and his condition worsened. He had little desire to eat. No nourishment was getting into his system.

He wrote to Céleste admitting for the first time that he was afraid of dying.

It didn't help that the mighty *Australasian*, the ship that he was travelling on, broke down in the dock at Ceylon and could not sail on. Other passengers were transferred to smaller boats for the onward journey. But Lionel was too ill. He had to wait until the big ship was repaired.

After the *Australasian* took to sea again, Lionel's condition worsened. From 11 September onwards he wrote of this in his short, two- or three-paragraph letters. There was no let-up all the way to Melbourne, where he arrived on 17 October. He was now convinced of his impending death. But his genuine fears, based on his poor condition, were allayed when he was with friends such as the Faucherys, who welcomed him back warmly. They were pleased to have such an illustrious character in their ranks again, and this lifted his spirits a fraction, though his health did not improve. He made a special effort to look presentable when the colony's governor paid him a personal visit, something he appreciated, and a vindication of his decision to leave France, where he was not nearly as well respected.

Despite his terrible condition, he went straight to work in an act of noblesse oblige for a compatriot in deep trouble. A French soldier named Soirit was condemned to be hanged for killing his mistress, 'who had been unfaithful to him'. There was no such thing as 'a crime of passion' under British and Australian law, whereas under French law it would mean leniency and a reprieve from the gallows.

'Although half-dead I dragged myself to the governor to implore his pardon,' Lionel wrote. The pardon was granted at eight that evening. 'I was so ill that this good news nearly killed me. But it was a happy beginning for my work in Melbourne.'

Lionel's illness was diagnosed as dysentery, a dreaded disease of the lower intestine caused by bacteria or unknown parasites. It had begun with diarrhoea after Aden and never abated, and was now marked by inflammation. He was passing blood and mucus.

On 16 December, he wrote to Céleste from Melbourne, 'I have read and re-read *The Gold Thieves* ten times; I have lent it to everybody. How magnificent you are and what willpower you had to give me such joy!'

This was the first time he had opened up about her writing and his appreciation of it.

'I am sorry that I did not help you in your studies,' he went on, 'but I was far from expecting this great transformation in your mind.'

Lionel now seemed resigned to his fate. He did not mention his illness but instead referred to feeling 'fine'.

'A lot of our friends have died here in a very short time,' he added. 'Well, in this world, what must come, comes. Do not forget me. I adore you and dream only of you.'

On the morning of 21 December, he tried to leave for work but was forced to return to bed. His doctor did not think he was dying. Then on 26 December, the medical opinion changed. He had only days to live. The next day Lionel called his sometime vice-consul, Édouard Adet, a French importing merchant, as well as Fauchery, to witness his will. Adet was to act as his executor.

Lionel had calculated, accurately, that after his debts were paid off he would leave just short of 395 pounds, not the fortune he would have hoped for. But he was pleased he would not be leaving Adet, and ultimately his wife, a financial mess.

Lionel showed that his dearest last thoughts, and those he wished to record for posterity, were for Céleste. He wrote in the will:

> *My only regret in leaving this life is dying far from my wife, and not leaving her in the situation that I would have wished her to have.*

Lionel, Count de Chabrillan, died two days later on the morning of 29 December 1858, his best friend Fauchery by his side.

The Age of 1 January 1859 reported on the count's funeral and procession from his Collins Street home and office to St Francis's Cathedral for a 'solemn' requiem mass. The governor, the mayor, the chief justice, the commander of the forces and many other dignitaries were present. The hearse was drawn by four horses and followed by fifty Frenchmen, including Fauchery, on foot, along with twenty other carriages. The coffin was covered in the French flag, with Lionel's cocked hat and sword placed on it. After the service, the procession meandered on to the Melbourne Cemetery. There Lionel was with about 500 people in attendance, but not the one person he would have wished to be there.

Letters from Lionel arrived posthumously in January 1859, but Céleste had no idea he had died. The string of plaintive, short missives saw her put her house at Poinçonnet up for sale. But France was experiencing a property slump and it did not attract a buyer. Nevertheless, Céleste was prepared to depart despite her doctor forbidding her to undergo sea travel. Anne-Victoire was, as ever, also against her going, though she did accompany Céleste to Paris, where she was meant to rest.

Céleste received more letters from Lionel in February, and she hoped upon hope that the downcast reports of his medical condition were, at least in part, disguised pleas for her to join him.

Céleste became more and more contemptuous of her mother from them being in such close proximity. Anne-Victoire's negativity irritated her, as did her complaints about everything in life, her possessive attitude towards Céleste and her wish that her daughter not go to Lionel. Céleste began to use every excuse to leave the apartment, even in the harsh winter conditions, and meet other people. She was introduced to Mr Marc Fournier, the director of the Porte Saint-Martin Theatre, which produced popular plays and musicals.

'I really enjoyed *The Gold Thieves*,' he told her. 'It would make a fine play. If you want to have a try at writing it, I would read it straightaway.'

This gave Céleste a boost.

'I can't promise anything,' Fournier added, 'but I may well produce it.'

'I'm too ill to sleep so I might as well write,' Céleste said.

This was also against her doctor's instructions regarding her recovery. She was not supposed to put herself under pressure of any kind. But she set about this new assignment with her usual fervour and produced five acts of the play in five nights. Friends to whom she showed it gushed over it. Fournier, who would have to make a commercial decision, was not so enthusiastic.

Céleste thought she could make the transition from book prose to playwriting. But like many before and since, she found the conversion tougher than it looked. Her prose was descriptive; the play demanded more of a visual sense and comprehension of stagecraft. Fournier said she should leave it until she was well and suggested that some of her playwright friends could assist in the adaptation. Céleste felt let down by the knowledge that another dimension of fame, and a source of modest extra funds, would not be coming her way as quickly as she wished.

On 7 March, she received Lionel's last letter. He seemed content, even resigned to his condition.

'I had a terrible premonition last night,' Anne-Victoire told Céleste when she visited her on 24 March.

'About what?' Céleste asked. 'Lionel? Me? What?'

'I don't know.'

The doctor arrived at the same time and distracted Céleste from probing her mother more. He had heard Anne-Victoire's remarks.

'You women don't make my work any easier,' he said with a smile. 'It's hard enough dealing with the natural, let alone the supernatural.'

He examined Céleste.

'You're making good progress,' he said, and glancing at Anne-Victoire, added, 'and you'll only become sick again if you travel. Don't think of going to Australia for the foreseeable future.'

On his way out, the doctor met the postman. He took the only letter to be delivered and returned with it to the house. It was postmarked from Australia.

'This is not the count's handwriting,' he said sombrely to Céleste.

She tore open the envelope. Lionel's wedding ring fell to the floor. She picked it up. There was also a lock of hair inside the letter. Céleste fainted.

'I heard the sound of my head hitting the tiled floor,' she recalled later, 'but I felt no pain.'

When she regained consciousness her mother and doctor were by her side. The doctor read the long accompanying letter from Fauchery, which told, in at times dramatic terms, of Lionel's last days: how a priest heard his confession and administered the sacraments; how he made his will; and how he was lucid and with a minimum of pain at the end.

The letter was of little comfort at first. Céleste sobbed all through the reading. When the doctor had finished, she said with chilling certitude, 'I just want to die. There's nothing in the world I care about now.'

'My dear woman,' the doctor said, 'you have responsibilities to Solange.'

'It's all so meaningless now,' Céleste said through tears. 'It's over!'

Anne-Victoire was crying.

The doctor moved close to Céleste and whispered in her ear, 'Your mother is old! You're upsetting her dreadfully.'

Céleste was in shock. She remained in her room in a surreal, depressed state for a fortnight.

CHAPTER 45

Title Fight: Return Bouts

Céleste's recovery was aided by her desire to have Lionel's body brought home to France for burial. It was not the easy process she envisaged. The major problem was that not one ship's captain was prepared to take a coffin on board. Furthermore, Lionel's lawyer informed her that the body could not be exhumed in Melbourne. It was simply too hot and there was a real fear of epidemics that doctors of the time did not know how to treat or cure.

The situation galvanised her and gave her something to live for. She petitioned every relevant authority in France and the Victorian colony, but to no avail. As a last resort she wrote to Napoleon III, whose office sent a polite 'no' to interceding. Defeated but still with a Plan B, she sent bronzed iron ornaments and wreaths to Melbourne for Lionel's grave.

'I made a rough sketch for the workman of what I wanted,' she wrote in her diary. She also made a special trip to Bordeaux to instruct the captain of the boat taking the tomb artefacts to Melbourne.

Still quietly in despair over Lionel's death at just thirty-seven, and after five years of marriage and a relationship of twelve years, Céleste was consumed with organising dedications to him. Her next move was to see the chief editor of the highly respected newspaper *L'Illustration*. She persuaded him to publish a portrait of Lionel. Then she returned to Berry and stayed for a while at Solange's boarding school, the convent at Ardentes. While there, she obtained permission from local authorities to have two-metre-high iron crosses erected at the intersection of the two roads leading from Poinçonnet to Châteauroux forest. They were decorated with marble plaques bearing a gold-lettered memorial inscription to Lionel. Céleste was doing all she could to have him remembered in the region 'he had loved so much, and for which he had done so much good in happier times'. A local priest blessed the crosses and the event attracted a big crowd.

Céleste returned to Paris, now with a more rational and responsible attitude towards caring for the elderly Anne-Victoire and young Solange. She had almost no money left and her first stop was at Librairie Nouvelle to collect funds owing for the publication of her *Mémoires*, now grateful that she had not won the legal fight to have the second edition stopped. She made her peace with Monsieur Bourdilliat, who apologised for publishing the book in the first place, once he learned she was a married woman. To demonstrate his good faith he bought a novella from her, *Is He Mad?*, which she dedicated to Lionel.

This continual, sometimes frenetic activity had strengthened Céleste's mind, although she still had only half her normal physical strength and energy. She would take a seat or lie down at every opportunity, but kept on with this ritual, sad and depressing process of tidying up everything to do with her husband.

Céleste was summoned to see Ferdinand-Marie Viscount de Lesseps at the Ministry of Foreign Affairs, the man who had allowed Lionel to take leave after three years in Melbourne. He was embarrassed to see her looking so unwell, especially with what he had to discuss. De Lesseps, directed by the Chabrillan family, and in particular, Lionel's brother, wanted her to relinquish her title of Countess de Chabrillan. He asked about the circumstances of her marriage contract in England.

'It's impossible for you to keep the title and the name of a family who—'

'Who would like to destroy my marriage?' she said, cutting him off. 'Lionel thought of that, Count. He married me twice and no power on earth has the right or the ability to undo what he did.'

'But,' de Lesseps said, 'if we could come to some arrangement …'

'Never!' she said. 'It would be disrespectful to his memory. He has given me his name and I will bear it until my dying day. I will make sure that it survives me.'

'That's just what we want to avoid,' de Lesseps said, his pity evaporated and replaced by annoyance. 'You must spare yourself the arguments of a lawsuit, which …'

Céleste stood up to leave.

'Is that all you have to say to me, *Count*?' she asked.

'Yes, but surely it's enough to make you reflect on undertaking a course of action that could only do you harm.'

Céleste stared him down, repeating that she would keep the Chabrillan name and title.

'He knew who I was when he gave them to me,' she said, 'and since then I have done, and will continue to do, my utmost to bear them with dignity.'

De Lesseps, not wanting to face the Chabrillans without a win, attempted to bribe her.

'But you have no means of support,' he said.

Céleste scoffed. 'You will never be strong enough to break me, *Count*!'

'I'm authorised to offer you 6000 francs a year if you give up your title.'

'Thanks,' she said, 'but no thanks. There's no price the family can offer.'

She left de Lesseps's office fuming. Despite her frailty, she was invigorated by the prospect of a fight for her title.

A few weeks later, de Lesseps' failure to intimidate or bribe Céleste led the head of the Chabrillan family, Marquis Marie-Olivier, to again meet her to try to resolve the issue. Céleste had put on some weight and was looking closer to her best. She was thirty-four and on the way back to being one of the most sensual and beautiful women of the mid-nineteenth century. She would never match the stunning younger women in the demimonde and other social sets, but there was another dimension to Céleste in her maturity. While many of the top courtesans of her generation were fading or had faded into obscurity, she was still a name, or rather two names—Mogador and the Countess de Chabrillan. She was also an author with two big-selling books in France and a new reputation. Her intellect sparkled as much as her character and personality. The countess, growing with every experience, was a person to be reckoned with by anyone from the top to the bottom of French society. From one perspective, Céleste had taken a position of power and status with her successful conquest of Lionel. However, she had deepened and widened her own status by her hard work. This was not the woman of 1850 whom Marie-Olivier had tried to persuade not to marry his brother.

The marquis, neither a lothario, hard worker or achiever, had lived mainly off the family inheritance. Though he put on an act of distaste for his younger brother's less conventional life, especially his adventures as a miner and consul, his own life had never remotely reached the excitement of Lionel's. And there had never been anyone with the sex appeal, drive, ambition and achievements like Céleste among the women he knew. In Marie-Olivier's aristocratic circles, women were kept in their place; they were not driven to accomplish; they were definitely never to be seen as public figures such as in the theatre. The marquis would never have dealt with someone as forceful or charismatic as Céleste.

'I think you might agree that someone with your background would not normally marry into a family of standing like mine?' the marquis began when they met at her apartment. 'I trust you can see the situation from our point of view?'

'Quite. I agree that a Mogador should never marry a Chabrillan. Before our marriage, and when I could see the stress Lionel was under, I often advised him to marry someone of his own class, even if he had ruined himself.'

'So you see—'

'But may I be so bold as to remind you of your cousin, Monsieur de Choiseul-Praslin. He murdered his wife.' The marquis blanched. Céleste went on. 'It was a terrible scandal. Lionel told me every detail. How gruesome. How difficult for the Chabrillans.'

'We managed to keep it out of the press.'

'Yes, that was an impressive feat. But would you not agree that that event, if it had made the press, would be a far greater disgrace to the Chabrillans than I have been?'

'It would have been,' the marquis agreed.

'I humbly submit that my writing might even enhance the family name, not besmirch it.'

The marquis did not react.

'You see, my lord,' Céleste said, 'above all else, Lionel and I loved each other. Our backgrounds were not relevant to how we were together.'

The marquis thought for a moment. Against instinct, he seemed to be trying to be civil, even reasonable.

'Our family has always maintained certain discretions in private affairs.'

'Meaning?'

'Well, your dalliances with Prince Napoleon, for instance.'

'Wherever did that come from?' Céleste asked with a dismissive smile. She knew Plon-Plon would never tell him.

'I have my sources.'

'Pray tell who? If it was the actress Judith, she's always been fearfully jealous of me. She's been the source of malicious gossip because she was besotted with the prince.'

The marquis blinked. She had called his bluff.

'I can prove my relationship with him was nothing beyond friendship.'

Céleste excused herself, left the room and returned with letters between her and Prince Napoleon.

'Here, read a few of these,' she said with an easy gesture. 'Please tell me if they are the missives of lovers or just good friends.'

The marquis browsed them.

'You can see that he was inviting me to his fortnightly dinners at the restaurant Voisin,' she said. 'Prince Napoleon hosted them. I was just one of twenty guests. I would imagine that some of the much younger, more beautiful women may well have been his conquests. But not me.'

The marquis sighed.

'Céleste, you must understand that it is not me behind this effort to have you relinquish the title. There are others in the family who wish it.'

'Your sister perhaps? Please tell her there's no hope of it.'

'I hear you might be having financial difficulty.'

'Your hearing is sound,' Céleste said with a gentle smile. 'I have had trouble selling Poinçonnet. But I'll manage. I always do. Your offer via de Lesseps was not enticing.'

'If you want more, we can—'

'No, no, you misunderstand. I cannot be bought. I have learned to make my way around money. I hope you understand that it was I who pulled your brother out of financial messes here and in Australia.' Without rancour or rush, she outlined examples. 'Again, I submit that I far more than fulfilled my duties as a wife, especially in the hardships we encountered in Australia.'

The marquis retreated, falling back on the refrain that unnamed 'others' held sway in the democracy of Chabrillan, and that he was a mere member with one vote, which he said he would place with her retaining her title.

After the meeting, however, Céleste felt it had been a charade; a light, polite shadow-box before war was declared.

First salvo from the Chabrillans was to cut off her sources of income. *La Presse* had promised her twenty-five centimes a line for a new serialisation of one of her latest books, *Miss Pewell*, which had an Australian setting and was published in 1859. The marquis persuaded its editor, Émile de Girardin, not to publish the serialisation. De Girardin's feeble offer to her, as a sop, was to say he would have any of her future novels reviewed favourably. It was a blow to Céleste, who now felt the power of France's ultra-conservative aristocracy. Other publishers also shunned her after showing serious interest in her work.

She went to the Rue d'Amsterdam apartment of Alexandre Dumas Sr, who had always promised to support her.

Dumas greeted her with his usual effusiveness and glee, and admonished her playfully for her not having seen him for many months. He was genuinely affronted at the 'Chabrillans blocks' and the publishers' lack of courage But his own similar predicament didn't allow him to provide a brave contact in the publishing world.

'Is it possible for you to rewrite my novel *Emigrants*?' she asked. 'You could publish it under your own name and split the royalties with me.'

'No, I've done this with novices,' he said, 'but you already have a good name. But I have an idea. Why don't you dramatise your novels?'

Céleste demurred. On her mind was the rushed effort of *The Gold Thieves* that had been rejected by Marc Fournier at the Porte Saint-Martin Theatre. She mentioned it. Dumas dismissed the experience, saying that her five-act play would probably need reworking and guidance.

'Plays are ten times easier to write,' he said. 'You don't have to deliver descriptive passages or character portraits. You create the framework, the bare bones and instructions. Stage designers, directors and actors take care of the rest.'

He asked Céleste to send him the first draft she had done. She protested that it needed a solid second draft. He told her not to worry, he would set one of his 'ghosts', writers from his stable of hacks, to work on it.

Dumas then pre-empted the process by telling Marc Fournier he was supervising the rewrite. Fournier agreed to accept the revised work sight unseen, and planned to produce the play.

Céleste was most unhappy with the rewrite. She stormed around to Dumas's apartment. He laughed at her fury. She insisted he sit down with her and go through it. In the end, he agreed it had been 'butchered' by his ghost and he rewrote the five acts himself. Dumas then took her to meet the secretary of the Society of Dramatic Authors, Monsieur Peragallo. He was the most powerful figure in French theatre. His hands were on the purse strings of the industry. The society collected all authors' royalties from the theatre managers and producers. Peragallo's role was to disburse the royalties due to the authors. He, too, had read *The Gold Thieves* and did not need any convincing that it would make a box-office hit. He was also taken with Céleste. Peragallo was aware of the efforts to stop the play being performed in Paris's main theatres and her impecunious state of affairs, and was sympathetic. He advanced her 1500 francs against the royalties she would receive from *The Gold Thieves.*

But in the short time since Fournier had said yes to the project, he had been visited by a lawyer representing the Chabrillans. Fournier pulled out, much to the anger and chagrin of Dumas. Dumas sent the play to Montparnasse's Gaîté Theatre director, Monsieur Harmant, who loved it. He had cast it and was preparing for a rehearsal when the Chabrillans, tracking Céleste's every move, struck again. She received her play in a mail parcel with a letter from Harmant expressing regrets that he could not produce it.

Céleste was consoled by the fact that big-name, experienced theatre people had all wanted the story initially. At least she knew it was not being rejected on creative grounds. It was easily stage worthy. But she had to leave the problem for a while to secure her financial position. Down to her last francs, she had no choice but to mortgage the house at Poinçonnet. She stayed at her daughter's convent for two months until the funds came through. Then she returned to Paris, where her first act was to visit Peragallo to repay him the 1500 francs he had advanced her against royalties she would not now receive for her play.

'No, no,' an amazed Peragallo said. 'The money is yours until you receive royalties for the play.'

He had never had an author offer to repay the society *before* the play generated royalty income. Peragallo asked what her plans were, given the manoeuvring by the Chabrillans.

'I have no choice,' she replied. 'I will go into theatrical management and produce my own work.'

Peragallo smiled. 'You, Countess, are capable of anything,' he said, 'except dishonesty.'

CHAPTER 46

Author–Actor–Producer

Céleste went in search of a theatre and found the rundown, abandoned Folies-Marigny in the Avenue Gabriel off the Champs-Élysées. It had been made famous for staging operettas from 1855 to 1858. The great mime Deburau had then leased it for his shows from late 1858 to 1861. Céleste took over the lease for 9000 francs a year, with a quarter of that paid in advance. She went straight to work on repairs and decorations with a verve born of someone who believed she was always destined for the theatre world.

Her passion forced her to take one of the big gambles of her risk-prone, hard-working career. She sold her house at Poinçonnet, paid off the mortgages and other debts, and used the remaining 14,000 francs to renovate the theatre and set up her first production. Being a woman precluded her from going into theatrical management. She assigned a proxy, ex-journalist Monsieur Alain, who was rejected by the Minister for Arts, and judged by some friends she spoke to as an unworthy character. Undaunted, Céleste met with Prince Napoleon, who, like Dumas, had always supported her. He wrote to the minister, who granted the authorisation for Alain, along with a written warning of sorts: 'I wish you every success and hope that you will have no regrets.' It indicated that he expected a problem concerning Alain.

Céleste worked long hours in the weeks before the opening night to make it a full house. There was great support from her female friends of the demimonde, the courtesans and actresses with whom she had remained popular. Glamorous women, including the biggest names of the era, such as Adele Page, Augustine Bellinger, Cora Pearl and Anna Deslions, turned up looking their best. They competed with each other for press attention, wearing eye-catching dresses which left little to the imagination, extravagant hairstyles and expensive jewellery with diamonds predominant. They were accompanied by wealthy men, mainly from the elite and Lionel's class, who, while looking good themselves, were mere escorts or accessories for the women. Céleste had engineered the appearance of these female superstars, knowing it would further upset the Chabrillans, especially as they would also know many of the male invitees.

The now 37-year-old Céleste's first show, on 19 April 1862, was of three one-act plays. The lead play was a comedy, *Bonheur aux Vaincus*. The third play was set in Melbourne in 1853 and ended with a satirical song, which would not have had anyone in the audience rushing to make the next boat trip there:

Cursed, Melbourne, I have no regrets leaving you;
Never in my life have I seen a more dreadful country;
The north wind burns you; the mosquitoes are an absolute plague;
And I'll spare you any mention of all those things that devour your skin;
No, no more travelling in those miserable faraway lands;

Let's go back to shore, repeating this carefree refrain;
Viva la France! *Land of happy days; Land of prosperity;*
Land of love.

She was the producer, writer and star and took the name Madame Lionel. She would never have used Mogador, although that would have assured big box-office revenue, for even though Mogador was last at the Hippodrome in 1848, the name was legendary. Céleste had made a new reputation as an author, but not yet in theatre production. She would have loved to have used her name as a countess but did not want to further antagonise the already riled and vengeful Chabrillans, who had their spies everywhere and were already plotting ways to stop her current venture. The compromise of 'Madame Lionel' would have infuriated the family but left them no room to manoeuvre legally.

The family had been caught by surprise. The shows were successful and received fair reviews. Céleste moved on. She now sacked her proxy, Monsieur Alain—who was as incompetent as the warnings had suggested—and replaced him with a more reputable former theatre manager.

Around this time her relationship with Alexandre Dumas Jr strengthened. He was the same age as Céleste and making his own way in literature and the theatre. He had begun with a good run of books, twelve up to that point. His father gave him the same advice he'd given to Céleste: write plays, they were more lucrative. He, too, heeded his father's words and by 1862 had had nine plays produced. He asked Céleste if she could release a leading lady, Céline Chaumont from her contract so that she could perform in one of his productions, *L'Ami des Femmes*. Because of her friendship with him and his father, she granted the big request.

'I shall be eternally grateful to you for this,' Dumas Jr told her.

Seemingly unstoppable despite the Chabrillans' spoiling tactics, Céleste produced two of her comedies, *On Guard* and *A Compromised Man*, followed by a musical comedy, *In the Breton Way*.

Céleste's creativity knew no bounds. She was invited to put on a one-act play at the Théâtre des Champs-Élysées on 19 July, which she called *En Australie* (*In Australia*). In it she demonstrated a lingering negative feeling regarding her experiences Down Under, with the lines: '… the women are only appreciated when they are as strong as men. They saw wood, split logs, groom horses and do the washing and cooking for relaxation.'

It was condescending and a sharp generalisation, yet in some ways a fair comment about the pioneering life.

Next, she decided to produce operettas, given the earlier success of her theatre, the Foiles-Marignys', in that field, and hired the conductor/composer Hervé. Hervé had been involved in a scandal in his private life and had recently been prevented from putting on his own shows. He was grateful to be employed by Céleste, who sympathised with his plight, which was not dissimilar to hers. She wrote her own operetta, *Militairement*, and hired another composer to create the music. This show was her biggest stage hit to date.

The Chabrillans had thwarted her efforts to publish books, but now they were confronted with a far more threatening situation. The theatre gave her more of the limelight, especially more attention in the press. The family had one nefarious line of action left: the press, who favoured her for her name and fame. The marquis bribed several journalists to attack her. Articles ignored the successful theatre productions and went for the man, and woman. The articles Hervé bracketed and Mogador as two of a kind—maverick, amoral and scandalous performers. The sordid elements of her past, right back to her days in the brothel and even prison, were raked over, distorted and full of inaccuracies. The orchestrated nature of the attack was obvious, with the 'bought' journalists taking on pseudonymous by-lines such as 'The Spider', 'The Scorpion' and 'The Mosquito'. The most defamatory article was from Monsieur Alain, her incompetent former front-man, who signed himself as '*Bete aux Veines*' (bad—or stupid—to the veins).

This avalanche of criticism had an impact on attendances. House numbers fell and debts mounted. Céleste had had times in her life when she had been frugal or extravagant. She had turned Lionel's affairs around several times and had shown a commendable, sensible fiscal prudence on those occasions. But now she was running a modest-sized operation in a fickle business. It put enormous stress on her to write, act and produce, the last being the most demanding of these jobs. She was responsible for the livelihoods of all those in her productions and she erred on the side of generosity in her terms of employment, fees and conditions.

Her venture almost collapsed and she was in debt for more than 12,000 francs. Her only assets were the scenery and costumes and the lease itself, which she managed to pass on for the amount of the debt. The new lessee also agreed to perform four of her plays a year for the next five years. Her agent said he would agree to terms with her creditors, which meant she could take her production on a tour of Northern France in the hope of earning some revenue and clawing her way back from this precarious position. But the shows did not break even. When she returned to Paris her agent told her she was likely to be declared bankrupt.

Céleste felt defeated and in despair. The shame for her was too much. In the past, she had always found a way for her and

Lionel to avoid such a calamity. She decided for the third time in her life to commit suicide. Again, she was methodical and clinical in her planning. She contacted her former lawyer and lover, Maitre Desmarest, whom she knew had become very rich since their affair. He was married but still infatuated with Céleste.

Desmarest had followed Céleste's career in print, on the stage and on the Paris rumour grapevine. Consequently, she found it easy to tickle his ego and seduce him again. After just a few days of reviving their intimacy, she told him she was going on a long tour. Would he see his way clear to giving Anne-Victoire a modest monthly allowance, at least until she returned? Smitten again and even more dazzled by her than before, Desmarest agreed.

Céleste had reverted to her old Mogador ways, believing that all her actions in this instance were for the 'greater good'. Her request was mere cigar money for Desmarest. Céleste had already paid for Solange's boarding school for the next three years. Satisfied that she had not left anyone destitute, she went home to kill herself. She felt at thirty-eight that she had fought the good fight and now it was time to join her beloved Lionel.

She placed his portrait beside her on the bed and took an overdose of laudanum, an opium and alcohol solution that she used occasionally for pain relief and to help her relax.

The maid found Céleste unconscious and called the doctor. She came round to him forcing her to drink black coffee. Once more she had failed to take her life. The doctor attempted to explain it as being a result of stress and depression. In his experience, patients often mistakenly overdosed on laudanum because of its soothing qualities, which delivered a gently euphoric state.

CHAPTER 47

Working-class Revival

Céleste made a quick recovery and faced the apparently inevitable bankruptcy. One night, after meeting her mother for coffee, she wandered alone past the huge theatre on 94 Rue de Belleville and, reading the billboards, noticed that many of the cast in the current show had worked for her at the Folies-Marigny. She could not resist going in to see them before the show. They were all pleased to see her and introduced her to the theatre manager/director, Monsieur Holacher, who invited her to join them for supper after the show.

'I've read *The Gold Thieves*,' he said. 'It's a fine read. Loved it! Have you thought of dramatising it?'

Céleste told him of the Dumas script and the situation. 'I must be honest with you. I've been blocked at every turn by the Chabrillans.'

'I care not for social censorship or power plays by aristocrats,' Holacher said. 'I care for art, and your story is strong, intriguing and real. It's fit for my theatre in this working-class district. It will be a hit.'

'But the Chabrillans …'

'Don't worry about them. They can't intimidate me.'

Holacher asked for Dumas's script, which the renowned author had turned into a rollicking tale that would have resonance with workers and their wives. Holacher loved the script and saw the potential. He particularly liked that Céleste's original work had female characters and she'd given them a more or less equal role in the story. Here was an aggressive melodrama that would appeal to both sexes. Inside forty-eight hours he had created a three-way deal between himself, Céleste and Dumas. The next day he began casting and offered Céleste a part, which was a shrewd move. It meant she would have a greater investment in the production and it would be a big marketing draw to attract a sellout audience.

Holacher convinced himself he would have a big hit on his hands. He spared no expense in re-creating an Australian bush setting, complete with campfires and horses and carriages.

The show opened on 24 May 1864 and once more Céleste's demimondaine friends turned out in force to add some glamour. But this time, the numbers did not need boosting by fashionable mates and acquaintances. Every one of the 1600 seats was taken. People were let in the back of the theatre, swelling the numbers and box office for a record take for Belleville on an opening night.[1]

Céleste was more nervous than usual. Holacher whispered to her to peek around the curtain at the audience. She felt invigorated by the response, which was hugely appreciative. People reacted to every emotional high and low. At the end of the five acts, there was tremendous applause and cheering.

The crowd called, 'Author! Author!'

Holacher stepped onto the stage and motioned for Céleste to come forward from the line of actors.

'Madame the Countess, Lionel de Chabrillan!' he announced.

The audience roared their approval. They knew her. Many would have read the memoirs, where she had been clear about her roots. Despite, or even because of, her title, they cheered louder. Céleste, Mogador, Madame Lionel, Countess. No matter how she was announced, she was one of them and a heroine. She was mobbed when, laden with bouquets, she left the stage door.

Céleste had never felt a more euphoric and alive moment than she did in the heart of Belleville that night. All the struggle and setbacks now seemed worth it.

Céleste braced herself for the reviews in the press. Would the journalists in the Chabrillans' pocket repeat their murderous attacks? But the pernicious colour pieces of two years earlier, which had stopped her theatrical enterprise, were not repeated. There was nothing new to exploit about Mogador. Instead, there were surprisingly objective and universally good reviews. They were so strong that the repertory Bellevue Theatre decided it could not change its program, as it usually did, after a week. *The Gold Thieves* ran for a record five weeks.

This time Céleste took off afterwards on a provincial tour, not to salvage the situation, but to add revenue to the Paris production earnings. Her agent made sure that money kept flowing to her, including royalties, and ten per cent of the net profits, which was not as good as gross, but meant more than an extra trickle for her bank account.

The tour of the provinces was a winner, taking in another 9000 francs for her. Bursting with enthusiasm, she took the play abroad to Holland and Belgium, which added another 14,500 francs to her personal coffers.

Céleste's fluctuating finances were on the rise again. Having just avoided bankruptcy less than two years earlier, at thirty-nine, she was financially secure for the moment.

As ever, she was generous to Anne-Victoire and straight after her international tour she visited her, where she was living in a modest home in Belleville, to give her some money. Céleste found her in acute distress. Vincent had died. Céleste was sympathetic until she learned that her mother had buried him in the family vault in the cemetery at Pré-Saint-Gervais. Céleste was angered and berated her mother. How could she, her daughter, ever contemplate being put to rest with the man who had frequently attempted to physically abuse her and who had split her from her mother? It was an idea that Céleste believed she would never come to terms with.

CHAPTER 48

Creative Transition; More Battles

Eventually, mother and daughter reconciled their differences and Céleste invited Anne-Victoire and Solange to live at the new property she had built at Le Vésinet, sixteen kilometres and less than a half-hour train ride north of Paris. Knowing the stormy history she had with Céleste, Anne-Victoire accepted but retained her home at Belleville.

Céleste demonstrated mixed emotions and some nostalgia concerning Australia by building the new two-storey home in the style of an outback squatter's house, complete with shady all-round verandah, tin roof and corrugated water tank. She even went to the trouble of planting some fledgling gum trees in the hope they would one day stand tall in the forest surrounding the homestead. She would have loved to emulate Napoleon's Josephine by transporting kangaroos and other fauna from Australia, but decided that the cost was too high. The house's registered name was 'Chalet des Fleurs', but Céleste nicknamed it 'Chalet Lionel'.

Céleste had created a soothing atmosphere, conducive to her work and an improved mental and physical state, but it was often not a happy household. Anne Victoire was now sixty-five and very much at odds with everything about Céleste's lifestyle. The mother wanted her dinner at 5 p.m. and to retire no later than 7 p.m. Céleste would finish work at that hour after being locked away writing and researching for most of the day. She was a young-at-heart forty-year-old who still wanted to throw parties or hold stimulating dinners, often with people specifically chosen because they would argue with each other. This was the writer's life she loved and it could not have been more contrary to her mother's sedate lifestyle. Anne-Victoire disapproved of it all, disliked Céleste's friends and was so out of her depth that she was drowning in her disgruntlement at them and their behaviour.

She reserved most spite for a young, brilliant composer, Georges Bizet, twenty-five, who lived nearby and whom Céleste befriended on her frequent train trips to Paris. Bizet was struggling after a dashing start to his career when, in 1857, he'd won the top music prize at the Paris Conservatoire, the Prix de Rome. After living in Italy for three years, where he'd spent as much time with whores as he did composing, he was living frugally in a hut and settling down to compose lyrical operas. They included *La Jolie Fille de Perth*, which had been adapted from Sir Walter Scott's novel *The Fair Maid of Perth.*

Bizet would use any excuse to call on Céleste. He was besotted with her and she had invited him to play on her fine piano as often as he liked. She always encouraged artists, and despite Anne-Victoire's complaints about the 'noise', he turned up, sometimes with friends, to play his compositions. Céleste had a good ear for music, which had been part of her life's fabric, and she predicted Bizet would develop into one of France's great composers. She invited him to her parties where singers and other composers performed, but he was shy and would disappear into the garden when called on to perform. Bizet felt more comfortable with just her company.

Coming home late at night from Paris, he would often see her upstairs study light on and tap on the downstairs window shutters. This would cause Anne-Victoire's poodle to bark and the house would be woken. After this happened a few times even Céleste lost patience and told him to desist. But one day he received good news about one of his operas, *Les Pêcheurs de Perles* (*The Pearl Fishers*), being accepted for production. Well lubricated after a drinking celebration with mates, he could not resist telling his now close friend the countess about his success. It was 2 a.m. when he reached her house and rapped on the shutters. Céleste had finished writing and was in bed. She got up and was just about to dash downstairs when Anne-Victoire opened a window above the front door. She tipped the contents of her chamber-pot on his head, telling him where to go in terms that would make a Belleville cemetery worker blush.

Undeterred, Bizet kept visiting his muse, Céleste, and they often walked arm in arm in the woods during breaks from their writing. Once after he had played an exciting composition for her, Céleste pressed close to him as they walked in the moonlight. She was enchanted. Bizet, already dreaming of a relationship with this still stunning woman fifteen years his senior, misinterpreted her clutching his arm as they strolled. He wondered aloud if she was coming on to him.

Céleste handled his infatuation with sensitivity, saying, 'I adore your talent and am proud of your friendship … but my admiration for you is absolutely platonic.'

Young Bizet pressed further for a relationship. Céleste let him down gently in the practised manner of the experienced courtesan.

'Let's wait until we see what happens to our pleasant and honest friendship … otherwise the chances are a hundred to one that we would quarrel.'[1]

In April 1866 Céleste's Le Vésinet home was ransacked while she was away. That was bad enough, but she saw it as a violation and a step too far when it seemed that the burglars had targeted all the mementos, presents and other items she had inherited from Lionel: most of his letters, signed bound books he had given her, his hunting pistols, his consul's dress sword, and his signet ring engraved with his crest. Most upsetting was the theft of the little ivory model of Christ he had gifted her when she and Solange returned to France from Australia without him on the *James Baines*.

Céleste's first thought was that the Chabrillans had instigated the burglary and nothing could ever make her think otherwise. They had failed to stop her career. Instead, thanks to their interference, it had been diverted to different creative outlets, which had only strengthened her reputation and highlighted her connection to the family name. They had not been able to break her financially, and short of having her murdered, they could not stop her advance. Striking this way was an attempt to take away all the connections she had to Lionel and to them. But she still retained her title, which was the most important link of all.

Devastated, she tried to sell the house in order to rid her of this violation of her soul and spirit. Again, the timing was not right. She could not get a reasonable price and so held on to the property.

Céleste remained in the public eye and of regular interest to the press. Four of her plays, as agreed and contracted by the new lessees of the Folies-Marigny, were produced. Three were hits though without the impact of *The Gold Thieves*. They were *En Garde*, *Un Homme Compromis*, and the musical comedy, *A la Bretonne*. Modest income from these augmented the royalties from *The Gold Thieves*, but her expenses were beginning to outrun her income once more. Fearing bankruptcy again, she sought other work and accepted an offer from the owner of Café-Concert du XIXé to appear for 100 nights at 100 francs, meaning an income of 10,000 francs, which was in the order of the returns from her recent tours.

Like many artists before and after her, she felt that it was important to take reasonable offers because they could never be assured they would be in favour for their work from one year to the next. She now had a strong reputation in the theatre as Madame Lionel, although most people still referred to her as Mogador, which seemed to stick no matter her endeavours. This café was similar to scores in Paris that put on shows from strippers and burlesque dancers to more sophisticated performances of opera singers and classical guitarists.

Céleste signed the contract as the countess. The owner promptly advertised on Paris hoardings and in the press that the café was putting on shows by the Countess Lionel de Chabrillan. Céleste was deeply disappointed. She threatened to break the contract but could not. The press loved the faux pas on her part and trotted out old references to Mogador 'prostituting the good name of one of France's oldest and most respected families'.

The Chabrillans—led by the marquis and his sister—reacted with outrage. From their perspective she was insulting them after the burglary at Le Vésinet. They contacted the Paris Prefecture of Police and either bribed or put political pressure on him. Céleste was summoned to the office of an inspector. On his desk was the 25-year-old file in which she had been registered as a prostitute at sixteen years of age.

'You are Élizabeth-Céleste Vénard, are you not?' the inspector asked in an officious manner, as if he were addressing a common street worker rather than a countess. Asking her to sit opposite him at his desk, he pointed out that she had signed the registry of her own volition. This meant that she could be arrested at any time.

Céleste, shaken but much more confident than the pathetic, abandoned teenage prisoner she had once been, remained quiet throughout this aggressive threat.

'Let me give you some friendly advice,' he said in a most unfriendly manner. 'Cancel your engagement to sing at the Café-Concert.'

'Have you finished?' she asked the inspector. Surprised, he nodded.

'Let me remind you, sir,' she said, 'that my husband, in conjunction with his friend Prince Napoleon, had my name removed from your registry.'

She pointed at the big, thick book with its yellowing pages.

'Check it,' she said. 'It was on the 27th of April 1852, which was twenty months before my marriage to the count.'

The prefecture either knew or was too dumbfounded to respond and open the registry.

'If the Chabrillans are not aware of the fact,' she told the inspector as she stood to leave, 'perhaps you will be kind enough to inform them of it.'

Céleste left the office, with the inspector still sitting in his chair. She was furious but had kept a cool dignity throughout this ordeal. But it would have depressed her, especially with all its bad reminders of those dark days a generation ago.

She was now more defiant than ever and secretly pleased that she was being billed under her true name.

Céleste at forty-one still looked good; 'handsome' being the most hackneyed description of the time. Her face was unlined;

her waist was thin, her bosom and derrière full and firm and in no way matronly; her long limbs were still in superb condition. For the café show, Céleste wore a frilled white satin dress with a pattern of scarlet poppies. It had very short, almost non-existent sleeves, which showed off her arms, always her most remarked on physical attribute. But it was her inner beauty—the character and personality—that came through and captivated audiences. Céleste had a real presence on stage or anywhere. She was 'charismatic' before it became a theatrical cliché, and she was closer to the original definition of charm and influence. Men were often mesmerised; women were inspired, particularly those who lived repressed lives as second-class citizens in a male-dominated world.

Her show was an autobiographical monologue called *Encore Moi*. She naturally sanitised her life, speaking about her careers as a dancer, equestrienne, actress and author. There was not a word about Guy, Vincent, prison, the brothel, courtesans or the Chabrillans. She did, however, speak glowingly about her one true love, Count Lionel. It may have seemed defiant to her critics, but she felt she owed more than just some acknowledgement to him. At no point did she play up her status as a countess. Instead, she stayed true to the integrity of events in that respect.

In the interval, she changed costume and returned to the stage in a more dramatic black velvet gown with a white lace cape and sang ballads, some her own and others contemporary hits. Even though her vocal skills did not match her writing, dancing or acting, she got away with mediocrity because she had already won her audience over.

The show was a great success. Céleste was surprised when the contract was not renewed, and believed that the unseen Chabrillan guillotine had fallen on her elegant neck once more. Certainly the owner had done strong business throughout the three months. He would not explain his decision, which to Céleste was explanation enough.

When Holacher, the Belleville Theatre director, approached Céleste about a follow-up to *The Gold Thieves*, she was ready and in the mood for a creative burst. She came up with *Les Crimes de la Mer* (*Crimes at Sea*), a melodrama about the adventures of a Breton sailor shipwrecked on the Australian coast. She had an oversupply of material. There had been monthly reports of shipwrecks all around the huge Australian coastline. She borrowed ideas from these, threw in some similarities to the mutiny of the *Batavia* off the coast of Western Australia in 1629 and stirred in her own upsetting experiences on two long trips. The new play debuted on 8 May 1869 and was nearly as big a hit as *The Gold Thieves.*

The audiences loved it. Critics, including political journalist Édouard Drumont, reviewed it favourably. His words of praise turned to flattery in person, when he offered to write and publish a mini-biography of Céleste. This seemed like a good idea at the time. She was riding high and wished to remain in the public eye. There had never been such a thing as bad publicity for Céleste, whom Paris loved reading about. She thought that something more controlled and positive would help, and perhaps modify her image among those who would always sneer at her achievements, such as the Chabrillans and their aristocratic circle.[2]

But Drumont proved to be unscrupulous. She ended up paying the cost of printing the book, while he pocketed the 300 francs she had given him to publish it.[3]

In early 1870, another benefactor, in the form of the Count de Naurois, seventy-eight, turned up unexpectedly. He had been a friend of Lionel's and had opposed his marriage to Céleste, whom he had never met. But when she starred in another of her hit plays, *Les Revers de l'Amour* (*Troubles in Love*), which ran for three months at his Théâtre des Nouveautés, he could not resist popping in to meet her.

Until Céleste's performance, the rundown theatre had been used for strip shows, which irked him and he avoided it. But *Les Revers* lasted for several months. It was a welcome change. Enamoured with her efforts, he invited Céleste to his home to view his art treasures. Céleste was delighted to meet his adopted daughter, Princess de Lusignan, who confided that her bored father needed a distraction, but not a sexual one, for he had declared he was past that. Céleste was pleased to be consulted. She then showed the very rich, sometimes charming, often grumpy old gentleman all his properties, including the theatre. He was appalled at their state of disrepair. Nouveautés, the market across the road, and the building which housed his newspaper, *L'Opinion Nationale*, were all rundown. With Céleste's discreet guidance and assisted by his daughter, the count had a new direction. He went to work engaging contractors, and enjoyed slipping down to the theatre and chatting with the cast and crew who were putting on another Céleste creation, *La Femme Américaine* (*The American Girl*).

Count de Naurois was so pleased with Céleste that when the manager/lessee of the theatre fell behind in his rent, he fired him and installed her instead.

CHAPTER 49

War Changes and Service

Céleste had never had it so good. It was 1870 and she was forty-five. She had her own theatre. She was starring in her own production. Money problems that had dogged her throughout her career were no longer an issue as long as she did not over-extend herself. She had a satisfactory private life with Desmarest an undemanding, part-time lover. Her dependent mother and daughter were settled and secure.

On 19 July 1870, her world was turned upside down by the Franco-Prussian War, when France was conned by the canny, belligerent Prussian Chancellor, Otto von Bismarck, into declaring war on Prussia. Von Bismarck had long planned to provoke a French attack. He knew it would be the spark to draw the southern German states—Baden, Wurttemberg, Bavaria and Hesse-Darmstadt—into an alliance with the Prussian-dominated North German Alliance.

In Paris, theatres, businesses and sporting events shut down. The good run at the Théâtre des Nouveautés ended abruptly. Count de Naurois, fearing an invasion of Paris and the appropriation of his property and wealth, was whisked away to England by his daughter. He gave Céleste a modest parting gift of 1500 francs and assured her that they would become reacquainted as soon as the war was over. Céleste took Solange out of the drapery shop where she worked and sent her to Le Vésinet, believing she would be safer there. Although the Prussians were a long way from Paris, Céleste was aware from her contact with her lawyer and radical politician, Léon Gambetta, that civil unrest in France would lead to bloodshed in French cities, perhaps as much bloodshed as fighting the well-organised Prussians would cause.

In fact, defeat for the French on 2 September 1870 led to internal strife and change. At Sedan on France's north-east border, the French Army was defeated by the powerful enemy, which took 80,000 prisoners, including the hapless Napoleon III, who was present to boost his troops' morale. His capture ended the Second Empire. On 4 September he was deposed and the Third Republic was declared by a Government of National Defence led by the new president, General Louis-Jules Trochu, along with Monsieur Jules Favre and Céleste's friend and dinner-party jousting opponent, Léon Gambetta.

Céleste could be forgiven for cursing her ill luck at a time when she had reached a grand peak in her career. But instead of retreating to mope at her misfortune, she did the opposite and thought of ways to defend France with the help of an organised women's civilian force. This would support the regular army and the stronger, often politicised and radical troops of the National Guard.

On the day the Third Republic was announced she sent a long and impassioned letter to the Governor of Paris.

> *There are in the capital thousands of energetic and strong women, belonging to all classes and particularly to the working class, who, at a word from you, are ready to form a legion.*

> *It could proceed by divisions to care for the wounded, to transport them on stretchers, prepare meals for the besieged. The women could also do their washing, look after animals, form a chain of rescuers in the case of fire … They would become the devoted servants of France … so that our ramparts shall not be deprived of one single defender …*

Céleste signed it 'Veuve Hubert, born in Paris in 1824'. Anticipating that the Governor of Paris, on a day of turmoil in the capital, was never going to sit down and write a reply, particularly to someone he'd never heard of, she sent the letter to several newspapers, signing it this time as '*Une Parisienne*'.

'Have you read this?' Desmarest asked after reading her piece in a morning paper. 'There's a proposal for a women's corps.'

'No I haven't,' Céleste said, wanting to hear his reaction.

'It's a model of generosity and intelligence.'

'A man must have written it, then.'

'No, I don't think so. It's signed by a woman. You should join this corps.'

'Really?'

'Of course. The government should organise it. Women cannot organise themselves.'

'Oh, you believe that, do you? Well, the disorganised woman who wrote it is me!'

Desmarest was stunned.

'I'm sorry,' he said, severely embarrassed. 'I had no idea.'

'Clearly!'

'I'll tell you what I'll do,' he said in an attempt to recover ground. 'There's a large empty office of mine at 17 Boulevard Saint-Martin. You can use it to start this … this legion.'

The editor of *La Presse* Émile de Girardin suggested the new organisation should be called Les Soeurs de France. Céleste liked it and it was adopted. It was officially founded on

15 September 1870 under the Civil Committee for the Means of Defence. Possibly missing the message, three men from the committee were appointed to direct it.

On 19 September, the Germans surrounded the city and erected a blockade.

Céleste had recruited 150 women by that date. They all wore the uniform she had suggested in her letter of 'a wool dress and calico bonnet; an apron with wide pockets to hold the necessary dressings for the wounded; and a shoulder bag containing provisions'. They also wore a brass number and the insignia of the Red Cross as armbands. By 21 September, the women had begun organising ambulance stations in empty houses on Paris's outskirts. This move had an immediate impact. Many soldiers' lives were saved. Céleste was now ubiquitous and fully involved with events on the frontline as well as in the suburbs, particularly in the north of Paris, where the Prussians were pressing hardest. There was more ill feeling towards the new French Government of the Third Republic than there was towards the Prussians, who had put the capital in a state of siege.

The Prussian blockade of Paris dragged on into November and December of 1870 and the beginning of a cold winter. The stalemate encouraged all the worst elements of humanity as black-market racketeers, looters and German spies destabilised the French position. As the new year approached, the winter became harder and exacerbated the dire situation for the city's defenders. Its water system was under stress as pipes and street pumps froze. Wood became scarce and fuel was almost non-existent. The Prussians applied a stranglehold on Paris.

Céleste's Soeurs de France were kept close to the action and she was as busy as any general, marshalling her troops for the behind-the-barricades work in saving lives and tending to the wounded.

On 1 December 1870 Céleste returned to one of her ambulance stations at Nogent, ten kilometres east of Paris, and helped nurse thirty-five wounded soldiers. The next day she saw French troops moving through the town on the way to the front. Céleste was soon working at a demanding pace as the wounded and dead were brought in. On 3 December she returned to Paris. Sometimes, although near to exhaustion, she would go to halls in Paris to recite her nationalistic poems and raise funds for her work.

On 5 December she was deeply saddened to learn of the death of good friend Alexandre Dumas Sr at the age of sixty-eight. Céleste took time off from her busy rounds of ambulance stations to attend his funeral and burial at his birthplace of Villers-Cotterêts, in Aisne.

CHAPTER 50

Commune with the Devil

Céleste's forty-sixth birthday on 27 December 1870 passed with little joy as the Prussian Army continued to defeat the French provincial forces that were organised and urged on by Gambetta. Favre travelled to Versailles on 24 January 1871 to discuss peace talks with Bismarck. The Prussian president agreed to end the siege and food convoys would be allowed to enter Paris on condition that the French Government of National Defence surrender key fortresses outside Paris. Knowing that Gambetta's provincial armies were most unlikely to break through and relieve the capital, Favre agreed to the terms. French President Trochu resigned the next day. On 27 January a most distressed Favre signed the surrender at Versailles, with armistice to come into force at midnight.

Learning of this, and that the Prussians were about to enter Paris, Céleste disbanded Les Soeurs de France. She could not stand the thought of seeing the Prussians march into her city, so she headed for Le Vésinet. There were no trains running and no other transports. She trudged the sixteen kilometres north through intermittent evidence of the invading armies' destructive path.

As she neared Chalet Lionel at Le Vésinet she began to expect the worst. Her fears materialised. The Prussians had occupied and looted her grand Australian-style home. She decided to have it repaired immediately, yet this soon became of less concern than the news that Solange, now just shy of twenty-two, had disappeared. According to the woman who had cared for her and the home, Solange had gone off of her own volition with Prussian soldiers. This at first surprised Céleste, although Solange was not alone in leaving with the conquering enemy. Mother and daughter had become increasingly estranged, with fault on both sides. Céleste's expectations for her adopted daughter had been too high and the girl resented her mother's fame and glamour, a situation exacerbated by her being adopted. Solange did not have Céleste's drive or intelligence. Not many people did. Also the girl reacted against her mother's pushing. Solange had been content with her work learning the drapery business, but she was rebellious and difficult.

Céleste made inquiries with the authorities, but was informed that it would be impossible to trace her. The victorious Prussian Army was not about to stop and search for missing French family members, especially unmanageable young adults. Céleste experienced a mix of emotions from distress to guilt over Solange's disappearance. On reflection, she could only hope that her adopted daughter would find happiness.

An armistice in February 1871 was meant to lead to peace, but it was only the signal for communists to start a bloody internecine war, using radicalised elements of the National Guard to fight the regular French Army. It resulted in the brief control of Paris by the radical Paris Commune from 18 March to 28 May, culminating in bloody confrontations that all but destroyed parts of the capital before the elected government led by Adolphe Thiers resumed power.

By the end of May 1871, the turmoil, death and destruction of war and internal political struggles, which had reigned in some form in France for nearly a year, was over. So also was a liberated, some would say decadent, era.

Looking back on it, the Count Albert de Maugny wrote:

> *A whole epoch! And what an epoch! Eighteen years of luxury, pleasure, recklessness and gaiety, of gallantry and incomparable elegance. It was a time … like an apparition of the eighteenth century. Then [after the Franco-Prussian War and the Commune period] a veil of mourning and sadness suddenly hid the décor; it all vanished again, into shadow and triviality … Who can remember without emotion, that swarm of pretty young women … happy to be alive, to flirt and to be admired? You see, the mould for those women is broken.*[1]

The fall of the Second Empire had changed the French, and in particular the Parisian, way of life. The royal court had disappeared, as had the aristocracy that had made the courtesans distinctive and special. The dandies were almost all gone. The emperor, who once said he enjoyed a woman as much as a good cigar after dinner, was no more. The life of pleasure now seemed banal and profligate. War had been a great leveller while it was on and after it had ended, everything got serious. The artists who had painted the courtesans, the poets who had been inspired to create verse, and the writers who had been driven to describe them were gone, dying out or out of favour.

Writer Maxime du Camp more or less supported the attitude that the Prussians had what they saw as the morals-free decades in France when he blamed '*les femmes interlopes*'—the female interlopers—for corrupting the solid middle classes, and some of the aristocracy. He reckoned the war had been lost because of it.

It was the generation who had lost themselves in a life of pleasure, du Camp believed, and therefore lost the Franco-Prussian War. They had changed the course of French history. 'For when France looked within herself for the men she needed, she saw emptiness, and she found no one.'[2]

In mid-summer 1871 the Count de Naurois returned with his daughter from exile in England. He renewed his friendship with Céleste and did not hesitate to fund the rebuilding of her Le Vésinet homestead. In an odd turn of events, she was asked by his business representative to repay 6000 francs that Naurois had advanced her when she became the director at his Théâtre des Nouveautés. Céleste was confused. She knew from his daughter that he sometimes did some irritating things over money, and Céleste put this strange demand—straight after funding the refurbishment of Chalet Lionel—down to his age, and perhaps some mental confusion. In order to pay him back she asked if she could mortgage the property in his name, which because of his huge wealth was always acceptable to the bank, Crédit Foncier. He did not hesitate to accept this arrangement, and thus had an indirect but legitimate interest in the Le Vésinet property.

After missing more than a year in the tenuous world of the theatre, Céleste's finances were again uncertain. But with her usual, undiminished drive and diligence, she set about resurrecting her shows. She decided on something simple and income-generating to begin with—a lecture tour of Belgium, commencing in Brussels on 3 April 1872. This seemed safer than another play, which could be a flop with fickle audiences. No one knew how other nations would react to anything in a newly arranged continental Europe, with the Prussian-dominated confederated German nation the new superpower.

Céleste was promoted as 'Madame Lionel de Chabrillan'. However, the Belgian press had no interest in a French countess. They dragged out her history as a top courtesan. Predominantly male audiences turned up expecting a risqué performance. Instead, they were given tales about the 'Wild West' of the Australian goldfields. Céleste, now forty-seven, was still a beautiful woman, but not the sensual coquette she had played at will in front of audiences a generation earlier. She received some catcalls, but restored the night by handling questions about her former life with aplomb. She went on with the tour, using the same format, and managed to avoid a financial failure.

These shows were not the attractive plays she had put on before the Franco-Prussian War. Nevertheless, the income generated allowed her to tread water. She worked hard and produced more plays, but they were flops. Once more she began to run into liquidity problems and she was forced to take out a second mortgage on the property, which increased Naurois's indirect interest.

During the summer of 1872, she returned to Le Vésinet and found that she was so far behind in her payments that the bank had put the house up for sale. It was sold to a neighbour, who had often asked Céleste if she would sell. Now, it seemed, the neighbour had acquired it by default. Céleste claimed that she had not received the summonses warning her this would happen. She had a strict honesty policy over all business matters and she accused the neighbour of having stolen the notices from her letterbox.

Céleste informed Naurois. He told her not to worry.

'Your neighbour is a scoundrel,' he said, 'but he shall not get your house. I'm one of your creditors. According to the law, I'm entitled to make a higher bid for it.'

He made the bid the next day, just before the property was transferred legally to the neighbour. Naurois informed her of his acquisition, but he had gone one better by buying all the land surrounding Chalet Lionel.

Céleste had been reading about the orphans in the two former French border provinces of Alsace and Lorraine, which had been taken over by the Prussians. She hurried to see Naurois, an idea forming.

'Why couldn't we build something for the orphans on that extra land you've bought?' she asked, focusing all her persuasive powers on him.

'Whatever made you want that?'

'I once told you of my deprived childhood,' she said, 'and my dark times at Saint-Lazare.'

'I admire your humanity, my dear, but it isn't just a matter of building an orphanage. There would be considerable politics involved. The Germans control the region.'

'I'm sure with your marvellous range of contacts, my dear Count, you could have those children released to live here.'

The count demurred. Céleste nagged him over it and he agreed to look into it with his political connections.

By late 1872, Anne-Victoire was no longer well enough to live on her own at Belleville and Céleste arranged for her to live in an eldery care home. She provided her with all the necessary comforts in her final years, and paid the rent of 100 francs a month. Anne-Victoire developed dementia, which led her to complaining bitterly to her daughter until she died on 24 February 1874, aged seventy-seven.

As her will dictated, Anne-Victoire was buried next to Vincent in the family grave at Pré-Saint-Gervais. Céleste shuddered at the thought of being placed near Vincent herself. She had never forgiven him for molesting her, and blamed it, not without reason, for the early life she had been pushed into. Céleste was made to feel so miserable and lonely by the prospect of being laid to rest in such company for eternity that she swore never to return there, until she, too, was dead.

CHAPTER 51

Muse and Munificence

In 1875, Céleste's close friend Georges Bizet produced his finest, most commercial opera at the Opéra-Comique. Some critics savaged it and branded it as 'shocking', which of course generated interest. The big-drinking, chain-smoking and overweight Bizet, ill and depressed by the critical response, died of a heart attack at age thirty-seven, almost exactly three months after the opening performance. This was when *Carmen* became a stupendous success, and Bizet never knew. He had lived for his work and had been inspired by people such as Céleste, who believed in his talent and urged him to keep producing. Bizet always said his output and mild acclaim were rewards in themselves. He never seemed to suffer from recognition deprivation, although it was known that he had the highest expectations for *Carmen*.

'The gypsy heroine is little more than a splendid animal,' Paul England wrote in his book *Fifty Favourite Operas*, 'irresistible in her sensuous beauty, superb in her physical courage, knowing no law higher than her own desires. Carmen's amours are rarely of more than six months' duration'.[1]

Many critics then and later suggested that Bizet based the character on Céleste, who early in her career fitted most of this description.[2] He loved whores and he was so enchanted by Céleste that he wanted to give up his girlfriend for her. Céleste was rarely out of the press and his mind. They lived close to each other for more than a decade, but according to her, never had sex.

Bizet's early demise prompted Céleste to turn to her creativity for solace. She wrote the play *Ambition Fatale* with such manic drive that she caught bronchitis and ended up in a nursing home, the Maison Dubois. But the nurses could not stop her frenetic scribbling. By the time she was well enough to leave she had finished and sold the play to the Théâtre Beaumarchais, which produced it at the end of 1875. She did not stop writing and returned to a remote Australian setting for another book, *The Two Sisters*. It had one memorable line: 'Dreamers don't go to Australia; dreamers would not have time to dream there.'

The Australian experience may have been harsh for her, but she was extracting everything from it to help her make a living.

Céleste had moved from being productive to prolific. The book's sales were modest, but she was keeping her name before the press and public. It prompted Céleste's publisher to convince her to bring out a new set of memoirs, *Death at the End of the World* (*Un Deuil au Bout du Monde*), covering her wedding, the boat trip to Australia and her life in Melbourne and the goldfields. It was 1877, twenty years after she had returned to Paris from her Australian sojourn.

She had been thinking about publishing her memoirs from that time ever since her tour of Belgium five years previously and she had been refreshing her memory of the experience with the odd talk in Paris. It was an about face after all her protests two decades earlier about the republishing of her first set of memoirs. But she felt comfortable with this book and her fears about the Chabrillan family's reprisals had subsided. It was scandal-free and gave her a chance to reiterate Lionel's efforts to make sure their marriage was valid. It covered their lives in Australia, and expressed the factual experience from which she drew her themes in the fictional *The Gold Thieves*.

Death at the End of the World was published under the name Countess Lionel de Chabrillan, a defiant reminder to the Chabrillan family. Just to make the point even stronger, she agreed to the publisher bringing out a third edition of the original memoirs.

The family had won many of the early battles in thwarting her career in publishing and the theatre, but she was winning the war in reminding France of her marriage and her grand love affair with Count Lionel. The new book also kept her name in the press and generated welcome extra income.

Céleste finally convinced her benefactor the Count de Naurois to approach the Count d'Haussonville, who was in charge of helping the people of Alsace and Lorraine, with her suggestion about an orphanage at Le Vésinet. Haussonville knew the Chabrillans and refused to facilitate the building work. Naurois was not used to being rejected, especially over such a humane and charitable project. He persisted. Haussonville accepted the proposal on the condition that Céleste would not be on the list of patrons. Céleste never wished accolades for the charity. She agreed to this and building began. While she was overseeing it, the nuns, the Sisters of Saint-Charles, who would bring up the twenty orphans, approached her about the construction of a small chapel for them. Céleste made sure their wish was granted.

The chapel was consecrated on 22 August 1877 with a fair sweep of France's aristocracy represented. However, only one member of the Chabrillan family attended—Céleste herself, even though she had not been invited. She lived a stone's throw from the chapel and orphanage and it was easy to creep into the woods nearby and observe the ceremony. When the guests began to disperse, Naurois beckoned her to meet the nuns and orphan girls, explaining that Céleste was their true guardian angel.

This description flattered and humbled Céleste, for she was forever being reminded in commentary and art that many viewed her as more of a fallen angel. In 1878, 26-year-old French painter Henri Gervex produced a superb oil on canvas he called *Rolla*. It depicted a young, beautiful prostitute lying asleep on her back on a bed with an aristocratic-looking fellow—very much like Alfred de Musset—gazing out the brothel window at Paris rooftops. Gervex said he was inspired by a long poem by Musset. The text recounted the destiny of a young, debauched and idle 'Jacques Rolla' (read Musset himself) who fell in love with Maria, a teenager who escaped from a life of misery by going into prostitution. The poem was written a few years before Musset met Céleste, but the girl depicted in 1878 by Gervex bears a very close resemblance in face, body, colouring and circumstance to a young Céleste. Gervex knew her. He had read her memoirs and the perennial stories about her in the Paris press. He had read of Céleste's relationship with Musset. Again, as with Georges Bizet and the inspiration for *Carmen*, he would have had the well-known Mogador in mind when he painted the girl.

Similarly to *Carmen*, this outstanding creation caused feverish controversy. The bureaucracy banned the work from the opening of the Salon de Paris, a place for the best artists to exhibit. The judges saw it as 'immoral'. The post-Franco-Prussian War era was generating a degree of conservatism as if in repsonse to the idea that, as the Germans had suggested, France's softened morals had helped in its defeat by the more rigid, disciplined Prussians.

Naurois became ill suddenly in 1878 and called his good friend Céleste to his deathbed to say goodbye.

'I'm going to leave you 1200 francs a year,' he told her, 'which will be held in trust by my stepdaughter. There will be an additional 800 shares, which will need a final payment in a few years.'

Céleste expressed her gratitude.

'No, no, my dear,' he said, his eyes filling with tears. 'My whole fortune would not have been too much of a reward for the happiness you have given me.'

He was buried in the chapel he had funded at Le Vésinet.

Naurois's death left Céleste feeling isolated. Close friends, family, dependants and benefactors were dying or disappearing with such alacrity that she had a sense of being alone. It began with Dumas, and was followed by Solange, Anne-Victoire, Bizet and now Naurois. Her relationship with Desmarest, who had retired, had fallen away. She could no longer use the apartment in which he had set her up. Nor could she live at Le Vésinet, which was now incorporated into Naurois's estate. She had grown to enjoy the secluded life and thought she would miss Le Vésinet, but she still preferred Paris, if she had to make a choice. She took a small room in the Passage de l'Opéra.

Céleste's method of getting over the losses and loneliness was to write. She laboured over the play *M'ame Nicole*. She still had the energy but was not flavour of the decade anymore. Young playwrights who had not experienced the period from 1830 to 1870, and who had been influenced mainly by the morbid impact of the Franco-Prussian War, were preferred. Nevertheless, she broke through yet again when this play was produced by the Folies-Dramatiques in 1880, the year she turned fifty-six. Céleste's run seemed almost over and it had been a good one of twenty-six years—a generation—since her memoirs had burst onto the literary scene in 1854.

During the two years since leaving Le Vésinet, she often made the short train ride to see the nuns and the orphan children. Once more her whimsical, spontaneous nature took over and she decided to buy another home there but found herself cash-strapped. She consulted her long-term friend Alexandre Dumas Jr.

'Why don't you think about selling the copyright to your ten novels to Michel Lévy, the publisher at Calmann-Lévy? I've done it. We struggling authors need all the help we can get.'

'I must consider it,' Céleste said, more than interested.

'Mind you, it hurts. You'll never again receive royalties.'

'I'm not worried about that. Most of them aren't generating funds.'

'Don't forget, you can't pass on the copyright to any dependants in your estate, or anyone you have bequeathed.'

'I'm not concerned. I have no children, siblings or family.'

'What about Solange?'

'I haven't heard from her in nearly a decade. I heard rumours that a German soldier had taken her away. I hope she's happy.'

'You realise that books can generate royalties for seventy-five years after your death?'

'They're not creating royalties now. How could they that far into the future?!'

'You wouldn't consider keeping the copyright for *The Gold Thieves*? It's done so well as a book and play.'

'It's lost its appeal,' Céleste said despondently. 'There's no momentum.' She thought for a moment and laughed. 'The only one copyright I really don't care about losing is for the memoirs.'

Céleste sold all the copyright to the publisher and in the deal it bought another book from her, *Marie Baud*. The payment allowed her to buy the property at Le Vésinet, which she called Chalet des Fleurs. She found it difficult to maintain and ended up subletting two rooms to a young, struggling photographer. Céleste believed in him and the potential for this new and fast-growing creative area. When his operation flopped, she recognised the usual inability of artists to run a business, and took it over. She told him to produce the photos and organised a Paris company to do the development and printing.

Soon afterwards, Céleste fell ill again, this time from accidental coal poisoning. Dumas Jr rushed to see her at Le Vésinet and suggested strongly that she again enter the Maison Dubois nursing home. When she demurred he understood it was because she was, as ever, short of funds. The upkeep of the Chalet des Fleurs and her Paris pied-à-terre had drained her finances. Dumas paid for the sojourn and said she should always see him if she needed help. Céleste wrote to thank him for his generosity and kindness.

He then sent her a huge bunch of red roses and white lilacs.

Dumas Sr and Dumas Jr had always seen the inner beauty and soul of this unusually tenacious, spirited and gifted woman, who had often fought against the odds.

CHAPTER 52

Battling On

Céleste's illness gained unwanted press attention. Newspaper jackals swarmed with the thought that she might be dying since coal-gas mishaps had taken many lives. She was pestered by inquisitive visitors and the odd journalist, who wanted to see Mogador or check if she would survive. Yet in this case any publicity was good publicity. It revived interest in a celebrity author, who had slipped from view over recent years. But it did not help her sell another play. Her finances were running low and now at sixty, she did not have the contacts or benefactors of previous decades, which had helped her to somehow find the resources to keep doing what she wanted. After leaving the nursing home she sold Chalet des Fleurs and retreated to the bedsit in Passage de l'Opéra. Illness on illness had worn down her physical and mental resilience and she thought it might be time to enter a retirement home. On the advice of Dumas Jr, she applied for admission to the home run by the Society of Dramatic Authors. Dumas Jr, French poet and playwright Camille Doucet and Michel Lévy at Calmann-Lévy sponsored her. The society's secretary invited her to a meeting.

'There's no doubt, Madame, you have had a verifiable career of some distinction,' he said.

'And there have been no complaints or legal proceedings against me.'

'This is true. For most this would be sufficient accreditation. Nevertheless, there is your past.'

The dead hand of the Chabrillans was evident as ever. But this time not due to pressure from a lawyer's visit. For a secretary who had never written anything, and who would never understand the writer's life, Céleste's past would just not do for the elite society. It was not about to dispense largesse to Mogador, despite her literary output.

'Monsieur,' Céleste said to him, 'I thought that even murderers condemned in penal servitude were sometimes reprieved after thirty years.'

'Insolence does not aid your cause, Madame.'

'Insolence? Your probes have been both insolent and insulting!'

Céleste would wait for the society's verdict. Predictably, she was turned down. Dumas Jr was surprised and irritated. He wrote telling her how brave and worthy she was. But he observed that people like the secretary and the society's board were blind to everything she had achieved and done except what she had written in her memoirs.

'It appears that today, lying and hypocrisy are small faults,' he said, 'but that frankness is a crime.'

Céleste struggled on and managed in 1885 to put on her play *Pierre Pascal* at the Théâtre de l'Ambigu. She was now a curio for journalists a generation younger who had only read about the risqué period during the mid-nineteenth century. One was the talented critic, essayist and satirist Charles Chincholle, a noted contributor to the newspaper *Le Figaro*.

He wrote a biographical colour piece. It was balanced but predictably dwelt on her background.

'This evening towards midnight at the Ambigu,' he wrote, 'an actor will stand in front of the prompter's box to announce: "Ladies and gentlemen, the play that we have had the honour of presenting to you was by Madame La Countess Lionel de Chabrillan."

'Who bears this name? All Parisians know this is the former dancer of Bal Mabille. It is Mogador. What has become of Mogador? How does she live? This is less well known … her hair is now white and she is always simply dressed.'

The journalist noted that her marriage in England would not have had much validity if the Count de Chabrillan, 'in his passion', had not had it registered at the Chancellery of France.

'There is no need to speak here of her errors between her girlhood and marriage. They can be read in the *Memoirs of Mogador.* It's more important to remember that the young countess resolved to bear her husband's name with dignity. In order to insult her today, one must go back to her past. She does not conceal it … For more than thirty years the countess has been trying to kill Mogador. She never succeeded.'

Michel Lévy, who'd shown great loyalty as publisher and friend to Céleste throughout her career, consoled her for being rejected by the society, saying she was far too vibrant and productive to fade away in the old writers' home. Lévy said that he would publish her in the future if she kept working. He encouraged her to do another volume of her *Mémoires.* She took up the offer and went to the offices of Calmann-Lévy to borrow all her manuscripts to help with research for the new volume. She noted in her diary that it was 12 July 1895 when she bumped into Dumas Jr at the counter in the foyer. He was fifteen days short of his seventy-first birthday, and she was seventy. Céleste was shocked. His appearance had deteriorated. Noticing her reaction, he said, 'I have changed a great deal.'

'Oh no!' she replied.

'You've become short-sighted,' Dumas Jr said.

He remarked that he had heard Calmann-Lévy might be publishing the last volume of her memoirs. Was it true?

'It's not certain,' Céleste responded. 'I'm going to read my books and diaries and then reflect before I commit.'

'You're not overly enthused?'

'I don't wish to go through the long battles again, like the ones I had over the earlier volumes. On the other hand, a fresh volume would give me the chance to right all the wrongs; to put the record straight once and for all.' She paused and added ruefully, 'And I could do with the advance.'

'I advise against it,' Dumas Jr said. 'Guy de Maupassant regretted doing his final memoirs.'

'But if I'm compelled to write them …?'

'By all means put them on paper, then destroy the manuscript.'

'Why?'

'For the sake of those that you name.'

'Most of them are dead.'

'I'm here, too, to collect all my manuscripts, books and plays so I can research it all and write a final manuscript. I'll call it *La Route de Thebes*. I'm doing it only for my own personal pleasure. Then I'll destroy it.'[1]

'I don't think I could put such effort into a book and then throw it away. But now you've told me what you'll do …'

'We shall not have the courage,' he said with a laugh. 'You won't burn the manuscript of your *Mémoires*; nor will I that of my *La Route de Thebes*.'

They collected their weighty parcels and left together by carriage, chatting.

'You've taken good care not to be forgotten,' he said. 'I've never known another woman who has been talked about as much as you.'

'Mostly badly,' Céleste said drily.

'Not always. Your devilish willpower is still quite amazing, but I have none left anymore.'

'Take a rest before you write the last one.'

'I can't. Even in my sleep I'm haunted by the thought of the work I cannot finish.'

The carriage clattered on for a few minutes before he spoke, 'I don't believe in the afterlife. Do you?'

'Yes.'

'But surely with Darwin's Theory of Evolution ...'

'Oh, please! You're going with the chatter of the intellectual classes. Atheism is popular at the moment. Just a theory.'

'You believe in heaven?' he asked sceptically.

'I believe in a better world and that kind of distraction prevents it. Belief is a consolation for all human beings, since we're all condemned to die.'

'So thought of the afterlife is a comfort for you?'

'It is.'

'But it's not necessarily reality.'

'I prefer to avoid it.'

Dumas died four months later, on 27 November 1895, and never finished his final book. Céleste was devastated. She went to his home to pay her respects, placing in front of the coffin a bunch of red roses and white lilacs, the same flowers he had sent her when she came out of the nursing home. After praying for

Dumas Jr, she was about to leave when she had a shock. Facing her was a man who was the image of Dumas Sr. She wondered if she was seeing a ghost, but soon learned that the man was one of Dumas Sr's several illegitimate children.

'My heart,' she told her diary when she returned to her bedsit, 'is like a cemetery in which there is no longer room to erect anymore crosses.'

CHAPTER 53

The Extended Goodbye

Perhaps through boredom, Céleste, at seventy-three in 1898, became involved on the fringe of the so-called Dreyfus political/espionage affair which divided France (and to an extent still does). In December 1894, the month Céleste turned seventy, a young artillery officer, Alfred Dreyfus, of Alsatian and Jewish descent, was convicted of treason for allegedly passing military secrets to the German Embassy in Paris. He was sentenced to life in prison. Evidence came to light in 1896 that someone else—Ferdinand Esterhazy—was the real culprit. But high-ranking military authorities tried to suppress the new evidence and succeeded in exonerating Esterhazy in a military court, in a trial lasting just two days. Dreyfus then faced further trumped-up charges.

In 1898, famed writer Émile Zola wrote an open letter headed '*J'Accuse*' to a Paris newspaper in support of Dreyfus, and this put pressure on the government to reopen the case. In effect, from then on the public either lined up for or against Dreyfus. He was attacked by mainly anti-Jewish, anti-German, right-wing, pro-military Catholics, and supported by left-wing radical republicans. Céleste backed Édouard Drumont, who ran an anti-Semitic newspaper/propaganda sheet, *La Libre Parole*. It is not clear if she truly supported his position, although she had expressed the odd ignorant anti-Jewish stereotype, prevalent at the time, in her memoirs. Her main reason for supporting Drumont was to extract from him the 300 francs he had pocketed after promising to publish the biography of her nearly thirty years earlier. Drumont, desperate for high-profile names in his corner, agreed to pay her back the money when he could, starting with 100 francs. This put Céleste in the anti-Dreyfus camp, but when Drumont had paid back the 300 francs with interest, they had a falling out and she branded him untrustworthy. She also condemned his dirty tactics and false commentary concerning Dreyfus.[1] But she later resumed an acquaintanceship with him.

In 1899, Dreyfus faced a new trial which ended in another conviction and a ten-year sentence. But then he was given a pardon and set free. Eventually, all the accusations against him, including Drumont's specious diatribes, were found to be baseless.[2]

Céleste kept writing well into her seventies, despite some severe drawbacks such as poor eyesight and less mobility. She was surviving, though not with the zest for life that had propelled her through her turbulent existence. She could no longer afford a secretary or maid. Her friends were dying off with depressing regularity. When Michel Lévy died, she lost her biggest professional supporter and felt her writing career was finished. She kept writing her memoirs but with no enthusiasm to see them published, partly because of the negative remarks from Dumas Jr. Nevertheless, she created several more manuscripts for plays, even though theatres rejected them. Producers felt she was out of touch with the new theatre's needs and audiences.

Céleste was becoming a living apparition of the past and she knew it. One journalist in 1899 even portrayed her that way in an article he wrote in the journal entitled *Une Revenante* (a ghost), which regurgitated all the romance and the sordid details of her glory days at Mabille and the Hippodrome. Journalists were now harking back with nostalgia to a raunchier, more exciting era, and Mogador was a key symbol of it. Much to her chagrin, this was overriding her five decades of creative output. Sex and sensuality were winning out over sense and substance. Only her memoirs were being mentioned in the press and she considered them her least substantial work.

The press's attitude to Céleste, was exemplified on 1 December 1902, a few weeks before her seventy-eighth birthday when she fell down the stairs and injured her knees. This put her in hospital and once more the newspaper hyenas circled. There was a moment of pathos when she pleaded tearfully with a journalist to refer to her books and plays, her real-life profession, rather than to Mogador. She showed him her range of books. The journalist demonstrated some respect and obliged, although he could not resist dwelling on her days as a courtesan.

At eighty years of age in late 1904, she was frightened to live alone in her bedsit in an area that was becoming increasingly violent with robbery and murder. With guidance from Drumont, who seemed to have kept their link going despite their disputes over the Dreyfus affair, she applied for a room in an old people's home in Montmartre, La Providence. It was not a place for the poor or for invalids. Céleste knew and loved the lively Montmartre area, with its elevation and sloping streets that afforded wonderful views of Paris. She liked the preponderance of cafés and theatres that reminded her of her very early life in the Boulevard du Temple. She did not fancy walking up the hills, which were more like climbs for her now, especially where La Providence was situated. But this was a minor drawback. Céleste wanted to be a member of this comfortable retreat, which she knew would be her last home.[3]

She had to prove she had the income to pay the 1800 francs a year demanded for her lodging. The annual gift from the Count de Naurois, a stipend from the Society of Dramatic Authors, another annual payment from the society of composers for her many operettas and songs, some assistance from a French heiress friend Husna de Crepeney, and a final payment from Calmann-Lévy in addition to some cash in the bank got her over the line. She had enough left over for the occasional café meal out in the Paris she loved so much.

Céleste spent her final years wishing she could die rather than fade away and referred to life in general as 'this absurdity between the cradle and the grave'. But she never seriously considered committing suicide again. She had no passion for it. Nor were there the stressful circumstances which had driven her to try it earlier. She didn't even care if she was buried in the family vault with her mother and Vincent.[4]

The life of a brilliant and determined woman, 150 years ahead of her time, ended on 18 February 1909. Her tombstone at Pré-Saint-Gervais was rendered in the simple yet creative style that summarised with genius the main loves and elements of her eighty-four years. One word, CÉLESTE, adorned the marble plaque on her tomb. Below was engraved a countess's coronet pierced by a quill. There was no sign of Mogador.

Notes

All quotes, except otherwise noted, come from Céleste Vénard's memoirs and diaries.

Sources of memoirs and notes

Céleste Mogador, *Adieux au Monde, Mémoires de Céleste Mogador*, 5 vols, Locard-Davi et de Vresse, Paris, 1854.

—*Mémoires de Céleste Mogador*, 2nd edition, 4 vols, Librairie Nouvelle, Paris, 1858.

—*Mémoires de Céleste Mogador*, 3rd edition, 2 vols, Librairie Nouvelle, Paris, 1876.

—*Un Deuil au Bout du Monde, Suite de Mémoires de Céleste Mogador*, Librairie Nouvelle, Paris, 1877.

—*The French Consul's Wife: Memoirs of Céleste de Chabrillan in Gold-rush Australia*, Introduction and translation of *Un Deuil au Bout du Monde,* by Jeanne Allen & Patricia Clancy, The Miegunyah Press, Melbourne University Press, 1998.

—*Memoirs of a Courtesan in Nineteenth-century Paris*, Introduction and translation by Monique Fleury Nagem, University of Nebraska Press, Lincoln, 2001.

Chapter 2

1. Rue du Pont-aux-Choux (Street of the Bridge of Cabbages). Vegetables, including cabbages, were grown on the edge of the nearby canal. The apartment where Céleste was born and lived for the first eight years of her life still stands. An electronic sign in the window when the author researched the area said, 'Love is in the air.' Half the front door's window is ornate wrought iron.
2. The attempt on King Louis-Philippe's life was made by Corsican Giuseppe Marco Fieschi. He attacked the king with a self-built weapon made of twenty-five gun barrels fastened together. Fieschi shot from the third level of 50 Boulevard du Temple. One bullet grazed the king's forehead.

Chapter 4

1. Roland Perry, *The Queen, Her Lover and the Most Notorious Spy in History*, Allen & Unwin, Australia, 2014, p 126.

Chapter 7

1. The pseudonym of Amantine Lucille Dupin, 1804–76. She happened to be from Berry (where Count Lionel de Chabrillan had his estate south of Paris). She was famous for popular, romantic novels set in regional France.

Chapter 9

1. The Tahitian queen of the Pomare dynasty was Aimata (1813–77). She reigned as Pomare IV after her brother, the king, died.
2. Céleste received this nickname in September 1844. She was nineteen. In that year the Moroccan city of Mogador was fired on by the French fleet.

Chapter 10

1. For more on this famous theatre see Nicole Wild, 'Théâtre Beaumarchais' in *Dictionnaire de la Musique en France au XIX Siecle*, Fayard, Paris, 2003.
2. The Hippodrome was where the Place de l'Étoile is now, at the entrance to Avenue Kleber. This was one of several open-air arenas that were well patronised in Paris from 1845, when the Hippodrome began, to 1907.

Chapter 11

1. The Duke of Osuna represented Spain at the marriage of Napoleon III to the beautiful Spanish aristocrat Eugénie de Montijo in 1853. Spanish writer Juan Valera wrote of the way Mariano's extravagance reached a pinnacle from 1856 (when aged forty-two) to 1862 in St Petersburg, where he made a huge effort to spend his enormous wealth on wine, women and roulette. At fifty-one, he finally deigned to marry a German princess less than half his age, and they had no children. After a life of degeneracy and monumental self-indulgence, he died, aged sixty-seven, in 1882 (Nicolas Hobbs, *Grandes de España*, in periodic publication, Instituto de Salazar y Castro, Spain, 2007).

Chapter 14

1. Berry is a province in central France. The Chabrillans were pretenders to the throne of Monaco in the twentieth century.

Chapter 15

1. The marquis was sixty years of age, which was not young in the 1840s.

Chapter 19

1. The barricade was at the end of Rue des Filles-du-Calvaire.

Chapter 21

1. Cholera has been a scourge throughout world history. Descriptions of it were found in the fifth century BC in Sanskrit. Study by the British physician John Snow from 1849 (the year the maid Caroline contracted the disease) to 1854 led to significant advances in epidemiology. An effective oral vaccine was only created in the second half of the twentieth century. Cholera still affects up to five million people annually and up to 130,000 die from it.

Chapter 23

1. Presuming this directive to mean for quite a long time, the Jew, Ahasuerus, found himself propelled by an unseen force that would not let him find a place to rest.

Chapter 26

1. The philosophical works of Jean-Jacques Rousseau (1722–78) were among the most influential in the world in the eighteenth century and continue to be so. They included *The Social Contract* and *Émile*, both published in 1762.

Chapter 27

1. Alexandre Dumas Jr's 1848 novel *La Dame aux Camélias* was adapted into Verdi's celebrated opera *La Traviata*.
2. Prince Napoleon, or Joseph Charles Paul (1822–91), was the son of Napoleon's brother, Jerome, King of Westphalia. He was an arts patron, and his fortnightly dinners at the restaurant Voisin were legendary for their glamorous guests.

Chapter 29

1. Alexandre Dumas Jr 1824–95 was the illegitimate son of Alexandre Dumas and dress-maker Marie-Laure-Catherine Labay. His father took him from his mother and educated him. The distress this caused Dumas Jr saw him write about tragic female characters. In his play *The Illegitimate* he expressed the belief that if a father sired a child, he should marry the mother. He wrote twenty-five plays, one unfinished, and fifteen books.

Chapter 30

1. Edgar Holt, *Plon-Plon, The Life of Prince Napoleon*, Michael Joseph, UK, 1973, pp 72–3.
2. Françoise Moser, *Life and Adventures of Céleste Mogador* (*Vie et Aventures de Céleste Mogador*), Albin Michel, Paris, 1935, pp 143–4.

Chapter 31

1. Françoise Moser, *Life and Adventures of Céleste Mogador* (*Vie et Aventures de Céleste Mogador*), Albin Michel, Paris, 1935, p 147. Also Roland Perry, *The Queen, Her Lover and the Most Notorious Spy in History*, Allen & Unwin, Sydney, 2014.

Chapter 35

1. The book caused a big stir in Paris, but nothing in Melbourne to begin with, despite Céleste's dramatic claims in her memoirs about Lionel reading newspaper accounts of it in local papers before he even disembarked in Melbourne. The morning paper had only a reference to the *Croesus* being late. But contrary to the account in her memoirs, there were no alarms in *The Argus* or *The Age* about the ship being lost and all on board presumed drowned. Céleste's memoirs imagined obituaries for the count and references to his notorious wife. They were never written or published. Using dramatic licence, she spiced up the memoirs occasionally but not enough to destroy their integrity or credibility. It seemed part of her prejudice, based on ignorance, about the locals and her own insecurity about being married to a count.
2. From 1851 to 1857 there were mass desertions to the goldfields. At one point in 1854, ninety-seven vessels coming from Hong Kong and England did not have enough sailors to leave port. In the end, shipping companies were offering sailors as much as seventy-five pounds for the return trip to first entice them to make the outward journey, and second, influence them to make the return trip. Even so, once boats reached Australia, there were thousands of desertions over the decade until 1860.
3. A palanquin—a carriage for 'important people'—is a covered seat on poles carried by four men.
4. Where Princes Bridge at Flinders Street is situated now.

Chapter 36

1. Baroche redeemed his somewhat idle, under-achieving image (compared with his high-profile politician father) when he joined the Franco-Prussian War in 1870 in command of a battalion of 5000 soldiers. He died in action leading his men into battle. Victor Hugo

delivered a back-handed remark when he said, 'On that day, the death of the son made one forget the life of the father.' (See the *Dictionary of French Biography*.)

Chapter 37

1. Céleste's second set of memoirs were derived from her copious notes on her trip to Australia and the two and a half years she spent there. She called them *Un Deuil au Bout du Monde—A Bereavement (or Death) at the End of the World.* This had a double meaning. She had a passionate hatred of Victoria. In one sense she meant that it was akin to death to be there. In another, she was thinking about her husband, who is buried in Melbourne. The book was published in 1877, two decades after the experience, which meant she had time to reflect on her diary entries and compose her work with hindsight and a little 'shaping' of the narrative and editorial, assisted by the newspaper clippings she collected. Some experiences of other people reported on in her second book were included as if they were hers.
2. There are no reports of this incident in any papers in Ballarat or Melbourne. No pictures were published. Patricia Clancy and Jeanne Allen in their introduction to *The French Consul's Wife* appear rightly sceptical about this mine 'event'. They point out that the governor's wife, Lady Hotham, was widely praised when she and her husband visited in early September 1854. Was Céleste's entry a fabrication? Possibly, and she may well have had enough English to read the newspaper accounts and 'incorporate' them into a personal account. However, she did visit the goldfields on several occasions. It was fashionable (and still is) for visitors to be taken down the mines.
3. The count's proclamation appeared at Sovereign Hill, Eureka, on 3 December 1854.
4. There was conjecture over whether or not the drummer boy, John Egan, had actually died. Some reports suggested he died much later, in 1860, because of injuries sustained in the battle with miners. A memorial was erected to him in Ballarat Cemetery, and remained there for fifty years after the incident.

Chapter 38

1. Before Australia, Antoine Fauchery fought in Poland in 1848 and was imprisoned in Magdeburg. In 1852 he sailed for Melbourne on the *Emily* and joined the gold rush at Ballarat. After his café venture, he returned to the goldfields as a store owner at Daylesford. This venture

also fell well short of profitability so he returned to France in 1857. His only modest 'success' was to published eight *Letters from a Miner in Australia* in serial form in *Le Moniteur Universal.* On returning to Paris, he edited the letters into a book published by Poulet-Malassis et de Broise. It gave an intense and colourful view of Melbourne and the goldfields. He then gained a grant from the French Government for an official photographic assignment to India, Australia and China.

Fauchery returned to Melbourne with his wife. In 1858 he worked at a Collins Street studio and published *Sun Pictures of Victoria.* He later wrote *Letters from China* (*Lettres de Chine*), which was where his charmed, struggling yet up-beat life ended in 1861 after a short illness.

2. Joanna Richardson, *The Courtesans*, Castle Books, New Jersey, 2004.

Chapter 41

1. Writer and poet Henri Murger had presented a Left Bank student's tale of a prostitute, *grisette*, in his book *Scenes de la Vie de Bohème.* It was the basis for the opera *La Bohème* by Puccini.

Chapter 47

1. The Belleville Theatre at 94 Rue de Belleville still operates, on a smaller, more modest scale, in a down-market part of the Belleville district.

Chapter 48

1. Bizet and Céleste met in 1865 and remained good friends for life. He struggled for another seven years until 1872, when he wrote the music for Alphonse Daudet's play, *L'Arlésienne*, before creating his best known opera, *Carmen.*
2. Even today there is a certain snobbery from French aristocratic ranks concerning Céleste. In their eyes, someone with her background has no right to break into their circle. There is disregard for her achievements and exceptional life.
3. According to Moser, the mini-biography was published by La Hune but no date or detail is given.

Chapter 50

1. ZED, *La Société Parisienne*, Librairie Illustrée, France, 1888, pp 94–5.
2. Maxime du Camp, *Paris Ses Organes, Ses Fonctions et Sa Vie dans la Second Moitié du XIXe siècle*, vol 3, Hachette, France, 1876, p 453.

Chapter 51

1. Paul England, *Fifty Favourite Operas*, Bonanza Books (Crown), New York, 1985, p 436.
2. *The New Grove Dictionary of Music and Musicians*, Oxford University Press, UK, vol 2, p 755.

Chapter 52

1. Alexandre Dumas Jr's last work, *La Route de Thebes*, was never finished. Céleste kept diaries from 1895 until her death. They were repetitious and disclosed nothing new.

Chapter 53

1. Françoise Moser, *Life and Adventures of Céleste Mogador* (*Vie et Aventures de Céleste Mogador*), Albin Michel, Paris, 1935, pp 242–3.
2. In 1906 Dreyfus was exonerated and reinstated as a major in the French Army. He served throughout the Great War (1914–18) and ended his service as a Lieutenant-Colonel. He died aged seventy-six in 1935.
3. La Providence still stands and remains a notable old persons' home. It has recently been refurbished and is known as La Providence Maison de Retraite. Montmartre is now thriving more than ever and the area is one of Paris's main tourist attractions. It is a short walk from Paris's red-light district Pigalle and the Moulin Rouge.
4. Céleste's remains were exhumed in 1993 and placed in the cemetery at Poinçonnet. The local Historical Society thought it appropriate, given her life and relationship with Count Lionel. Perhaps it was also because she had expressed such anguish at being in the same burial place as the hated Vincent.

Céleste Vénard, Countess de Chabrillan

Céleste Mogador, *Memoirs of a Courtesan in Nineteenth-century Paris*, University of Nebraska, 2001.

Adieux au Monde, Mémoires de Céleste Mogador, 5 vols, Locard-Davi et de Vresse, Paris, 1854.

Mémoires de Céleste Mogador, 2nd edition, 4 vols, Librairie Nouvelle, Paris, 1858.

Mémoires de Céleste Mogador, 3rd edition, 2 vols, Librairie Nouvelle, Paris, 1876.

Un Deuil au Bout du Monde, Suite de Mémoires de Céleste Mogador, Librairie Nouvelle, Paris, 1877.

NOVELS

Les Voleurs d'Or, Michel Lévy, Paris, 1857. Translation: Lucy and Caroline Moorehead.

The Gold Thieves, Sun Books, Melbourne, 1970.

La Sapho, Michel Lévy, Paris, 1858.

Miss Pewell, A. Bourdilliat, Paris, 1859.

Est-il Fou?, A. Bourdilliat, Paris, 1860.

Un Miracle à Vichy, Vichy Bougagard fils, 1861.

Mémoires d'une Honnête Fille, A. Faure, Paris, 1865.

Les Deux Soeurs Emigree et Deportees, Calmann-Lévy, Paris, 1876.

Une Méchante Femme, Calmann-Lévy, Paris, 1877.

La Duchess des Mers, Calmann-Lévy, Paris, 1881.

Les Forçats de l'Amour, Calmann-Lévy, Paris, 1881.

Marie Baude, Calmann-Lévy, Paris, 1883.

Un Drame sur la Tage, Calmann-Lévy, Paris, 1885.

PLAYS

Bonjour au Vaincu, 1 act, Théâtre des Champs-Élysées, Paris, 19 April 1862.

En Australie, 1 act vaudeville, Théâtre des Champs-Élysées, Paris, 1862.

Quarelle d'Allemond, 1 act, Théâtre des Champs-Élysées, Paris, 28 October 1863.

Les Voleurs d'Or, 1 act, Théâtre de Belleville, Paris, 28 May 1864.

L'Armour de l'Art, Théâtre des Folies-Marigny, Paris, Alcan-Lévy, 4 June 1865.

Chambre à Louer, 1 act, Théâtre des Folies-Marigny, Paris, 20 October 1865.

Un Homme Compromis, 1 act, Théâtre des Folies-Marigny, Paris, Alcan-Lévy, 4 September 1865, 1868.

Les Crimes de la Mer, 5 acts, Théâtre de Belleville, Paris, 8 May 1869, Morris pere et fils, 1869.

Les Revers de l'Amour, 5 acts, Théâtre des Nouveautés, Paris, 3 April 1870.

L'Américaine, 5 acts, Théâtre des Nouveautés, Paris, 3 April 1870.

La Plaideuse, 1 act, Théâtre de l'Ambigu-Comique, Paris, 26 December 1874.

L'Ambition Fatale, 5 acts, Théâtre Beaumarchais, Paris, 15 April 1875.

Le Bonnet d'Une, 1 act, Paris, 1876.

Entre Deux Balcons, Théâtre des Fantaisies-Parisiennes, Paris, 7 March 1880.

Ma'am Nicole, 3 acts, Théâtre des Folies-Dramatiques, Paris, 4 July 1880.

L'Armour et la Rose, 3 acts, Théâtre des Arts, Paris, 1880.

Pierre Pascal, 5 acts, Théâtre de l'Ambigu-Comique, Paris, Paris, 4 August 1885.

Cordon, Revue, Théâtre Pépinière, Paris, 26 December 1886.

OPERETTAS

Nedel, 1 act, Théâtre des Champs-Élysées, Paris, 23 May 1863.

Militairement, 1 act, Théâtre des Champs-Élysées, Paris, 28 October 1863.

En Garde, 1 act, Théâtre des Champs-Élysées, Paris, 14 January 1864.

Les Pierrots en Cage, 1 act, Théâtre des Folies-Marigny, Paris, 9 September 1865.

A la Bretonne, 1 act, Théâtre des Folies-Marigny, Paris, 10 September 1868.

La Tiretire d'Yvonne, 1 act, Paris.

Note: Céleste wrote twelve poems and seventeen songs.

Bibliography

Adcock, W.E., *The Gold Rush of the Fifties*, W. Cole, Melbourne, 1912.

Allen, Jeanne and Clancy, Patricia, *The French Consul's Wife*, Melbourne University Press, Melbourne, 2003.

Chisholm, A.R., 'Céleste de Chabrillan and the Gold Rush', *Meanjin Quarterly*, Australia, June 1969, pp 197–207.

Clarietie, Jules, *La Vie a Paris*, Charpentier, Paris, 1907.

Claudin, Gustav, *Mesn Souvenirs, Les Boulevards de 1840–1870*, Calmann-Lévy, 1884.

Diguet, Charles, *Les Jolies Femmes de Paris*, Librairie Internationale, Paris, 1870.

Du Camp, Maxime, *Paris, Ses Organes, Ses Fonctions et Sa Vie Dans la Second moitié du XIXe Siècle*, Hachette, Paris, 1876.

Dumas, Alexandre, (Junior fils), *La Dame aux Camélias*, 4th edition, Michel Lévy, Paris, 1852.

Girardin, Mme Émile de, *Le Vicomte de Launay, Lettres Parisennes*, Michel Lévy, Paris, 1852.

Haldene, Charlotte, *Daughter of Paris*, Hutchinson, London, 1961.

Holt, Edgar, *Plon-Plon: The Life of Prince Napoleon*, Michael Joseph, London, 1973.

Leclerq, Pierre-Robert, *Céleste Mogador, Une Reine de Paris, Biographie*, Hutchinson, London, 1961.

Montez, Lola, *Lectures of Lola*, CC Bart (editor/writer), Woodfall & Kinder, London, 1858.

Moser, Françoise, *Life and Adventures of Céleste Mogador* (*Vie et Aventures de Céleste Mogador*), Albin Michel, Paris, 1935.

Perry, Roland, *The Queen, Her Lover and the Most Notorious Spy in History*, Allen & Unwin, Sydney, 2014.

Richardson, Joanna, *The Courtesans*, Castle Books, New Jersey, 2004.

Seymour, Bruce, *Lola Mentez, A Life*, Yale University Press, London, 1996.

Wild, Nicole, 'Théâtre Beaumarchais' in *Dictionnaire de la Musique en France au XIX Siècle*, Fayard, Paris, 2003.

ZED, *La Société Parisienne*, Librairie Illustree, Paris, 1888.

1848 Revolution 141–5, 154–5, 159

The 1852 Revue 213

Index

Note: C = Céleste.
An 'n' after a page number indicates an endnote.

A

Adele (maid) 172
Aden 301
Adet, Édouard 303
Adieux au Monde: Mémoires de Céleste Mogador 200–1, 204–5, 219, 239, 248–9, 261, 280, 284–7, 309
Adolphe (C's boyfriend) 59–60, 62–3, 65–7, 74–5, 78
The Age 304
Aimata 368n
Alain (C's father) 15
Alain, M. (proxy manager) 318–20, 322
Albert, Prince 30
Alex (Denise Onze's boyfriend) 50, 60
Alsace 347, 351
L'Alternative du Paradis (brothel) 40, 44–8
Ambition Fatale 350
L'Ami des Femmes 320
The Argus 271
aristocrats 90, 113
Aumont, Louisa 66–7, 72–5
Australasian (ship) 302
Avenue de Saint-Cloud 212

B

Bakery Hill, Victoria 258
Bal Mabille 69–71, 75–6
Ballarat 253–5, 257–60, 269–70
Ballarat Reform League 258–9
Ballarat Times 269
Baroche, Ernest 250, 261–2, 370n
Bastille Day Ball 267
Batavia (ship) 335
Bathurst 208–9
Beaujon Hospice 168
Belgium 326
Bell, Sally 269–70
Belleville Theatre 372n
Bellevue Theatre 326
Bellinger, Augustine 319
Bell's Life in Sydney 265
Benard, Michelle 24, 29, 35
Bentley, James 257–8
Béranger, Pierre-Jean 212
Berry
- during 1848 Revolution 145
- C convalesces in 294
- C stays at convent in 309
- C's sense of isolation at 246
- Dumas on 298
- as home of de Chabrillan family 368n
- Lionel helps stonemason from 244
- Lionel organises house in Poinçonnet for C 188, 204, 211–12
- Lionel's country estate in 128, 135, 175

Bertrand, Jacques 217
Bettini, M. (opera singer) 91–3, 96–8, 104
biography 335
Bismarck, Otto von *see* von Bismarck, Otto
Bizet, Georges 3, 329–30, 349–50, 352, 372n
Bonaparte, Josephine 64
Bonaparte, Louis Napoleon *see* Napoleon III
Bonheur aux Vaincus 319
Bordeaux 221, 308
Boulevard du Crime, Paris 14
Boulevard Poissonnière 173
Bourdilliat, M. (publisher) 204, 219–20, 309
Bourges 212
Bresival (gambler) 150
Brididi (dancer) 71–4, 112
brothels 42

C

Café Anglais 1, 78, 112–14, 206
Café-Concert du XIXé 332
Café de France 142
Café Estaminet, Melbourne 263–4
Calmann-Lévy 354, 356, 358–9, 365
cancan 76
Cape of Good Hope 236
Cape Town 238
Carmen 349, 352
Caroline (maid) 167–71
Cavaignac, General Louis 155
Chalet des Fleurs 355–6
Chalet Lionel 328, 345
Chartists 145, 258
Châteauroux 135, 295–6
La Chaumière 58–9
Chaumont, Céline 320
Chinatown, Melbourne 251
Chincholle, Charles 357–8
cholera 169–70, 369n
Chopin, Frédéric 78
Collingwood, Melbourne 243–4
A Compromised Man 321, 332
copyright 354–5
courtesans 67, 90–1
Couture, Thomas 3, 212
Crédit Foncier 345
Crimes at Sea 335
Les Crimes de la Mer 335
Croesus (ship) 227–30, 232–8, 250, 370n

D

d'Agoult, Marie, Countess 264
Les Dames aux Camelias 204
dance halls 69–71, 76, 269
dancing 196, 265
dandies 112–13
Daudet, Alphonse 372n
de Brillard, Mademoiselle 164–5
de Chabrillan, Lionel, Count (C's husband)
  arrives in Paris from Melbourne 291–2
  asks C to live with him 158
  business dealings 262–3
  C sends ornaments for grave of 308
  cares for C during sickness 134–5, 295
  challenges reporter to a duel 271
  compliments C on her writing 303
  confronts Richard Maylam 190
  contracts dysentery 301–3

courts C 121–4, 126–7
death 303–4, 306–7
decides to try fortune in Australia 197–8, 208–9
discusses memoirs with C 249
draws up marriage contract 221
falls ill 187–8
financial woes 145–6, 157–8, 175–6, 194–5, 274–6, 281, 288
as French Consul in Melbourne 218–19, 231, 243–4, 251–2, 258–60, 264, 267–8, 271, 280, 302–3
friendship arrangement with C 188–9
gains leave due to C's efforts 282–3
gives C ivory crucifix 278, 331
gives condolences to Lady Hotham 268
has tombstone made for Duke d'Esclignac 244
insists on dismissing maid 163
insults C 193
joins National Guard 144, 154
keeps second mistress 122–3, 125, 132
life with C at the chateau 160–3
life with C in Melbourne 240–3
marries C in London 222–6
meets C 115–18
moves to Victoria Heights 245
obliged to go to ball without C 263
opens office in Collins Street 260
persuades C to return to him 173–5
persuades Montez to flee 270
placates peasants 146
plans to marry without telling C 164–5
pressured by family to leave C 162–3
proposes marriage to C 197, 217–18, 220
reads C's novels 293
receives inheritance 130
rescues C from oafs 4, 115–16
returns to Ballarat 258–9
returns to Melbourne 296–8
returns to Paris from Australia 214–17
rides from Sydney to Bathurst 208–9
sails to Melbourne with C 227–39
seeks out C's detractors 271
separates from C 165–6
sets up C in an apartment in Paris 163
sets up house for C in Poinçonnet 188–9
spurned by family after marriage 294–5
in Sydney 208
takes C out to dinner 119–21
takes C to his castle 135–9
takes Charlotte Odene as mistress 190, 192, 194
turns up in Paris unannounced 133–4, 144
vicissitudes of love 181, 183–5, 190–1, 208–9
wounded by C 193–4
de Chabrillan, Louise, Marquise 283, 292, 295

de Chabrillan, Marie-Olivier, Marquis 117, 188, 223, 311–14
de Chabrillan, Marquis 128
de Choiseul-Praslin, M. (murderer) 312
de Crepeney, Husna 365
de Girardin, Delphine 200
de Girardin, Émile 200, 219, 314, 339
de Lesseps, Ferdinand-Marie, Viscount 282, 310–11, 314
de Maugny, Albert, Count 344
de Maupassant, Guy 359
de Montijo, Eugénie 368n
de Motholon-Sémoulville, Countess 294
de Musset, Alfred 3, 51–7, 160, 352
de Napoli, Roland, Count 116
Death at the End of the World 350–1, 371n
Deburau, M. (mime artist) 318
d'Esclignac, Duke 240, 244
Deslions, Anna 319
Desmarest, Maitre
  as C's lawyer 198–9, 210–12, 219, 279–80, 284–6
  encourages C to write memoirs 198–200
  reads C's letter in paper 339
  relationship with C 210, 323, 337, 353
Un Deuil au Bout du Monde 350–1, 371n
d'Haussonville, Count 351
Diggers' Right Society 258
Doucet, Camille 200, 356
Dresden 264
Dreyfus affair 362–3
Dreyfus, Alfred 362–3, 373n
Drumont, Édouard 335, 363–4
du Camp, Maxime 344–5
Dumas, Alexandre Jr
  adapts novel for opera 369n
  advises C not to publish final memoirs 363
  advises C to seek admission to home 356–7
  attends *The 1852 Revue* 213
  C's impressions of 212
  death 360–1
  literary output 369n
  meets C in old age 359–60
  opposes rule of Napoleon III 250
  pays for C's convalescence in Maison Dubois 355
  raised by father 369n
  relationship with C 320–1
  reviews C's performance 213
  suggests C sell her copyright 354
  as a writer 204
Dumas, Alexandre Sr
  advises C to try writing fiction 203, 253, 255
  C rejects advances of 298–300
  C sees illegitimate child of 361
  consulted by C for literary advice 314–15
  death 341
  dramatises C's novel 324–5
  encourages C as a writer 287
  gives C advice about publication of memoirs 220
  opposes rule of Napoleon III 250
  reads C's manuscript 200
  relationship with C 202–3, 208
  relationship with Lola Montez 265

reviews C's novel 204, 290
success as a writer 202
visits C during illness 298–9
Dupin, Amantine Lucille 368n
Duplessis, Marie 204

E

Edmond, Charles 280–1
Egan, John 371n
The Emigrants 291
En Australie 321
Encore Moi 334
England, Paul 349
Equator ritual 234, 240
Esterhazy, Ferdinand 362
Eureka Hotel, Ballarat 257–8
Eureka Stockade 258–60, 268

F

The Fair Maid of Perth 329
Farewell to the World: The Memoirs of Céleste Mogador 200–1, 204–5, 219, 239, 248–9, 261, 280, 284–7, 309
Fauchery, Antoine 263–4, 271, 277, 303–4, 307, 371–2n
Favre, Jules 338, 342
Ferry, Gabriel 290
Fieschi, Giuseppe Marco 367n
Fifty Favourite Operas 349
Le Figaro 357
financial speculation 262–3
Flaubert, Gustave 290
Fournier, Marc 305–6, 315–16
France
1848 Revolution 141–5, 154–5, 159
coup d'état by Louis Napoleon 205
Dreyfus affair 362–3
Franco-Prussian War 337–45
Paris Commune 343–4
Second Empire 338, 344
Second Republic 141, 154
Third Republic 338
Franco-Prussian War 337–45
Françoise (courtesan) 92–3
Freemasons Ball 267
French Army 343
French Consulate, London 225–6
Frisette (C's friend) 1–2, 112, 116, 129–30, 142–3, 148

G

Gaîté Theatre 316
Gambetta, Léon 338, 342
gambling 126–7, 148–53
Gatineau, Louise Josephine 264
Georges (Lionel's friend) 129–30
Gervex, Henri 3, 352
Gilbert, Marie *see* Montez, Lola
gold rushes, Australia 198, 208–9, 370n
The Gold Thieves 272–3, 280–1, 288–91, 293, 303, 315–16, 324–6, 332, 351, 354
Grace (horse) 87–8
Grand Imperial Hotel, Melbourne 270
The Great Britain (ship) 246–7
Guichard, Robert 79–80
Guizot, François 143

H

Harmant, M. (theatre director) 316
Heaven's Alternative (brothel) 40, 44–8
Henri (Lionel's friend) 129–30
Hervé (composer) 321
Hippodrome 80–8, 94–6, 98–100, 102–3, 320, 368n

Hirondelle (ship) 251
Holacher, M. (theatre manager) 324–5, 335
Holland 326
Un Homme Compromis 321, 332
horse racing 80–8, 94–6, 98–100, 102–3
Hotham, Sir Charles 259, 263
Hotham, Lady Jane 268, 371n
Hughes, John 255–7
Hugo, Victor 370–1n
Humffray, John 258

I

L'Illustration 309
In Australia 321
Is He Mad? 309

J

James Baines (ship) 278–9, 331
Janin, Jules 291
Jean (Russian prince) 131, 133–4, 140–2
Jerome, King of Westphalia 369n
Jockey Club, Paris 125
Jocottet, M. (publisher) 219
La Jolie Fille de Perth 329
Josephine (C's friend) 92
Judith (actress) 313
July Monarchy 141

L

Lachmann, Thérèse 172
Lalor, Peter 260
Lassagne, Alphonse 181
Laurence (C's benefactor) 60–2
Laurent, Franconi 81–4
le Grand, Toulouse 65
Le Havre 140, 247
Le Marais, Paris 13, 155
Le Vésinet 328, 331, 342–3, 345, 351, 353–5
lecture tour 345–6
lesbianism 29–30, 50
Letessier, Caroline 172
Lévy, Michael
  buys C's first novel 280–1
  buys C's second novel 291
  C sells copyright of work to 354
  death 363
  Murger complains to 287
  sponsors C's application to home 356, 358
Librairie Nouvelle 204, 219, 284, 309
La Libre Parole 363
Lionel, Madame 320, 332
Liouville, Maitre 284–5
Lisbon 228, 232
Liszt, Franz 264–5
litigation 210–12, 279–80, 285–6, 288
London 184–6, 222–6
Lorraine 347, 351
Louis-Phillipe, King of France 15, 64, 141, 145, 367n
Lusignan, Princess 336
Lyon 10–11

M

Madame Bovary 290
Maison d'Or 174
Maison Dubois 350
Malmaison 64
M'ame Nicole 353
Manceau, Louis-Édouard 243–4
Manet, Édouard 212
Maria II, Queen of Portugal 232
Marie (maid 1) 105, 108, 134, 138, 155, 162–3

Marie (maid 2) 222, 241, 244–5, 250, 276, 278
Marie Baud 355
Martin (Lionel's friend) 133–4, 136–7
Maylam, Richard 172–4, 180, 182–8, 190–2, 194
mazurka 78–9
Melbourne 238, 240–6, 250–1, 263–4, 266–7, 319–20
The Memoirs of Céleste Mogador 200–1, 204–5, 219, 239, 248–9, 261, 280, 284–7, 309
Mettray 286
Militairement 321
miners 253–5, 257–60, 269
Miss Pewell 291
Mogador (C's stage name) 74, 76, 79, 320, 368n
Mont Saint Michel 36
Monte Cristo (journal) 290
Montez, Lola 264–6, 269–71
Montmartre 364–5, 373n
Moser, Françoise 225
Mourier, M. 178–81, 196
Le Mousquetaire 204
Mullois, Father 286–7
Mureut, Jacques 251
Murger, Henry 204, 287, 372n
My History 265–6

N

Napoleon III (Louis Napoleon Bonaparte)
  captured by Prussians 338
  declines C's request 308
  Dumas opposes rule of 220
  flower display in honour of 267
  marries Eugénie 368n
  organises coup d'état 205
  reads C's memoirs 286–7
Napoleon, Prince (Plon-Plon)
  attends C's party 212
  C solicits support of 262
  declines to help C in bid to stop publication 220–1
  helps C remove name from register 206–7
  holds fortnightly dinners 369n
  opposes C's marriage to Lionel 220
  as Queen Victoria's confidante 225
  relationship with C 206, 208, 313
  secures temporary annulment of contract 280
  supports C's theatre venture 318–19
  warns Lionel about C's memoirs 248
National Guard 144, 154, 338, 343
Naurois, Count de 336–8, 345–7, 351–3, 365
New South Wales 198
novels *see* writing

O

Odene, Charlotte 190, 192, 194
Odry, Jacques 181
On Guard 321, 332
Onyx (ship) 251
Onze, Denise
  accompanies C to registry 47
  asks Madam for more freedom 58
  farewells C 34
  introduces C to life as a prostitute 45–6, 49–51

relationship with C 27–30, 121–2
suggests C consider prostitution 30–1, 34
visited by C before death 195
opera 349
Opéra-Comique 349
operettas 321
L'Opinion Nationale 336
orphanage, at Le Vésinet 347, 351
Orsuna, Duke of *see* Téllez-Girón, Mariano, Duke of Osuna
Ozy, Alice 172

P

Page, Adele 196, 228, 319
Paris 13–159, 163–221, 279–365
Paris Commune 343–4
Passage de l'Opera 353, 356
Passage du Havre 214
Paul, Joseph Charles *see* Napoleon, Prince
Paurent-Pichat, Léon 291
Pearl, Cora 319
The Pearl Fishers 330
Les Pêcheurs de Perles 330
Pederlini, M. (opera singer) 91
Pedro (horse) 82–5
La Pepine 148–51, 153
Peragallo, M. (Society of Authors) 315–17
photography 355
Pierre Pascal 357
Place de la Madeleine 122
plays *see* writing
Plessis, Alphonsine 172
Plon-Plon *see* Napoleon, Prince
Poinçonnet
C convalesces at 295
C mortgages house at 316
C sells house and pays off mortgage 318
C tries to sell house at 304, 314
C's remains placed in 373n
house seized by creditors 195, 204, 211
Lionel organises house for C in 188–9
polka 72–3
Pomare *see* Sergent, Lise
Port Phillip Bay 238
Porte Saint-Martin Theatre 305
Pré-Saint-Gervais cemetery 365
La Presse 219, 280, 290, 314, 339
prostitutes, life of 1–4, 49–51
prostitutes' register 88, 178, 206–7, 332–3
La Providence 364–5, 373n
Prussian-French War 337–46
public execution, Melbourne 256–7
publishing 204–5, 281, 309, 354

Q

Queen's Theatre Royal, Melbourne 267

R

Raoul (factory owner) 7–11
Rede, Robert 258–60
reformatories 286–7
Regnier, M. (magistrate) 35, 46–7
Les Revers de l'Amour 336
Revue de Paris 291
Rolla (painting) 3, 352
Romantic Age 172
Roqueplan, Nestor 290
Rousseau, Jean-Jacques 369n
La Route de Thebes 359

Royal Commission on goldfield issues 259
Royal Melbourne Hospital 243
Rue d'Alger 279
Rue de la Chaussée-d'Antin 204
Rue de l'Arcade 148, 151
Rue de Londres, 42 158
Rue du Pont-aux-Choux 367n
Rue Geoffroy-Marie, Paris 105
Rue Joubert 204–5

S

Sabatier, Apollonie 172
Saint-Lazare Prison, Paris 23–35
Saint-Louis Hospital, Paris 61
Sand, George 52, 160, 212
Sandridge 239
Sapho 291, 293
Scènes de la Vie Bohème 204
Scobie, James 257
Scott, Sir Walter 329
Second Empire 338, 344
Second Republic 141, 154
Sedan 338
Seekamp, Harry 269–70
Senard, Maitre 285
Sergent, Lise (Pomare) 71, 75–6, 98, 109–11
shipwrecks 251, 335
singing 332–3
Smith, John Thomas 267
Snow, John 369n
Society of Dramatic Authors 315–16, 356, 365
Les Soeurs de France 339–40, 342
Soirit, M. (soldier) 302
Solange (C's goddaughter)
accompanies C back to Paris 276–8
accompanies C to Australia 230, 238, 241
accompanies C to London 222
C pays for boarding school for 323
C stays at convent of 309
C takes responsibility for 177, 205, 218, 279
circumstances of birth 168–71
disappears during war 343
helps to run house in
Melbourne 245
holidays with C and Lionel in Paris 293
invited to live at Le Vésinet with C 328
placed in convent by C 280
sent to Le Vésinet during war 338
tutored by C 267
South Africa 238
Sri Lanka 301–2
St Francis' Cathedral, Melbourne 304
St Kilda, Melbourne 246–7, 261
suicide 107–8, 323
Sydney 208–9
Sydney Morning Herald 265

T

Tayleur (ship) 251
Téllez-Girón, Mariano, Duke of Osuna 89–91, 96–8, 104, 368n
The Hague 104, 119
theatre
C appears in dance revue 78–9
C as theatre manager and producer 318–23
C begins work as an actress 177–81
C collaborates with Adele Page 196

C performs at Café-Concert du XIXé 332
Dumas reviews C's performance 213
effect of Franco-Prussian War on 337
Folies-Marigny produces four of C's plays 331–2
production of *Ambition Fatale* 350
production of *Crimes at Sea* 335
production of *M'ame Nicole* 353–4
production of *Pierre Pascal* 357
production of *The Gold Thieves* 324–6
production of *Troubles in Love* 336
Théâtre Beaumarchais 78–9, 350
Théâtre de l'Ambigu 357
Théâtre des Champs-Élysées 321
Théâtre des Folie-Dramatiques 178, 180–1, 189, 196, 354
Théâtre des Nouveautés 336–7, 345
Théâtre des Variétés 196, 212
Théâtre Folies-Marigny 318, 321, 324, 331
Thiers, Alfred 344
Third Republic 338
transport, in Melbourne 250–1
Trochu, Louis-Jules 338, 342
Troubles in Love 336
The Two Sisters 350

V

Valera, Juan 368n
Vénard, Anne-Victoire (C's mother)
attends horse-race to see C 99–100
C arranges aged care home for 347
C checks on during Paris riot 155–6
C makes plans to look after 323
C sets up tobacco shop for 189
C supports financially 327
closes dress shop 129
death 347
finds apprenticeship for C 18–19
has premonition 306–7
invited to live at Le Vésinet with C 328–9
learns of C's decision to become a prostitute 46–7
lives in C's house 249
moves to Paris 13–14
negativity of irks C 249, 305
opens dress shop with C 105, 109
opposes C going to Australia 305
persuades Lionel to eat 295
prevents C from returning to Melbourne 298
relationship with Guy Vénard 5–12
relationship with Vincent 16–19, 28–9, 33–4, 37–42, 129, 249
remains dumbstruck at dinner 300
secures C's release from prison 31–5
tips night bucket on Bizet 330
visits C after accident 101–2
visits C in Paris 279

visits dying father 20
writes complaining letter to C 249
Vénard, Guy 5–12
Versailles 64, 342
Victoria (Australia) 198, 231
Victoria Heights, Melbourne 245
Victoria Parade, Melbourne 256
Victoria, Queen of Great Britain and Ireland 2, 30, 145, 225, 267
Villers-Cotterêts 341
Vincent (mason)
buried in family vault by C's mother 327, 347
C has crush on 15–16
C's mother listens secretly to 38–9
death 327
encounters C after riot 156
lies to C's mother 33–4, 37–8
lodges in same building as C 14–15
maltreatment of C by 19–20, 22, 28–9, 39, 41
reassures C after assassination attempt 14–15
relationship with C's mother 16–19, 28–9, 33–4, 37–42, 129, 249
rents apartment from C's mother 189
tries to marry C off 41
von Bismarck, Otto 337, 342

W
Weber, Madame (pianist) 231–2
women, social position of 42, 318
women's corp, Franco-Prussian War 339–41
writing
C considers transition to playwriting 305–6
Dumas advises C to try writing fiction 203, 253, 255
memoirs 200–1, 204–5, 219, 239, 248–9, 261, 280–1, 284–7, 309, 350, 358–9
novels 272–3, 280–1, 287–91, 293, 301, 303, 309, 350, 355
plays 287, 305–6, 315, 319–21, 331–2, 335–6, 346, 350, 353–4, 357, 363–4

Z
Zizi 122–3, 125, 132
Zola, Émile 362

Acknowledgements

My attention was drawn to Céleste Vénard in 1990 by the late filmmaker Tim Burstall, who suggested I write her biography. I prepared a proposal, which was rejected in 1999 by a French literary agent, whose cryptic comment was that the courtesan period of ascendency, 1830–1870, has been 'done to death' and 'who was interested in Melbourne's "Wild West" anyway?'. I wondered about her response then, and looking back it occurred to me that she may have been influenced by the attitude of the French aristocracy to Céleste and her grand tale. At the time I recall leaving the agent's office near the Eiffel Tower, catching the metro and getting off at Montparnasse, where there is a long underground tunnel walk dominated by slick wall advertisements. One ad was for *Les Cages aux Folles*, which was playing at a theatre called Mogador. As it turned out the theatre had nothing to do with Céleste, but I took it as an omen, an inspiration to have the book published, somehow, eventually. I engaged agent Jo Butler at Camerons in late 2014 and she found publisher ABC Books. So a quarter of a century after being introduced to the fascinating countess, the story had a home. I acknowledge all those along the journey, even the French agent who dismissed it.

Also to be thanked are Dr Annette Dezarnaulds and her husband, Peter, for their most helpful guidance and assistance in Paris. Annette has a PhD in French literature and her comprehension of the story and Paris's history was invaluable. Others whose thoughts, inspiration and advice were helpful included translator Frederique Lallement, Leon Levin, Narelle Levin, Hannah Levin, Tony Maylam and the late Tim Burstall.